Mustang Survivors

Paul Coggan

Midland Publishing

This book is dedicated to
my daughters Kathryn and Helen

Mustang Survivors
© 2003 Paul Coggan
ISBN 1 85780 135 0

Published by Midland Publishing
4 Watling Drive, Hinckley, LE10 3EY, England
Tel: 01455 254 490 Fax: 01455 254 495
E-mail: midlandbooks@compuserve.com

Midland Publishing is an imprint of
Ian Allan Publishing Ltd

Worldwide distribution (except North America):
Midland Counties Publications
4 Watling Drive, Hinckley, LE10 3EY, England
Telephone: 01455 254 450 Fax: 01455 233 737
E-mail: midlandbooks@compuserve.com
www.midlandcountiessuperstore.com

North American trade distribution:
Specialty Press Publishers & Wholesalers Inc.
39966 Grand Avenue, North Branch, MN 55056, USA
Tel: 651 277 1400 Fax: 651 277 1203
Toll free telephone: 800 895 4585
www.specialtypress.com

Design concept and layout
© 2003 Midland Publishing and
Stephen Thompson Associates

Printed in England by
Ian Allan Printing Ltd
Riverdene Business Park, Molesey Road,
Hersham, Surrey, KT12 4RG

Contents

Front cover: *Tom Patten's beautiful P-51D-25NA 44-73543/N151TP* Swettie Face *holds steady for the camera while conveying a sense of power and elegance.* Uwe Glaser

Title page: *Three of today's Mustang Survivors: P-51D-20NA 44-72145/N51PT* Petie 3rd *leads the P-51D-30NAs 44-74458/N351DM* Sizzlin' Liz *and 44-74524/N151HR* Dakota Kid. *Uwe Glaser

Below: *Some 50 years after being flown by Captain Raymond Littge DSC of the 487th FS, 352nd FG, P-51D-20NA 44-72216/G-BIXL turns back the years and roars to life.* Bob Munro

Introduction
and Acknowledgements

My love affair with the Mustang began as a teenage crush at a local airshow. I wondered what that fantastic-shaped red and white aircraft was that was flying around with the Red Arrows Gnats at the Rolls-Royce Hucknall airshow. The front cover of *Air Pictorial* a few months later answered my question. As it happens, that Mustang survives today. Flown by Charles Masefield, it was painted in a striking red and white paint scheme with a white cheat line. It looked much sexier than the Gnat jets it flew in formation with.

Now, almost 35 years later, I make my living from researching and writing about these 'old aeroplanes'. I prefer to call them classic and vintage. Some of my non-aviation friends express surprise that such an 'old plane' can command a purchase price well in excess of a million dollars, and sadly, this material world in which we dwell automatically makes it a hefty status symbol. I am very lucky, for even after all these years I still get a massive buzz from seeing a Mustang fly by, and an even bigger buzz from seeing one stripped and on its way back to flying condition. In the process I have met some fascinating people and made some very good friends. I've laughed and I've cried with the best of them.

Though, from any angle, North American's finest looks good, in the air it looks better. Yes, purposeful killing machine it remains, but today it sometimes turns on the pilots who love to fly it rather than the enemy it was once unleashed against. Fortunately, even against a backdrop of increased flying hours, accidents are becoming less frequent. Sadly, over the years, I have seen many friends and acquaintances lose their lives in Mustangs, and other warbirds too. I have reluctantly come to accept the fact – explained by a good friend and long time 'Mustang Survivor' – that it 'goes with the territory'.

Many people cannot understand the fascination. But if you have flown a Mustang you can understand how even the most experienced pilot may get carried away. It looks good, it feels good to fly – yet it still kills with brutal and unforgiving efficiency.

Few would disagree that the North American Mustang has a phenomenal historical record. When friends spar with me and ask why I don't (as an Englishman) agree the Spitfire is better, I simply say, 'Didn't see many Spitfires still in military service in the

early 1980s…'. It usually becomes the final comment on the matter! Fewer still would disagree that the Mustang is one of the finest fighters ever produced. In the early years of the 21st century it still excites and it is still much sought after, this time not by the enemy or fighter pilots, but by collectors who want to own a real piece of aviation history. The Mustang is truly legendary.

As I was going through my Mustang files in preparation for this book, I quickly began to realise that 'old Mustangs never die'. An old friend, Clive Denney of Vintage Fabrics, gave me a relatively recent reminder of this. Upon the crash of a P-51D in Switzerland, Clive innocently commented: 'Paul, this must be the third time that aircraft has been destroyed.' He was right.

For me, the Mustangs being operated today are still creating history. They are an important part of aviation heritage today. They are still creating history as they are

rebuilt, restored and often remanufactured. My views on replication and resurrection are well known and documented. To accurately document a Mustang in this new millennium requires an open mind. As always, I maintain that an aircraft identity should be based on the major structure that carries the all-important Manufacturer's data plate. No matter how many different sets of wings are used, how many tailcones the aircraft has gone through or how many engines the aircraft has utilised in its life, the identity is still that carried by the fuselage centre-section. There are those that do not agree, and those that wish I would change my views. Fortunately, the majority of Mustang afficianados appreciate my reasoning.

Using this yardstick, there are those aircraft (surprise, surprise) that are not what the paperwork says they are. In years gone by it was necessary to use old identities to register an aircraft with the Federal Aviation

Administration or the relevant civil aviation authority. In this respect, most restorers and rebuilders acted in good faith. Some did not, but I have no wish to mount a witch-hunt. Despite this caveat the vast majority of Mustangs carry their true military identity, and fraud is not widespread. A genuine and interesting provenance does indeed affect the value of the aircraft.

Since the first edition of *Mustang Survivors* (Aston Publications, 1987), the art of Mustang restoration has improved dramatically. After reviewing the 1987 edition I decided that the same format would not work for this latest tome. After all, there are only so many ways you can say 'transferred to 4th FG', 'was posted to 4th FG' or 'was assigned to 4th FG' before it becomes monotonous.

With the increase in the numbers of people and organisations involved in restoring the Mustang to flying condition, I decided to abbreviate all the civil histories, ask the publisher to include many more pictures (and lots in colour) and explain the who, how and why of Mustangs being restored today. I hope you enjoy the result.

When I wrote the original edition of *Mustang Survivors* I did not feel that the P-51 had an airworthy future beyond my lifetime. With the implementation of new techniques to restore and rebuild Mustang structures and the much higher standards of Mustang restoration, I now hold a different view. The more critical Merlin engine items are being manufactured, and those that are running out will soon also be replicated. Fuel is a more critical item but even the future supply of this is being looked into.

The Mustang will never die, at least in my lifetime. So, let's torque the talk and Fly Warbirds!

Acknowledgements

With any major project there are always a multitude of people to thank, and *Mustang Survivors* is no exception.

To my friends Lee Lauderback (Stallion 51), Michael Oakey (Editor, *Aeroplane Monthly*), Nigel Gill (Regional Area Manager at Andrews Sykes plc), Stephen Grey (The Fighter Collection), Philip Makanna (GHOSTS), Phillip Warner, Tom Smith, Thierry Thomassin and Uwe Glaser for their constant support and intense personal encouragement (some of which was combined with threats of physical violence if I didn't get this finished!) at a time when I needed it most. They are all busy people but they made time for me.

When I look back it seems incredible that I have spent more than 30 years researching the P-51 and other warbirds and writing endless articles and a few books, many of which document the rise and (sadly) demise of so many historic airframes. It never ceases to amaze me how generous the network of owners and enthusiasts is when it comes to assisting with detail.

Undoubtedly, major thanks must go to the three people that kindled my Mustang enthusiasm in the early days. Harry Holmes acted in an almost fatherly way when he was at Hawker Siddeley Aviation at Woodford, feeding a schoolboy with information from the ATC logs on HS.748 test flights that I'd seen over my home. Some years later, by sheer coincidence, our paths crossed again and he encouraged me once more, fostering my enthusiasm for the Mustang, about which he is also passionate. Jerry Scutts, the accomplished and well-known aviation researcher and writer, was my mentor early on and planted the seeds for my early publishing activities. I vividly recall a seemingly bizarre meeting with Jerry in a backstreet public house in London with a stripper performing in the background, but now I realise this was a most relevant introduction to aviation publishing! Since then I have seen many scantily clad ladies revealing interesting curves and in various states of undress, though I should stress that these have been of the older metal-and-wood variety.

William T Larkins responded to my requests for help and information with numerous long letters full of detail, accompanied by a series of packets of archive and then contemporary Mustang photographs, many of which appear in this latest work.

All three helped me compile and promulgate my first warbird list, The *Mustang Index* that appeared in 1973.

I am also indebted, over many years, to Gene Boswell of Rockwell International, who supplied me with countless North American Aviation photographs from the old North American Aviation Inc archives. Gene felt that not enough was being done to preserve the archival material; I am sure many people will appreciate his foresight in the future.

When I decided to include a chapter about owning and operating a Mustang it seemed logical to turn to some of the people I'd had the pleasure to meet that fell into this category. Had I attempted to write this myself I would have been immediately disqualified, for my chances of ever owning a P-51 are slim indeed. I was overwhelmed by the response of the majority of the people I approached to contribute, so my thanks to the following for making this a most worthwhile chapter: Ed and Connie Bowlin (I had the pleasure to fly with Ed and Connie in a B-25 in 1999 and they make a great pilot team), Robert Converse (*Huntress III*), Stephen Grey (The Fighter Collection), Chris and Lorraine Gruys, Chuck Hall, Bill and Marcia Hane (*Ho! Hun*), Steve Hinton (fastest Mustang pilot), Vlado Lenoch (*Moonbeam McSwine*), Ed Lindsay (Cavalier), Dan Martin (*Ridge Runner III*), Tom Patten (*Sweetie Face*), Brian Reynolds (Olympic Flight Museum), Anders K Saether (*Old Crow*), and Mike VadeBonCoeur (Midwest Aero Restorations Ltd).

For this latest Mustang chronicle, many people have helped with information and supplied photographs to add to those from my own collection. To everyone who helped I would like to say thanks. They are: Gregory Alegi, Chris Armstrong, Peter N Anderso Norm Avery, Gerry Beck (Tri-State Aviation Candace Bennage (Stallion 51), Arthur Ber ley, Roger Besecker, Tim Bivens, Ian Brod (New Zealand Fighter Pilots Museu Wanaka), Simon Brown, Bonnie Caldara (Caldarale Aircraft Refinishing), Gene Chas James P Church, Mark Clark (Courtesy A craft), Joe Cupido, Robert S DeGroat, Cli and Linda Denney (Vintage Fabrics), John Dilley, Phil Earthey, Martin Espin (The Fight Collection), the late Jeff Ethell, Nigel Foste Erich Gandet, Chuck Gardner, Kev Grantham, Wayne Gomes, Dave Goss (Gos Hawk Unlimited), David K Gosser, Alan Gr ening, Anthony Harmsworth (Assista Editor *Aeroplane Monthly*), Maurice Har mond, Pat Harker, Paul Hunt, Dave Jon (RAAF Museum), Rod Kenward, Tryg Johansen, John Kerr, James Kightly, Ro Lamplough, Martin Lardner (Martin A craft), Brad Lauderback, Pete and Richa Lauderback (Stallion 51 Maintenance Ope ations), Terry Lawless, Bob Luikens, Der Macphail, Dave McDonald, Barry McKe Callum Macpherson (Editor, Pacific Wing John Morgan, Frank Mormillo, Coert Mun Bob Odegaard (Odegaard Aviation), Di Odgers, Brian O'Farrell, James Parks, Richa Paver, Steve Penning (Aerocrafters), Di Phillips, EAA Founder Paul Poberezny, E Quenardel, Richard Rasmussen, Boardma Reed, the late Robb Satterfield, Henry 'Butch' Schroeder, John Seevers, Micha Shreeve, James Shuttleworth, Tulio So Frank Strickler, Square One Aviation, A Teeters (Cal Pacific Airmotive), Ed Tot Jerry E Vernon, Philip Wallick, Bud Wheel (Allison Competition Engines), Sandy We man (Sky Harbour Aircraft Refinishing Angela West (Stallion 51), Jim Wincheste and the staff at the RAAF and RNZAF Mus ums. Without these people this work wou be pictorially poorer.

Escalating insurance rates are constan cited as one of the reasons some of the Mu tang survivors do not fly. Unfortunately, t blame often stops at the desk of the profe sional insurance broker. I have known B Cannon for years and it took him exactly s minutes (following an email) to say I would help with words on the subject insurance. Over the years, Cannon Aviatic Insurance Inc has supported and sponsor many warbird-related events and Bob is all-round good guy. Sound advice is worth lot, and I thank him for taking time out write the chapter on insurance.

Finally, to my best friend and soul ma Debra, my love and thanks. Not only did s watch me disappear behind files and hea of photographs for hours on end, she su plied calm in times of stress; without h help this new book would simply not ha appeared.

If I have forgotten anyone the omission not intentional, and I apologise in advanc

Paul Coggan
November 2002

Keeper of the Keys

Foreword by Lee Lauderback

With slide rules and engineering genius the North American P-51 Mustang was designed and built in just a little over 120 days. Conceived as a weapon of war to defend democracy this remarkable aircraft went on to arguably become the premier fighter of World War Two. Today the Mustang is approximately 62 years old and if the remaining airframes could talk, what terrific stories they could tell!

One can only imagine the different pilots, the different places, and the various missions each of these Mustangs experienced during the war years. Although few of the actual aircraft returned after World War Two, their legend was to continue with new Mustangs coming off the assembly line. These Mustangs would see combat in Korea, primarily on air-to-ground missions but occasionally going up against next-generation aircraft such as the MiG-15. After Korea the Mustang would continue its military service with the Air National Guard units across the United States. In 1985, after almost 45 years of military service, the Mustang would finally retire as a combat aircraft, last operated by the Fuerza Aerea Dominicana. Yet this was just the ending of a chapter in the history of this remarkable aircraft. The story was to continue.

The Mustangs being surplussed during the late 1950s offered civilian pilots a chance to fly this high-performance fighter, and so they did. For just a fraction of the original $56,000 cost these Mustangs took to the skies in civilian hands. They were used as sport aircraft, and for air racing, airshows, and many other unique applications. However, unlike their military counterparts, most of the pilots were not properly trained and the accident statistics were very high, pilot error being the cause in most cases. Annual losses approached 10% of the remaining airworthy Mustangs, and the aircraft were inexpensive and easily obtained. They were just surplus military junk to so many people, out for a spin and left to the elements to age away; a sign of the times in our new 'throwaway society'.

But time changes all things, and the future of the Mustang was no exception. A new breed of owner was to begin a professional approach to the maintenance and operation of this fantastic fighter. The civilian paint jobs were replaced with original combat paint schemes, most paying tribute to the warriors who flew Mustangs in combat.

Names such as *Angels' Playmate*, *Old Crow*, *Glamorous Glen III*, *Hell-er-Bust*, *American Beauty*, and *Slender, Tender & Tall* would once again grace the skies. At times, ageing Aces such as Col Bruce Carr, Col Bud Anderson and Gen Chuck Yeager would have the chance to once again wear their favourite aircraft, but for the first time far from war. A chance to enjoy the freedom they fought so long and hard for.

As the airframes aged, Mustangs underwent complete restorations. Businessmen for the first time saw the true value of these aircraft and made substantial investments in time and money to return them to pristine condition. Every nut, bolt, and rivet would be replaced, and the airframes polished with tender loving care. The aircraft were transformed into national treasures, to take their rightful place in history.

Pilots began to take a professional attitude towards initial and recurrent training. Investments of time and money to really learn this high-performance machine have begun to turn around the high loss rate due to accidents and allow the numbers of Mustangs to grow for the first time since initial production. The stories of 'torque rolls on go-around' and 'excessive rudder required for take-off' are beginning to fade as more people begin to understand the proper procedures to use; procedures learned in the dual-cockpit, dual-controlled TF-51 Mustangs such as *Crazy Horse*.

From combat days to airshows, flown by the likes of R A 'Bob' Hoover, the Mustang has constantly been in the public eye. In 1999, for the first time in history, rows of extraordinary Mustangs were viewed by four generations during the 'Gathering of Mustangs and Legends'; combat veterans mixed freely with the public. Children marvelled at the 65 time capsules. The event was an unprecedented collection of Mustangs and the Gladiators who took them into combat.

Today the P-51 Mustang has a bright future, or so it would seem. But do not get complacent, as there are other enemies that even today threaten these aircraft. Enemies within our own ranks not armed with bullets, but with rules and short-sightedness that would remove the Mustang and other historical aircraft from our nation's skies forever. This fight will not be fought in our aircraft in some far-off country, but in the United States Congress and hopefully we will win this battle also.

I am truly blessed to fly the Mustang almost every day for the past 15 years. To have the opportunity to give back some of what the Mustang has given me; to share the Mustang with so many others that would never have had the chance to experience the performance and handling qualities of this thoroughbred. But I remind myself often that I am just the 'keeper of the keys'. These treasures must move on to the next generation, not because they are awesome to fly but because they represent what so many fallen Patriots gave their lives to defend. They represent the ultimate freedom.

I hope you enjoy this terrific volume *Mustang Survivors* and when you go through its pages, stop for a moment and listen to the stories these Mustangs have to tell.

Mustangs Forever,
Lee Lauderback, 2002

Lee Lauderback of Orlando, Florida began flying in 1966 at the age of 15. Shortly after graduation from college, Lee started to work for the noted professional golfer and businessman, Arnold Palmer. For 16 years, Lee headed up Mr Palmer's flight operations as chief pilot and director of flight operations, piloting his Learjet, C-I, C-II, C-III series Citation jets, and MD500E helicopter.

Currently, Lee is chief instructor and demonstration pilot in the P-51 Mustang. Additionally, he is also one of the pilots for the USAF Air Force Heritage Flight Program and a civilian instructor for the Navy Test Pilot School at Patuxent River, MD where test pilot students and instructors fly the Mustang.

Also a certified flight and ground instructor for airplane (single and multi-engine), instrument, helicopters and gliders, and an FAA Pilot Proficiency Examiner, he does acceptance flight-testing in various warbirds, helicopters, and turbojets.

Amassing in excess of 17,000 flight hours in all types of aircraft and helicopters, including over 5,000 hours in Mustangs, Lee has also flown the F-15 Eagle, F-16 'Viper', and F/A-18 Hornet. Additionally he has over 2,000 hours in sailplanes, has competed in many soaring contests and has held several sailplane records.

Even in his spare time Lee goes flying; he is an accomplished falconer, and can often be found flying hawks and falcons.

Web Resources

The advent of the internet and associated world wide web have opened up a whole new area for information, hard data and latest news reports. A request punched into one of the search engines (the author uses Sherlock software on the Macintosh and the pure search engine Google located at **www.google.com**) will reveal a host of both professional and amateur websites. Some are valuable resources put up by dedicated individuals, others are just mass breaches of copyright which take little effort to produce!

Undoubtedly the most Mustang intensive website is Curtis Fowles' effort located at **www.mustangsmustangs.com** which not only covers the North American Mustang but the Ford Mustang car too, hence the double-barrelled name. Don't be fooled, however, because the two subjects are properly separated and the site contains several thousand photographic images from a multitude of sources as well as up-to-date information on the world's Mustang population. It also has a discussion forum where you can ask questions related to the P-51, post information or just keep an eye on the latest Mustang happenings around the globe.

If you are looking to purchase a Mustang **www.barnstormers.com** is a good starting point for general warbird sales, but if a dedicated professional broker is what you are looking for then Mark Clark's long established and knowledgeable Courtesy Aircraft is most definitely the place to go at **www.courtesyaircraft.com**. For those who need a wider degree of coverage often turn to the now famous yellow newspaper *Trade-A-Plane* which also has a website full access to which can be exercised if you have a subscription to the printed edition of *Trade-A-Plane* newspaper. Not surprisingly, **www.tradeaplane.com** is the address for this resource.

The brainchild of the author, **www.warbirdindex.com** is another excellent warbird website which often contains Mustang topics and a first-rate forum (called warbirdtorque) where you will get useful information and answers to your technical questions (depending on their depth!).

Boeing took over all the history files fo the P-51 from Rockwell International an their website has basic information a **www.boeing.com/companyoffices/history bna/p51.htm**; it also has a contact addres for more specific enquiries.

For professional flight training and lots o Mustang 'goodies', Stallion 51's website a **www.stallion51.com** provides just what yo are looking for along with up-to-date info mation on what the world's premier warbir training facility is up to at present.

The Mustang is also prevalent in the worl of Unlimited Air Racing and one of the be: websites to help keep tabs on this activity located at **www.pylon1.com**, where you wi also find links to the regular Mustang air rac ing teams' websites.

A periodic search into any of the bigg€ search engines will reveal the latest crop o websites dedicated to the Mustang.

Website www.mustangsmustangs.com includes 44-72086/N789DH and 44-63057/N51E in its list of P-51D survivors. Robert S DeGroat

Chapter One

Airframes

Where Did They Come From?

In the last ten years the art of Mustang restoration has developed considerably. The thirst to own and fly an example of North American Aviation's finest piston-engined fighter has not diminished in the least. The number of companies involved in the area of Mustang restoration and operation has increased in line with the number of aircraft being restored and flown. So, where did these airframes come from? How did so many survive to be operational today as warbirds?

The late 1950s and the advent of more modern jet equipment saw hundreds of Mustangs withdrawn from USAF service and sent to the scrap yards. Fortunately, the Mustang was very much a part of the US Military Aid Program of the day and so not all the surplus stock went to the smelters. It is the aircraft that were phased out of USAF service, reconditioned and sent to foreign air arms that provided the lions' share of the Mustangs extant today. The huge spares stock held by the USAF was used to support the MDAP efforts. Of those Mustangs that did make it into civilian hands, many survive today as civilian-operated warbirds.

P-51D-30NA 44-74607, photographed over San Francisco Bay on 15 October 1949, shows the Mustang in one of its final roles for the United States – that of a National Guardsman. This is one of thousands of Mustangs that went to the scrap yards. William T Larkins

Some of the Air National Guard Mustangs did live to fight another day. In service with the Illinois Air National Guard, P-51D-25NT 44-84961 was saved to become a historic Mustang in its own right. Modified with a Griffon powerplant, it later became the famous RB-51 Red Baron. It is now owned by Steve Hinton as N7715C and operated in stock configuration. The Warbird Index

The Royal Canadian Air Force began taking delivery of the P-51D as early as 1947 and it was quickly put to good use by this air arm. The RCAF examples provide the majority of identifiable and original survivors. When the RCAF surplussed these airframes in the late 1950s, 87 went to warbird owners and two to museums.

Of the other Commonwealth countries, New Zealand used the P-51D, pressing some 30 airframes into service with the RNZAF. In 1958 the 19 survivors were put up for disposal by tender and only a few were left intact following disposal. Of these, two are flyable, one in the US (45-11507/N921 with the Weeks Air Museum in Florida) and one in the UK (45-11518/G-MSTG with Maurice Hammond at Eye in Suffolk), and a third

example is being rebuilt in the UK (45-11495 with Philip Warner in Cheltenham, Gloucestershire). Remarkably the other ex-RNZAF P-51Ds were broken up by the ANSA Company – they had paid between NZ$50 and NZ$160 per aircraft! One other aircraft still languishes in the open in New Zealand with John Smith of Mapua (45-11513).

Neighbouring Australia not only used the Mustang, it had the Commonwealth Aircraft Corporation Pty (CAC) licence-build the airframes. The year 1942 saw the Australian government actively seeking a replacement for the Curtiss P-40, which was hard at work with the RAAF in the Pacific. Initially 690 Mustangs were to be manufactured under licence by CAC and to be powered by Packard Merlin engines (also to be built by

CAC). However, the first 80 aircraft were to be assembled from components supplied directly by North American Aviation and shipped to Australia. One hundred sets of components were dispatched, the first 20 of which were used to organise production tooling at CAC and provide spare parts. These aircraft were designated CA-17 and the first example, serialled A68-1, was taken on strength by the RAAF on 4 June 1945 (this aircraft is a survivor – located in the United States as N51WB). After the victory over Japan the original Mustang production figure for the RAAF was cut back to 350 aircraft, though in the end CAC actually manufactured just 200 Mustangs (including the 80 aircraft assembled from NAA components). Interestingly the RAAF later received

P-51D-25NT 44-73254 was taken on charge by the RCAF on 7 June 1947 as 9571 and remained in service until 1960 when it was purchased by Aero Enterprises. It went on to become N6328T and is now owned by Donald Weber of Baton Rouge, Louisiana. Author's collection

P-51D-30NA 44-74908/N1070Z, looking in very rough condition when in the ownership of Intercontinental Airways of Canastota, New York in the 1950s. Formerly 9273 in RCAF service, it went on to become N151BP and is now owned by the Palm Springs Air Museum. via J E Vernon

P-51D-25NT 45-11495/NZ2406 arrived in the UK in 2002 as the basis of a restoration project for Philip Warner of Cheltenham Gloucestershire. Author's collection

P-51D-25NT 45-11507 was registered ZK-CCG to Ron Fechney in April 1958 after serving with the RNZAF as NZ2417. It first flew in civilian hands following restoration at Christchurch, New Zealand on 29 November 1964. It is now operated by Kermit Weeks in Florida as N921. Jim Winchester

The Australian War Memorial's P-51D-20NT 44-13106/A68-648 was restored by Bob Eastgate and is seen here shortly after rollout following restoration. It was previously an instructional airframe with the Royal Melbourne Institute of Technology. Chris DuVe

Trans Florida Aviation (later Cavalier Aircraft Corporation) was largely responsible for prolonging the life of the Mustang through its military refurbishment programme. Illustrated is P-51D-25NA 44-73454 in civilian colours as N2051D in 1968. It was later sold to Gordon Plaskett who restored it as a warbird. It is now owned by Richard Bjell. William T Larkins

P-51D-20NA 44-72059/N6150U at Brownwood, Texas in July 1965 when owned by the MACO Financial Sales Corp. Previously with Sweden's Flygvapnet and the Fuerza Aerea de Nicaragua it later went to the Fuerza Aerea Bolivia and is now being rebuilt by Glenn Wegman at Fighter Enterprises in Florida. Dick Phillips

P-51D-30NA 44-74391/N38229 seen just after being acquired from the Fuerza Aerea Guatemalteca by Don Hull. It was later acquired by Wilson 'Connie' Edwards and stored until sold on to Woods Aviation LLC of Carefree, Arizona in May 2001. Today it is registered as N351MX. The Warbird Index

additional NAA-built aircraft. Just 15 of the CAC-built aircraft survive today: 12 are airworthy (five located in the United States), one is in store and two are being rebuilt to fly.

Perhaps the most famous of the ex-RAAF Mustangs are the six CAC-built aircraft used to test the effects of blast damage as a result of an atomic bomb explosion. The six aircraft were carefully parked up at the Emu Claypan and subjected to the impact of atomic bomb shockwaves. The effects were numerous but all the aircraft survived to be recovered and put up for disposal by tender. They all found their way to the United States!

Similarly, in 1956 the RCAF put their Mustangs up for disposal and of the 87 aircraft offered and taken up by civilians, the majority (71 airframes) were sold to James H Defuria and Partners of DeWhitt, New York, with a further two aircraft going to museums. Today, 30 of these ex-RCAF Mustangs are flying and another five from this batch are being rebuilt to fly. Many have been restored more than once, several have received major repairs to damage caused in flying accidents, and some are just used as a paper identity.

Undoubtedly, a key factor in extending the life of the P-51 Mustang as a warbird was the work undertaken by Trans Florida Aviation (later known as the Cavalier Aircraft Corporation) to rework Mustangs for use in later Military Defense Aid Programs.

Several air arms across the world used the Mustang in front-line service, many of the aircraft being processed by Cavalier. When these aircraft were in turn replaced by more modern jet equipment, they were turned over to the civilian warbird market.

As early as 1963 Will Martin of the MACO Sales Financial Corporation purchased at least 12 Mustangs and a huge quantity of spares from the Fuerza Aerea de la Guardia Nacional de Nicaragua. Though some of the aircraft crashed on the ferry flight to the United States, eight are still regularly flown, seven in the USA and one in the UK. These aircraft all came from the Swedish Flygvapnet, and included a couple of original USAAF 8th Air Force combat veterans.

Perhaps the most famous and colourful Mustang recovery operation was undertaken by Wilson Connell 'Connie' Edwards of Big Spring, Texas in August 1972. Edwards negotiated the purchase of ten mainly Cavalier-modified Mustangs from the Fuerza Aerea Guatemalteca (FAG). For many years the core of this group of aircraft remained stored and sheltered from the elements at Big Spring, with Edwards gradually releasing an airframe every so often. In actual fact this was good for the warbird movement, for it preserved airframes in stock condition, i.e. untouched since being surplussed. There was also a substantial spares and Merlin engine holding with these Mustangs.

Soon after the FAG relinquished their aircraft, the Fuerza Aerea Salvadorena took the same option. Purchased by a consortium lead by Jack Flaherty of Flaherty Factors Inc., Monterey, California, the arrangement saw a further ten (mainly) Cavalier Mustangs and another spares cache change hands. The bulk of the airframes were ferried back to the United States in 1974, after the type had effectively been retired from military service a year earlier. These aircraft provided a welcome boost to the already growing civilian warbird and Mustang populations in the United States.

In 1978 English businessman Robert J Lamplough visited Israel and undertook a major recovery operation, which saw four historic Mustangs imported to the UK. The aircraft had been in a variety of locations in Israel and though they were in relatively poor condition, they were essentially complete and made good restoration projects. The four aircraft, serialled IDF28,41,43 and 146, were put in containers and shipped to the UK where they were initially assembled at the IWM airfield at Duxford. Robs selected IDF43 as his own project and involved the author in researching the history of this aircraft. IDF41 was sold to Noel Robinson and partners and was transported to North Yorkshire where it was to remain until 2001. It was exported to the United States the same year, in pretty much the same condition it was in when it was acquired from Robs Lamplough. IDF146 went to the Andrewsfield 'Rebel Air Museum' for a time as an exhibition centrepiece. IDF28 went to RAF Watton in Norfolk where the author and a small team set about restoring it to static exhibition standard. Sadly the project was never finished as the author was posted to Scotland, but some valuable preservation work was undertaken which improved the structural integrity of the fuselage.

Shortly after Robs Lamplough's foray into Israel, two now well-known collectors from California, Angelo and Pete Regina, recovered several major Mustang structures and fuselages including two D model units and a rare P-51B mainplane. Using the components rescued from Israel and a fuselage obtained from a film studio in California, both a P-51D and P-51B were restored.

Other activity in Israel included the rebuild of IDF38, later discovered to be an ex-Swedish Mustang (44-63864), by Israel Itzhaki, an Israeli Air Force colonel.

By the 1970s the Cavalier Aircraft Mustangs were starting to show their age and military air arms utilising them were replacing them with more modern jet equipment.

The Fuerza Aerea Boliviana (FAB) was one such user, having operated several Cavalier-reworked Mustangs supplied by the US Government under Project 'Peace Condor'. In 1977 Carnegie Holdings Limited of Edmonton, Alberta, purchased four Cavalier

Mustangs that included a rare TF-51D full dual-control aircraft and a further two original Mustangs, plus a multitude of spares. Major Jerry Westphal and Captain Butch Foster ferried two Mustangs into the United States in mid-1977 followed by two separate trips flown by Captains Les Benson, Butch Foster and Jock MacKay in two separate ferry flights. Neil McClain purchased the dual-control TF-51D plus two other aircraft; Ross Grady and Bill Bailey picked up the single-seaters. Florida resident George Roberts bought the remaining aircraft. All have since lost all trace of their colourful FAB service.

The MDAP-supplied Cavalier Mustangs from Indonesia's Tentara Nasional Indonesia Angkatan Udara (TNI-AU) were the next aircraft to be declared surplus to requirements by the air force in 1978. Stephen Johnson of Napa, California, and his father liberated at least 15 Mustangs and a substantial cache of spares the following year and imported them to the United States, where they were offered as complete aircraft and a series of 'starter kits'. The Mustangs were dismantled in Indonesia and containerised, after which they were shipped to the USA. The author corresponded with Stephen over a period of months and the data he supplied was invaluable. Even today the balance of the Indonesian airframes are being rebuilt, with three of the original aircraft recovered still under restoration. There are still several Mustang airframes in Indonesia serving as gate guards and museum pieces.

Undoubtedly the last great Mustang bastion was the Dominican Republic, which had already set a record for keeping the Mustang in continuous military service.

Remarkably, just as Johnson was containerising the Indonesian Mustangs, the Fuerza Aerea Dominicana (FAD) were just commencing their final Inspection and Repair as Necessary (IRAN) schedules on their surviving Mustangs. On 19 May 1984, after months of protracted negotiations, and having outbid some established players on the warbird scene, Brian O'Farrell and Armin Mattli acquired the FAD's entire Mustang stock including several large warehouses full of spare parts. When the author inspected some of the spares and ancillaries at a warehouse in Hialeah, Florida, the same year, it was obvious that the FAD engineers had been frugal in the use of their spares. Some of the smaller parts were still in their original NAA factory boxes and there were several rarer major structures as well as the nine airframes included in the arrangement. The spares cache included several mainplanes, stressed fuel tank doors, doghouse and afthouse sections, much sought-after spinner hubs plus a stock of original engine cowlings, many with signs of their Swedish Air Force (Flygvapnet) heritage, as well as thousands of smaller Mustang items.

One FAD aircraft, identified by a senior FAD officer as 44-72123 (a very historic airframe, formerly the mount of 343rd FS/55th FG, 8th AF pilot Edward B Giller and named *The Millie G*), remained in Dominica as a gate guard at San Isidro Air Base. As the majority of the FAD Mustangs came from ex-Swedish Air Force stocks, this was not the only historic airframe to be yielded by the recovery. Soon after the recovery, the author of this book discovered that FAD 1916 was formerly with the 352nd FS/353rd FG, 8th AF and had been flown as the personal mount

of Captain H Tordoff as *Upopa Epops*, coded SX-L. It is believed Tordoff scored 'kills' in the Mustang. Though it had no doubt gone through several IRAN programmes (including at least one via Cavalier), this particular Mustang had been in service with the FAD since its delivery on 31 October 1952, a total of 32 years. The aircraft is now registered to Flying Heritage Inc. in Washington, where it keeps distinguished company with several other rare and historic warbirds.

When Edgar Schmued designed the Mustang over 60 years ago, he did not envisage that the type would still be in front-line 'service' 44 years later, nor that surviving examples would be flying as warbirds well into the next millennium.

Photographs on the opposite page:

Project 'Peace Condor' supplied the Fuerza Aerea Boliviana with these five Cavalier Mustangs, delivered by Tactical Air Command pilots. Initially painted light gull grey, later they adopted a three-tone green/brown camouflage with light grey undersides. David K Gosser

Ross Grady at the controls of ex-FAB Cavalier Mustang 67-22581/C-GFUS What's Up Doc *at the CAF airshow in 1991.* Ed Toth

Below: *The Israeli Defence Force has been one of the most recent donors of Mustangs airframes for restoration to flying condition. Due to the clandestine method by which the IDF procured their airframes it has always been difficult to trace their individual histories. Robert Lamplough photographed this P-51D in a kibbutz playground in the late 1970s. It is understood the aircraft was retrieved later by an American collector.* Robert Lamplough

Two Fuerza Aerea Dominicana Mustangs still in service in 1980. As with the aircraft delivered to the Fuerza Aerea Boliviana, the Dominican Mustangs swapped a light grey finish for a green/tan camouflage scheme with off-white undersurfaces. Jeff Ethell collection

FAD 1900 seen at the Cavalier Aircraft Factory at Sarasota, Florida circa 1963. This may have been the same FAD 1900 recovered from the Dominican Republic by Brian O'Farrell in 1983. Author's collection

P-51D-25NA 44-73260 was one of the very last of the ex-Stephen Johnson cache of ex-TNI-AU Mustangs to be rebuilt. The airframe is seen here at Aero Trader in Chino, California in April 1999. Thierry Thomassin

Chapter Two

Mustang Engineering Drawings

Preservation of a Different Heritage

As a student of the art of Mustang restoration one of the questions I am most frequently asked is 'Where do I get a complete set of blueprints for the P-51 Mustang?' Researches in early 2002 revealed that several individuals are working on professional projects to increase the amount of Mustang data and drawings available to (very serious) enthusiasts and to Mustang restoration companies.

North American Aviation Inc Mustang production drawings for the P-51A, B/C, D, and H are available on microfilm from the National Air and Space Museum (Archives Division, MRC 322, National Air and Space Museum, Smithsonian Institution, Washington, DC 20560; phone 202 357 3133 in the USA). Ironically, according to renowned draughtsman Arthur Bentley in the UK these films were created from original drawings located in Canada, after all the American drawings in the United States had been destroyed. He also adds: 'My set of drawings on microfilm came from the NASM in the mid-1970s and include all versions of the Mustang from the NA-73 through to the P-51H. I acquired other information at the same time from various sources in the aviation industry. These were people who worked on the project at the time, and knew where to lay their hands on the data. This was during the period when all the traditional factory sites and research centres were still in existence with archives going back, undisturbed, to the wartime period. Sadly, from our point of view, all this has now changed. All these people have now retired, and no longer have the close contact with the people and sources, and due to industry consolidation and contractors relocating, or closing down altogether, much of the archives and data sources that were so helpful in the past have been lost. People – even the helpful and enthusiastic ones – with no real knowledge of what they contain, staff the departments that remain.' Arthur also points out that as no significant production versions of the Mustang were produced after 1945, the later drawing set is unlikely to differ in any great detail from the one from the NASM, apart from the later changes to equipment refinements post war (such as radio and instrumentation).

The NASM films, which are available for about $700 at the time of writing, consist of 25 reels of film. One reel is an index that is vital if you have certain parts or models you want to access. Generally the quality of the film is good but some recipients have reported some frames/drawings that are unreadable. Apparently a drawing containing the fuselage ordinates is not in the set. This is significant because it is referenced by many of the other drawings. However, most people that have purchased the films say the microfilm set is good value for money. Many people ask what is on the films. Basically the film is a library of parts, finished parts and assemblies. The latter two are more the rule than the exception. While many part dimensions are in the film, many more are not. Again, the film set is not a library of how to cut the parts, but more how to finish the parts and to assemble them into sub-assemblies. Anyone who believes you can build a Mustang from scratch by using these films alone is deluding himself.

From Bill Tolbert, who is also undertaking a project based on Mustang drawings: 'When a copy is ordered from NASM, they send their master, or more probably a copy of their master, to the laboratory and request a duplicate. The new copy is sent to the NASM customer. I've noted other copies like those found on the Internet may be copies of the duplicate, therefore, another generation of the original. I'm not saying this is always true, but that it is possible. I've learned of three people who possess Wright-Patterson generated copies that were purchased sometime in the 1980s. All complain of the index not being complete, not readable, whatever. My copy does not have these problems. It would be interesting to see both copies side by side. I just say, for those seeking copies of this film set, know the source.'

What about the physical content and make up of the films? Bill Tolbert again: 'Filming of the drawings was not for archival or historical purposes. Nor was it intended to be a "cookbook" on how to build the aircraft. The intent was to provide technical information on the Mustang to remote locations so that they could be more easily maintained. This is clearly spelled out in the discussion of the index on the first two pages. The filming process rendered many of the images slightly overexposed. Overexposure was not much of a problem for early mechanically focused viewers, but unfortunately, does present problems for today's film scanners. The technicians had other visual examples such as other aircraft on the line to access, too; and when questions arose that could not be handled locally, an infrastructure was in place to resolve the problem. Some 55 to 60 years hence, however, the technical information and resources on the P-51 are not as available! The following gives you an idea of the contents of the film set images.

- Photographed indexed images: 14,225
- Multiple indexed images from long drawings: 1,000 (approx)
- Index pages: 154
- Wing performance report pages: 380
- Aircraft performance calculation pages: 62
- Bomb Rack report pages: 25

'The film itself consists of 25 black and white 35mm spools. Each spool is some 100 feet long with no tractorfeed knockouts. Twenty-four of the spools are labelled "alphabetically" and the final one is labelled "Reports". Spool "A" contains the film index of 154 pages and the "A" drawing set. Spool "U" contains the specification reports.

'The film index is divided into two main sections. The first section is 70 pages and is a numerically ascending sorted list of the drawing numbers. This index is assembled in "matrix style" with "X boxes" provided in columns for the applicable variants. The film frame position column for the drawing is included at the end of each line.

'The second section, pages 70 to 154, is the alphabetical listing. This group is subdivided by major section such as wing, fuselage, empennage, etc, and are each sorted alphabetically with the drawing number attached. Both indexes are keyed on the drawing numbers. The drawings are in full-scale format, except where labelled otherwise.'

It is important to note that the NASM insist on a signed Document Use and Indemnification Agreement which states: 'Requestors of air and space craft drawings must execute an agreement with NASM indicating their intent to use the drawings and data supplied by NASM only for historical research, exhibition, model making, or non-profit restoration purposes. Requestors will also agree that the documents and data are intended solely for personal and non-commercial use, that these documents and data will not be used to create a replication of any aircraft, and that copies of the documents and data will not be reproduced, distributed or transmitted.' This signed agreement must be provided to NASM before orders for copying of drawings are accepted.

Gary Henry of Mustang Imaging in Refugio, Texas (www.mustangimaging.com) is re-lofting the fuselage drawings for the B and D models with available information. Gary says:

North American TF-51D-25NT Mustang
44-84745/N851D *Crazy Horse*

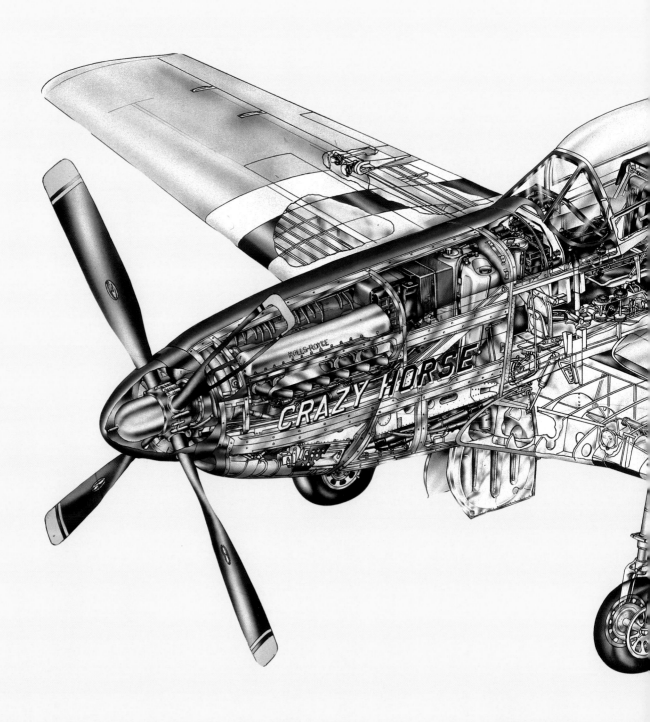

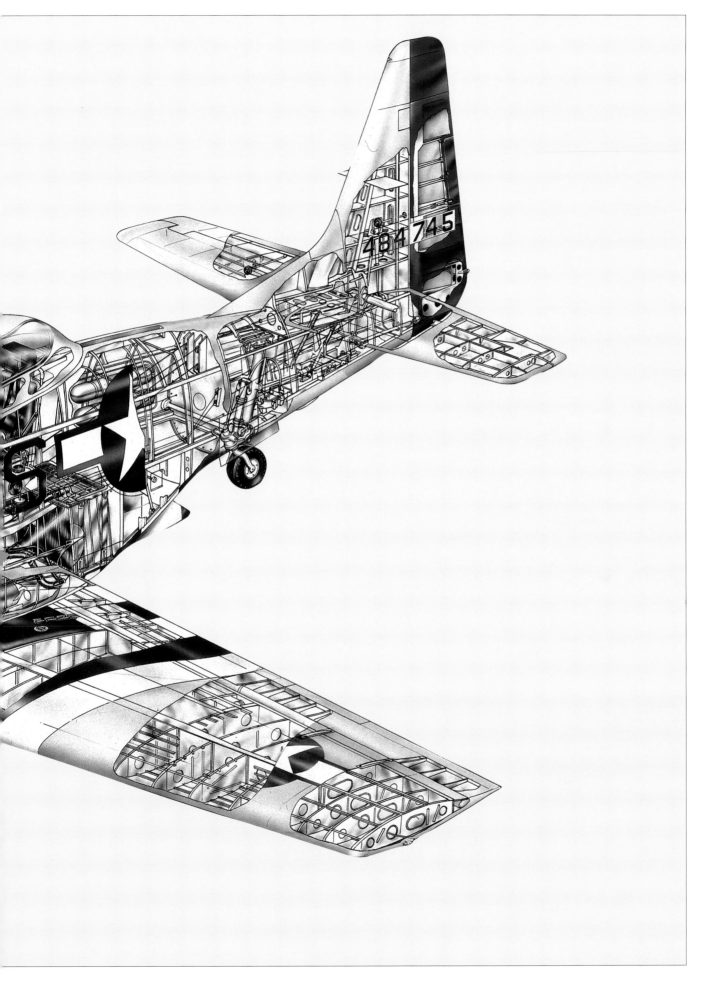

484745

'We are currently in the process of converting P-51 blueprints into full-size 3D Autocad models for plotting at any scale. This is an ongoing project and will grow in scope. Because of the interest shown and many requests for info, rather than take the time to respond individually, the website was started to answer frequently asked questions and gather feedback. Mustang Imaging will be offering drawings, documentation and information about the P-51A, B/C, D and H in the future. Considerable effort has been spent to ensure a high degree of accuracy in the drawings being generated.'

Gary has also spent many hours on his project, lofting the Mustang. He takes up the subject himself: 'Like a lot of aviation enthusiasts, I've had a love affair with the P-51 since I was a kid. After building many models and collecting all kinds of information over the years, I wanted to draw some plans that would be as accurate as possible for modelling, never having been satisfied with any drawings or plans available. Particularly frustrating was the lack of accurate fuselage cross-sections.

'The availability of the blueprints on microfilm from the National Air & Space Museum was the solution to the problem, or so I thought at the time. After obtaining the index for the set, it became apparent that the fuselage ordinate drawings were not included and since then the search for them has been fruitless.

'The "loft" drawings are important in that they are the benchmark for all of the drawings needed to fabricate airframe parts. The search for the drawings instead turned into a project to derive the fuselage ordinates as they had been during the original design. One of the first requirements was to get the microfilmed drawings into a format that would be easy to use and search. I found a company in Oklahoma City that had the capability of scanning microfilm into TIFF files that could be stored on CD. They also put the drawings into a database so that each reel (now a CD) can be scrolled through and the drawings viewed on a computer. Each drawing could also be printed out.

'There is software available that allows the user to load raster files such as TIFF files into Autocad and manipulate them so that any distortion can be eliminated. Also, the drawing files can be rescaled as desired. Once satisfied that the drawing is as accurate as possible, it serves as a backdrop for Autocad. The user can then trace over it, turning a raster file into a vector format file. This is how I originally started generating fuselage drawings for the D model. But I realised at the beginning that I should be working in 3D instead of two dimensions so a software upgrade from Autocad LT to full Autocad was in order – more money but a lot more capability!

'Another piece of software, called Loftsman (written by Peter Garrison), was also used. A lot of experimenting was performed to generate a fully lofted P-51 in Loftsman that matched the "tracings" I had produced in Autocad. Loftsman has the capability to accurately generate a P-51 because it employs the methods used at North American (conic sections). All that is lacking for Loftsman to do the job is the longitudinal control lines it requires. So, in addition to Autocad tracings and Loftsman, a third parallel effort was started, to derive the necessary longitudinal control lines.

'Roy A Liming was in charge of loft mathematics at North American Aviation Inc, when the Mustang was born. The method of conic lofting he employed allowed NAA to systematically generate a design that was defined by equations that could be used as a benchmark for model makers, tooling designers, et al to accurately determine the xyz co-ordinate of any point on the design. At the same time, it was felt that using second-degree curves yielded a body with the lowest possible drag.

'Two books written by Liming, one of which is *Practical Analytic Geometry with Applications to Aircraft*, contain a lot of useful information on lofting methods used to design the original model NA-73 as well as the methods used to re-loft the airplane into the P-51A, B, and D models. Using this info and some Autocad routines I wrote to generate the longitudinal curves, the final loft was arrived at. The end result of this lofting effort gives me a benchmark to use with the rest of the blueprints.

'The P-51 blueprints in Autocad open up a lot of possibilities. Multi-view drawings at any scale are possible. CAD files can be generated and used as input for CNC machines to cut blanks and templates and to run laser cutters. Since the project is done as a 3D model, any view from any direction can be plotted and used as a basis for illustrations and art work.

'There are some missing NAA reports that tabulate the loft equations used for all the P-51 models. I know that there were "master dimensions books" used by NAA engineers. It would be interesting to see how the final loft I arrived at varies from the original design. Most of it matches the original but there are areas on the cowlings that may be suspect. Maybe in the computerised world of today I'm trying to generate an accuracy that did not exist in 1940.'

Another professional project is being undertaken by Charles Neely in Visalia, California. His efforts have been directed at capturing accurate shapes, geometry, and dimensions. I believe that he has succeeded.

You may think that unless you are restoring a Mustang or want to build a piece of major structure, drawings are not really that interesting. However, when you get into the detail and see some of the drawings, it becomes more obvious that these items themselves are important artefacts, a legacy left behind by hundreds of dedicated professional draughtsman of a different era. Couple this dedication with that of today's crop of professionals and their desire to preserve aviation heritage of a different type, all combined with modern technology, and the prospects are exciting.

The original North American Aviation Inc production line at Inglewood, California, with D model Mustangs as far as the eye can see!
Gene Boswell, North American Rockwell

Chapter Three

The Mustang Restoration Industry

low was the North American Aviation Mustang originally manufactured? In simple terms it was mass-produced on a continuous production line that saw the fuselage go in at one end as a raw centre-section manufactured around four main longerons and a stressed skinned structure, with all the internal fittings and controls in place.

As the production process progressed, sub-assemblies were added to make the fuselage complete before it was mated to the engine at the firewall. This included the tailcone to which the empennage and vertical tail fin and tail feathers were attached and the radiator and plumbing/systems installed. The engine, engine mount and all engine cowling frames were finished as a complete unit before being attached to the fuselage and mainplane. Remarkably the fuselage structure was attached to the mainplane at only four points, and the engine was cradled in the engine mount and fastened to the fuselage with just four high-tensile bolts. The fuselage was then hoisted for attachment to the mainplane and the final fitting-out of the fighter before it was rolled outside

for engine runs, cannon testing and then flight tests. It is widely recognised that the Mustang, which at 1945 costings was priced at just over $50,000 per airframe, was one of the simplest wartime fighter aircraft to produce. It consisted of 36,000 parts held together by a staggering 25,000 rivets.

Today the Mustang restoration industry is a very different prospect from the 'cottage industry' days of the 1970s and 1980s. As this book is being written there are some 40 Mustangs being rebuilt to flying condition and 139 airworthy aircraft. All of these aircraft require support in terms of airframe, engines, parts, systems, instruments (and avionics) as well as consumables. The ownership circle and those wishing to fly the type are also expanding and as such, pilot training facilities are also in demand – Stallion 51, based at Kissimmee, Florida, have been offering a high-standard training programme for many years now (see Chapter 8: *Flying the TF-51 Mustang*).

The sources of original NAA parts are far from exhausted but some of the harder-to-find items have to be remanufactured in

Typical of many of today's surviving Mustangs, 44-73029/N51JB Bald Eagle saw military service in South America before being brought back to the USA, where its flying career has included several years as an air racer. Tom Smith

order to keep the fleet airworthy and assist those restoring aircraft to flying condition. The most popular airframe model tends to be the classic bubble-canopy P-51D variant, though more recently there has been a trend to modify single-place Mustangs into full-blown dual-control TF-51D Mustangs. This is basically so owners can share their aircraft with others, and in a few cases so non-pilot owners can actually fly their own aeroplanes under close supervision!

The Mustang rebuild/restoration process has now reached very high standards. Though there are many companies specialising in the restoration and reconstruction of Mustangs from parts, the basic process is the same. It is the attention to detail and the time spent preparing the sub-assemblies that sets the award-winning aircraft apart from the rest.

In 1993 a rare photo-reconnaissance ve sion of the Mustang, the F-6D, showed up the Experimental Aircraft Association Annual Convention at Oshkosh, Wiscons where it was entered for judging in the EA Warbirds of America annual awards by owner, Henry 'Butch' Schroeder of Danvill Illinois. Butch had discovered the almc complete aircraft in a garage in St Louis, a had spent some 12 years restoring it wi help from Mike VadeBonCoeur (the resto tion of this aircraft was detailed in a book the author called *Mustang Restored* pu lished in 1995 and no longer in print) wl went on to form his own company, Midwe Aero Restorations Ltd, shortly afterwarc For many, the standard set by this aeropla was a turning point. Even the EAA's ov officers and judges agreed that the F-6D s a standard for others to aspire to.

Since then the art of Mustang restorati has developed still further, and Mil VadeBonCoeur says further research in the state the aircraft left the factory in h revealed even more detailed informatic about paint shades, decal and stencil det. and a lot more. Mike runs Midwest Ae Restorations from his base at Vermili County Airport in Danville, Illinois where is preparing his latest restoration for its fi flight and commencing another.

So, where does the restoration proce commence? With the majority of 'bask case' Mustangs now restored and airworth there are few aircraft available for acqui tion and subsequent restoration. Many the airworthy Mustangs are now eith approaching or past their second resto tion. As with all flyable warbirds, flight safe is paramount. As such the structural integr of the airframe is imperative.

It is worth examining the history of rest ing Mustangs before we go on. Musta restoration for civilian operation began the early 1960s. By then some of the a frames were just over 15 years old and, pa ticularly if they had not seen arduo military service, required little work to g them back into the air. At this time the a frames were relatively plentiful, and spar availability did not pose a significant pro lem to safe operation. You could buy a Mu tang for a few thousand dollars. Today, ev the youngest original airframe is approac ing its 60th birthday. An increasing amou of the structural material has to be replac

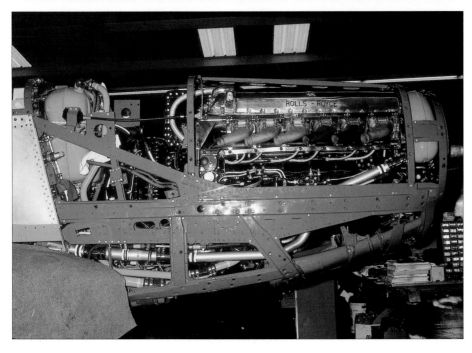

enable the Mustang to soldier on, and spares, though not critical in every area, are rarer and more expensive to procure. Though today's extant Mustang is worth between $850,000 and $1.4 million, the costs of maintaining such a thoroughbred have also risen significantly.

For restoration purposes, the Mustang can be divided into three major structural sections: the fuselage (including tailcone and empennage), the mainplane (wings), and the engine or powerplant (see Chapter 4)

The Fuselage

The fuselage centre-section, which carries the manufacturer's identity plate, is usually the starting point for most rebuilders. To maintain its structural integrity, the fuselage centre-section is usually secured inside a jig itself built to exact specifications from data available in original NAA drawings; there are now several drawings in use) for repair. The entire stressed skin structure contains the cockpit, oil and coolant radiators, and several other important sections. Compared to such contemporaries as the Supermarine Spitfire and Hawker Hurricane, the heart of the Mustang is a simple structure. The four extrusions, or longerons, run the length of the fuselage, from the engine firewall at the front end to the transport joint at the rear (at the junction with the tailcone) to which the empennage is attached.

In more recent years, the fuselage extrusions have been in most cases replaced during restoration, because they are both load bearing and known to suffer from stress corrosion largely due to their make-up and age. These factors make them prone to intergranular metal corrosion, which weakens the structure and could, in an advanced state, lead to total structural failure. The Merlin engine is bolted onto the engine mount in just four places, on the front end of each of the four longerons, with bolts that penetrate the armour-plate firewall. It is remarkable that the heart of the aircraft is secured to the aircraft with just four bolts.

The structure of the Mustang fuselage centre-section is based around four main extrusions that run the length of this unit. In simple terms these extrusions effectively hold the fuselage frames together and the stressed skin panels are riveted to the frames and longerons. Once corrosion attacks the extrusions, which are themselves stress loaded, they have to be replaced.

John Seevers has been instrumental in ensuring high-quality (certified) replacement longerons are available to undertake this important task. He takes up the story:

An unidentified TF-51 fuselage in the jig at Square One Aviation, Chino, California, after having new fuselage longerons installed.
Thierry Thomassin

Once the extrusions are fitted the fuselage can be removed from the jig. Author

'I've always thought the P-51 was an awesome aircraft and marvelled at its appearance, not to mention its sound. After my parents passed away I had the opportunity to purchase a project that had come from Indonesia. Serial number 45-11525 was stencilled on the side and the faint fuselage paint traces read "Texas Air National Guard". There was no data plate. Most of the pieces were there, but a lot had corrosion and problems. I decided to tackle the fuselage first, which needed four longerons. Upon investigation, I could not find that any were available and decided to make them myself. My background was well-suited to this as I am a Professor of Mechanical Engineering specialising in mechanical designs, manufacturing, and producing specialty mechanical devices. My hobby (passion) of airplanes was very helpful in "re-engineering" how and why the longerons were the way they were. I obtained a microfilm copy of the engineering drawings from Wright-Patterson and soon discovered that the prints were incomplete with respect to some important details, and had discrepancies with what was actually in my original North American-built fuselage. After studying the prints and the actual parts I was able to reconcile the differences. Then I built jigs and templates and refined the manufacturing processes to current standards and practices. A small production run was made and I installed all four longerons into my fuselage. They fit nicely so I guess I got it right. Since that time I have made several more production runs, and supplied longerons to many restoration projects worldwide. I take pride when I am told that my longerons "slip right in" and everything lines up, as it should. I keep certifications on all my material processes to document the product correctly. With the improved techniques in today's manufacturing processes, these longerons are truly better than those produced over a half-century ago. On occasions I have made the small upper longerons for the "hell hole" and the beams for the engine mounts to assist restorers in their projects. I am happy to offer advice based on my experience of working with longerons to anybody that is anticipating replacing any. I found some tricks that might save some grief later on.

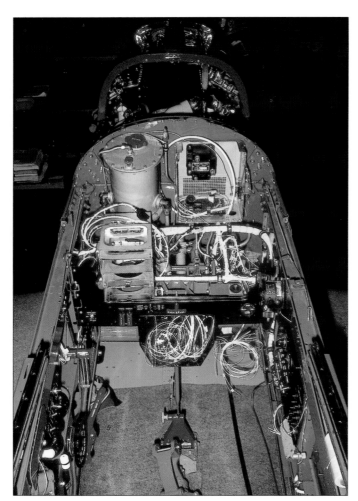

'I try to always have at least two complete sets in stock, so that I do not hold up any project. Since I left the Chino area I moved a few times and now live in McCall, Idaho.'

To install the new extrusions in the fuselage centre-section, the fuselage has to be placed in a special structure or jig. This maintains the structural integrity of the fuselage and prevents it twisting, ensuring a fit to the mainplane (to which it is fixed with four bolts), the tailcone, and the firewall/engine mount, once the longerons are in place. Most jigs have been proven having had a known 'straight' fuselage installed in them to ensure they work.

Once the basic fuselage structure is restored and painted internally, reassembly of the cockpit section, windscreen, canopy, seat (or seats, in the case of the TF-51), and fuselage systems including hydraulics, cooling and control systems, electrical wiring, and avionics can commence.

It is worth mentioning that the cockpit of the modern Mustang is one of two kinds. North American Aviation's original cockpit was painted cockpit green and fitted with standard wartime instrumentation. Today, cockpits are often painted light grey, which improves lighting conditions. Over the years, as the role of the aircraft has changed to that of a warbird and airspace has become more congested, some owners have adopted a more modern, ergonomic cockpit incorporating such equipment as GPS and extensive

radio fits. The instrument panel in some Mustangs looks more like that of a corporate jet than a World War Two fighter. Current instrumentation fits often include a comprehensive avionics package, and in some cases an electronic fuel flow system.

Comparatively recently, it has become more fashionable to restore Mustangs to a condition known as 'stock'. In other words, the aircraft is restored with authenticity in mind, to the point at which it looks exactly as it did the day it rolled off the production line. Restorers have even started replicating the original armament, including guns, camera guns, and a selection of bombs and rockets, based on drawings.

Henry 'Butch' Schroeder's F-6D N51BS set many precedents when it was judged EAA Warbirds of America Grand Champion Warbird (World War Two category) in 1993. Every little 'trinket', including all the special cameras, gunsight, flare pistol, and original armour plate (the restorers considered mocking this up with aluminium, but eventually decided to use the original and take the weight penalty) were incorporated. All of the original stencil markings on the airframe were either collected or reproduced over the 12 years Butch Schroeder and engineers Mike VadeBonCoeur and David Young spent restoring the aircraft. Although Mustangs had appeared with polished skin before, this one was absolutely immaculate. It set a trend.

Photographs, clockwise from top left:

The start of systems installation – again, Ed Shipley's P-51D-25NT 44-84634/N51ES at Pacific Fighters. Thierry Thomassin

Cockpit restoration under way on P-51D-20NA 44-72438/N7551T. The work was undertaken by Peter and Richard Lauderback at Stallion 51 Maintenance Operations. Tom Smith

Anders Saether's P-51D-25NA 44-73877/N167F was restored by Darrell Skurich of Vintage Aircraft Ltd, Fort Collins, Colorado. Darrell was one of the first proponents of light grey cockpit interiors and the cockpit was designed in close co-operation with the owner's requirements. Scandinavian Historic Flight

An interesting mix of old and new ideas – the cockpit of P-51D-20NA 44-63864/SE-BKG. This Mustang is scheduled for restoration by The Fighter Collection and the cockpit will be restored to full stock condition. The Warbird Index

A more stock cockpit is shown in this shot of Chuck Greenhill's P-51D-20NA 44-63655/ N5500S whilst being restored by Square One Aviation at Chino, California in 1998. Thierry Thomassin

The essential control positions are as per the stock Mustang but the cockpit of P-51D-25NA 44-72917/G-HAEC contrasts strongly with the cockpit green version. The Warbird Index

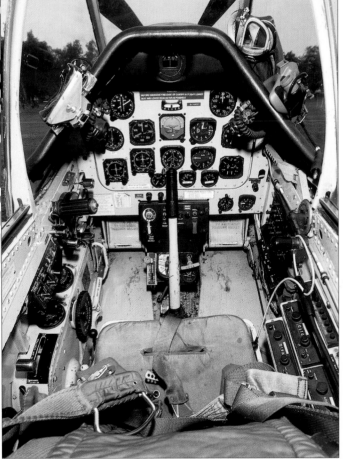

The Mainplane

It is almost always the fuselage that receives all of the detailing; in many instances the mainplane is relatively neglected in comparison. Structurally, the Mustang mainplane is a far more complex piece of engineering than the fuselage. Currently, three companies can repair a Mustang mainplane. Art Teeters' Cal Pacific Airmotive in Salinas, California – the first to get involved with the technique – has carried out many wing rebuilds and restorations. More recently, John Muszala's Pacific Fighters in Idaho Falls, Idaho, have been rebuilding Mustang wings.

North Dakota-based Bob Odegaard is also undertaking such work, and there are now several Mustangs airworthy with this repair work. For restoration, the mainplanes are separated in half and jigged before any major work is carried out. There is a trend for newly rebuilt Mustangs to carry replica armament, including guns (with moving parts) in the wings, inert bombs, and even replica rockets. Nelson Ezell and his team at Ezell Aviation in Breckenridge and Denton, Texas, have furnished one Mustang with ordnance it would have carried during the Korean War.

Another company supplied high-quality replicas of guns, and Brett Ward at Pioneer Aero Service in Chino, California, has a dwindling supply of original K-14 gunsights appropriate for the Mustang.

It is this sort of attention to detail that sets a 'Grand Champion' restoration apart from the average.

Everyone who has any experience with rebuilding or restoring Mustangs agrees on one thing: it takes time. For every hour actually spent working on the airframe, most will relate, you can spend three hours on the telephone chasing spare parts and specialist services. A rebuild is not for the faint-hearted. And, as restorers finish one aircraft, there is very often another waiting around the corner. The extraordinary thing about this is that the leading restoration shops say that they are still learning – learning how to do something differently next time, perhaps fit a particular part at a different stage or use a special paint or finishing agent in a different manner.

One exciting development is located in Florida, at Kissimmee on the appropriately named 'Merlin Drive'. Stallion 51 Maintenance Operations Inc is owned and operated by Peter and Richard Lauderback. They employ four other individuals, Martin Smith, Greg Wise, Mike Snyder and Scott Schirmer. Robert S Jepson, Jr, owns their current TF-51D project, formerly owned by Hess Bomberger as a single-control aircraft registered N6320T. This is a complete restoration. The fuselage was modified to TF configuration. The wing, tail section, engine mounts, flight controls, flaps and all cowlings are new. All components were rebuilt or purchased as new. Restorations typically take about two years to complete, which, when you consider the quality of work and the painstaking attention to detail, is a short time.

Besides restoring aircraft, Stallion 51 Maintenance Ops Inc also run routine maintain programmes on about a dozen other Mustangs, including the world-famous TF-51D *Crazy Horse*. This is practically a full-time job in itself.

Both Peter and Richard worked for Scott Smith and George Enhorning, starting out restoring their Curtiss P-40s and maintaining their Mustangs. Both P-40s were in need of total restorations. Scott Smith's P-40K was rebuilt to flying condition and is now owned by Evergreen Vintage Aircraft. George Enhorning's P-40K was 75% complete when he sold it. Twenty years later, Dick Thurman owns that aircraft – and Peter and Richard are working on it again!

As they were restoring the P-40s, they took apart George Enhorning's P-51D *Passion Wagon* and completely went through it. It got them hooked on the Mustang.

As the name suggests, Stallion 51 Maintenance specialises in the P-51. Peter and Richard have restored several Mustangs such as *Hell-er-Bust*, *Kentucky Babe* and *Slender, Tender & Tall*. One end of their hangar usually houses a restoration project and the other end is used for annuals and general maintenance. After 25 years in the industry they are still going strong. They say 'It's not easy, but we love it anyway. Well, most of the time!'

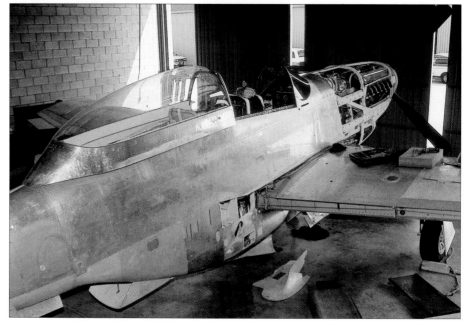

Mustang mainplane halves are mated together in the workshop of Cal Pacific Airmotive, Salinas, California. Art Teeters

Mating the mainplane to the fuselage requires a crane but again the two are bolted together in just four places. Square One Aviation restored this TF-51D-25NA for Doug Arnold of Warbirds of Great Britain Ltd. Author

Over the years a number of companies have specialised in providing restoration services to restoration shops and individuals, and in restoring aircraft and manufacturing new parts and major structures. One of the first companies to concentrate on the manufacture of major P-51 structures was Art Teeters' Cal Pacific Airmotive of Salinas, California. Art started in business in Eaton, Colorado in 1957, undertaking general aviation rebuilds and engine overhauls.

In 1976 Cal Pacific Airmotive Inc was formed at Salinas Municipal Airport. Two years later a customer asked if they could repair damage to a Mustang that belonged to a friend. That first repair job turned into a major restoration for the time. From that point they began building wings for the Reno Air Racers that included *Dago Red*, *Stiletto*, *Georgia Mae*, *The Healer* and *Precious Metal*.

From air racing, Cal Pacific's customer base became more orientated to museums and private collectors. Since then they have developed tooling and jig fixtures to rebuild nearly all of the sub-assemblies for the P-51A, B/C and D, and the rarer TF-51.

Recent work undertaken includes building up a TF-51, a P-51C and several P-51D sub-assemblies for completion by other shops. As an approved FAA Repair Station, Cal Pacific Airmotive have manufactured countless Mustang mainplanes and have refurbished and repaired several more, installing new wing spars and generally making safer new wings to keep the Mustangs airworthy well into the future. In 2001 Cal Pacific completed the restoration of an award-winning P-51C, N1204/42-103831 for Kermit Weeks in Polk City, Florida. The aircraft went on to win the EAA Warbirds of America Grand Champion award and Cal Pacific picked up the prestigious Golden Wrench trophy in the World War Two category warbird awards.

Another company that has made a significant contribution to Mustang restoration and reconstruction is Gerald Beck's Tri-State Aviation in Wahpeton, North Dakota. The company began by manufacturing new fuselage sections and undertaking major wing repairs and re-sparring projects, as well as restoring their own D model Mustang projects and several for customers. More recent projects have included the completion of the Confederate Air Force's rarer P-51C, which was turned around very swiftly and to a high standard; and as this book was being written the company told me they were tooling up to manufacture P-51A parts and structures. To date, Tri-State have worked on and made major contributions to 23 different Mustang projects. One of the first of these aircraft to be restored was Chuck Greenhill's P-51D 44-63350/N51TK, which received major damage in a forced landing. Work done to this aircraft included new longerons and fuselage repair, new tailcone, horizontal and vertical stabilizers, new doghouse, rudder and dorsal fin. The

wing had all spars replaced and all but three wing skins had to be replaced. The project was completed and the aircraft flown away in June 1996.

Hot on the heels of this project was P-51D 44-74524/N51HR for Hank Reichert. This was built up using mainly ex-FAD structures and components from Brian O'Farrell in Florida and the project was completed in May the following year. Next in line was a different version, a P-51C, which was restored for the Confederate Air Force. This aircraft, P-51C-5NT 42-103645/N61429, had been under restoration by CAF volunteers at various locations for many years and Tri-State came on board to get the aircraft airworthy. It was completely restored with new longerons, and skins on fuselage and tailcone. Odegaard Aviation did the wing, fitted with all-new spars and 90% new skin. The aircraft was assembled to flyaway condition and completed in June 2001. This aircraft, known by the CAF as 'the red-tail project' was painted in a 302nd FS, 332nd FG colour scheme and coded A 42 to represent the Tuskegee Airmen.

Top: *Humble beginnings. Peter and Richard Lauderback and team mate the fuselage to the wing of a P-51D. This is in great contrast to the custom facility which now houses Stallion 51 Maintenance Operations Inc at Merlin Drive, Kissimmee, Florida, where the company maintain ten Mustangs and have a constant stream of restorations passing through the facility.* Stallion 51

Above: *P-51A-10NA 43-6251/N4235Y during its restoration by Fighter Rebuilders at Chino, California.* The Warbird Index

Photographs on the following spread:

Art Teeters and crew at Cal Pacific Airmotive in Salinas restored Kermit Weeks' P-51C-10NT 42-103831/N1204 "Ina The Macon Belle", one of only four original P-51B/Cs, to exceptionally high standards. The attention to detail earned the company an EAA Golden Wrench award and the aircraft the coveted EAA Warbirds of America Grand Champion tag – hardly surprising when you look at the detail and workmanship both inside the cockpit and outside. All photos Tom Smith

Currently in the Tri-State workshops is P-51D-20NA 44-63476/N63476, an ex-Fuerza Aerea Uruguaya aircraft recovered from a lake in Uruguay. It has been completely rebuilt with a new fuselage, repaired tailcone and control surfaces. Odegaard Aviation have rebuilt the wing and all control surfaces as well as the engine mount and the restored aircraft is expected to fly in late 2002 or early 2003.

Tri-State have also undertaken the installation of dual controls in several Mustangs including 44-74466/N10607, 44-72051/N68JR and 44-63893/N3333E. Additionally, they have supplied numerous parts for overseas aircraft projects including Maurice Hammond's ex-RNZAF P-51D 45-11518/G-MSTG, and the Warplanes Fighter Pty CAC-built Mustang Mk.21 A68-110/VH-MFT which flew for the first time recently in Australia.

As mentioned earlier, Texas-based Ezell Aviation have restored several Mustangs, including examples from the famous Wilson 'Connie' Edwards P-51 store located at Big Spring in the same state. The most recent Mustang to be restored by Ezell Aviation was a P-51D-20NA for Richard Hansen (44-63663/N41749) painted in 55th FG colours as *Miss Marilyn II*. Research for the detailing of the aircraft was carried out by Chad Ezell. The same company also restored the beautiful Cavalier Mustang '44-10753'/N405HC *About Time* for the late Heber Costello.

In Chino, California, Elmer Ward founded Square One Aviation as a 'One Stop Mustang Shop'. Pioneer Aero Service was purchased from Joe Friedman in 1984 and was the forerunner of Square One Aviation. After operating the company for a couple of years, Pioneer Aero looked to invest in additional Mustang inventory. With this in mind they acquired the complete P-51 stocks from two notable individuals, Lefty Gardner and Gordon Plaskett. Following this acquisition, Pioneer Aero was able to make a bid for domination of the Mustang industry.

Shortly after this acquisition, Elmer Ward (owner of P-51D 44-72739/N44727 *Man O' War*) began planning the formation of a new company with the aim of restoring Mustangs

The massive wing jig at Square One Aviation. In the jig is the mainplane from Chuck Greenhill's P-51D-20NA 44-63655/N5500S.

At Square One Aviation the bolted-together mainplane of P-51D-20NA 44-63865/N151TF for Classic American Aviation, with the starboard wing fuel tank installed.

May 1992: Pacific Fighters begin the restoration of Ed Shipley's P-51D-25NT 44-84634/N51ES. Its first post-restoration flight was in July 1993. All Thierry Thomassin

Pioneer Aero Service purchased the P-51 stocks of several well-known collectors including several original Mustang fuselages, two of which are seen here in store in 1991. Author

A rare and clean-looking Cavalier Mustang Mk.2, N405HC was restored by Ezell Aviation of Breckenridge, Texas for Heber Costello. Sadly, Heber was killed in a non-Mustang related aviation accident only a few months after this photo was taken. Uwe Glaser

to the highest standards possible. Thus, in 1987, he directed Pioneer Aero Service to build a potential award-winning Mustang. Utilising original components from Pioneer Aero's inventory, they embarked on a project for Warbirds of Great Britain. Keeping in mind at all times originality as a baseline, the company also planned and undertook a revision of the cockpit layout and the instrument panel with the pilot in mind.

From 1987 Pioneer Aero Service rebuilt two P-51Ds and two full dual-control TF-51s. In 1995 a decision was taken to separate the parts business and launch a new company to run the rebuild business. This resulted in the creation of Square One Aviation. The latest project to emerge from Square One is Chuck Greenhill's P-51D 44-63655/N5500S, which is painted in spectacular 361st FG markings as *Geraldine*.

At Pioneer Aero Service, all parts sold are either original North American Aviation or remanufactured to original North American Aviation specifications from drawings or original parts. Pioneer Aero offer kits to update and overhaul hydraulic lines and reservoirs, coolant and oil lines, tail wheels, and to install replica guns. Additionally, Pioneer Aero say they are the only company with original Temco drawings, allowing them to manufacture Temco parts for the dual-control 'TF' version of the Mustang.

In Idaho Falls, Idaho, John Muszala's Pacific Fighters have also established an excellent reputation for restoring Mustangs. One of the first was a P-51D for Ed Shipley (44-84634/N51ES), which was flown to Oshkosh in 1993. Since then the company have worked on several more Mustangs, including a special project for Bill Allmon (P-51D 44-84900/N51YZ) which saw the fitting of much non-standard and historical equipment used on the aircraft when it was in service with NACA. More recently the company have undertaken structural work for the UK-based Fighter Collection's P-51C (43-25147/G-PSIC, approaching completion in the UK as this book is written) and have launched a new programme to recreate the rare and much sought-after 'razorback' Mustang. Apparently they already have their first orders for the latter.

There are several other companies and individuals who restore Mustangs and provide parts and major structures to the growing Mustang restoration industry. Glenn Wegman of Fighter Enterprises in Fort Lauderdale, Florida has been rebuilding Mustangs for many years – his latest project is a P-51D (44-72059/N951HB) for Vintage Aero Inc of Wilmington, Delaware. Dennis Schoenfelder, based in California, has been involved in quietly restoring Mustangs for many years now, including the aircraft recently acquired by film star Tom Cruise; a rare F-6K version (44-12840/N51EW) operated by Valhalla Aviation of Los Angeles.

At Falcon Field, Mesa, Arizona, Dave Goss of GossHawk Unlimited has also restored several aircraft including the famous E D Weiner racer '14' (44-72902/N335) for Violet Bonzer. Dave has also undertaken significant work on an original Temco TF-51D (44-73458/N4151D), working out some of the more modern modifications and cockpit items, replacing them with authentic items and stock equipment and generally improving the work previously done to the aircraft.

In California, Steve Hinton's Fighter Rebuilders have also done their fair share of Mustang restoration work over the years, including a very special P-51D – *Platinum Plus* – for the late John R 'Jack' Sandberg. Jack purchased 44-72051, an ex-FAD airframe, in 1988, from Brian O'Farrell. Also included were significant parts and new cowlings. It was Jack's intention to have 'the best Mustang' restoration possible and an extraordinary amount of effort went into personalising the aircraft for Jack's own use, including the building of a Merlin engine in his own shop, JRS Enterprises of Minneapolis, Minnesota. The aircraft was completed and flown regularly by Jack until his untimely death in a flying accident in the Unlimited Air Racer *Tsunami* in 1991.

Other companies that have worked magic on Mustangs include Fort Wayne Air Service of Baer Field, Indiana, largely under the control of John E Dilley. As you look through the Mustang histories you will see Dilley's name mentioned frequently. Their projects include TF-51Ds *Scat VII* (44-72922/N93TF), for Jim Shuttleworth, and *Mad Max* (45-11559/N151MX) for Max Chapman.

The list would be incomplete without a mention of Darrell Skurich of Vintage Aircraft Unlimited at Fort Collins, Colorado. Darrell has restored many aircraft to fly including the unique XP-51 owned by the Experimental Aircraft Association and now in the museum at Oshkosh, Wisconsin.

Jay Wisler of Warbird Parts in Tampa, Florida has been providing the 'trinkets' associated with detailing Mustangs (and other warbirds) since the 1970s and is an expert in locating hard-to-find items to complete the most stock of P-51s. Former Mustang owner Richard Ransopher, a retired airlines engineer based in Land O'Lakes, Florida, now specialises in North American Aviation types and can provide a multitude of North American Aviation spares, including hundreds for the Mustang.

As this book was about to go to press a German based company, Flug Werk GmbH announced they would be manufacturing major Mustang structures.

The company are now offering structural assemblies; complete wings, which will be followed by empennages and fuselages in the near future. Assemblies can be ordered individually to enable them to be incorporated into existing restorations and for repair work to original airframes. The Flug Werk structures conform to all North American Aviation specifications. Western materials, complying with all US airworthiness standards, are used throughout the construction of the airframe components.

The first mainplanes will be available at the end of 2003. They are ready to be mounted to an existing fuselage, or can be combined with the new-production fuselages/empennages right out of the Flug Werk production. Flug Werk will commence the construction of the fuselages approximately six months after construction of the first wing panels.

During the writing of this book I discovered several other companies which are about to embark on major manufacturing projects in support of the Mustang.

These are just a few of the dozens of people and companies working towards keeping the Mustang in the air. I wonder what the workers at North American Aviation would have said if they had known how many of the aircraft they were putting together in the 1940s would still be flying in the year 2002? Fly Warbirds!

Temco TF-51D-25NA 44-73458/N4151D has gradually been 'upgraded' to stock condition for its owner under the auspices of GossHawk Unlimited. Alan Gruening

P-51D-25NA 44-72902/N335, E D Weiner's famous racing Mustang, during restoration by Dave Goss of GossHawk Unlimited at Mesa, Arizona for owner Violet Bonzer. Alan Gruening

The same aircraft outside the GossHawk Unlimited facility following completion of the restoration work by Dave Goss and his team. Though most Mustangs wear military paint schemes, others are properly painted to reflect their air racing heritage. This is one such aircraft, having been raced and owned by the same family since 1964. Alan E Gruening

John Muszala (principal, Pacific Fighters) at the controls of P-51D-25NT 44-84634/N51ES Big Beautiful Doll *for engine runs*. Thierry Thomassin

Pacific Fighters' first P-51B fuselage in the jig at the company's facility in Idaho Falls, Idaho. Frank Mormillo

Two fine examples of the Mustang restoration industry's work close in on the camera. Up top is P-51D-20NA 44-72145/N51PT; below and behind is P-51D-30NA 44-74524/N151HR.
Uwe Glaser

Chapter Four

Mustang Powerplants

Past, Present and Future

The Rolls-Royce and Packard-built Merlin engine is universally acknowledged as one of the finest piston engines ever manufactured. Remarkably, over 50 years have elapsed since the last Merlin engine rolled off the production line, yet it is still in widespread daily use in warbird aircraft, not least of all the Mustang. Just as North American Aviation would never have envisaged their Mustangs would still be flying, Rolls-Royce probably never even considered that their beautiful Merlin powerplant would still be in front line service' in the 21st century.

For all Mustang operators the safe and efficient operation of the powerplant is critical to their own safety and well-being in civilian Mustang operations. To better understand what is happening to the Merlin engine today, a potted history of the powerplant is in order.

The overall success of this famous engine is built on one simple fact. Most will concur that by employing technology many years

ahead of its time, fuelled by the urgency of war, Rolls-Royce produced a piston fighter powerplant that is still without equal.

By the time the Battle of Britain was at its peak in August 1940, the Merlin had already undergone more than ten years of development, consolidated with thousands of hours of research by Rolls-Royce and its associated companies. Using some of the finest engineering and research staff in the world to develop the engine series, and with access to significant resources, the Merlin evolved at a record pace. With the prospect of a world war looming, Great Britain was heavily dependent on the development and production of what was then high tech equipment to meet the Nazi threat head on.

Today, in the early years of a new century, many engine specialists insist the Merlin remains state of the art for piston engine technology. Rolls-Royce ably met the challenge of creating an engine that would pro-

Oakland, 14 August 1980 – P-51D-25NA 44-73149/N6340T with the late John Crocker in the cockpit doing engine runs and Stephen Grey observing proceedings. William T Larkins

duce horsepower equivalent to its weight and displacement at high altitude, an area in which US piston engines of the time were found to be lacking.

Ironically, but not untypical of British industrial practice in the 20th century, the British government, through the Air Ministry, declined to fund a new engine in spite of the Schneider Trophy successes of the early 1930s. In December 1932 the Rolls-Royce Board, in the true sprit of British entrepreneurship, elected to finance the engine themselves as a private-venture project. Thus, early developments of the engine were designated P.V.12. No one could have envisaged that this step would contribute so significantly to the Allied victory in the air.

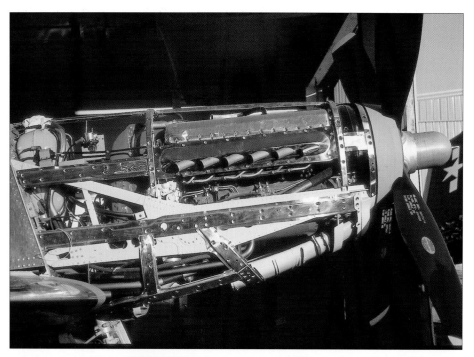

At this stage the Air Ministry recognised the engine's potential and decided to fund its development. The P.V.12 emerged as the now-famous Merlin. Various evolutions of the engine emerged until, in December 1935, the Merlin F was scheduled for production (with some modification) as the Merlin I for the Hawker Hurricane and Fairey Battle. Just short of 200 units had been delivered before it was realised that further improvements were required. Initially designated Merlin G, the Merlin II replaced the Merlin I on the production line in the first few months of 1937. Already the Merlin was developing just over 1,000hp at 3,000rpm. The new powerplant called for the modification of engine controls and installation for both the Hurricane and Battle.

By 1937 Ernest Hives had taken over the managerial control of Rolls-Royce's Derby works and sanctioned the production of a 'racing' Merlin. Initially this unit ran for some 15 hours at 1,800hp and some short bursts at 3,200rpm producing 2,160hp at 27 lb boost. This was conducted using 100-octane fuel. This was a turning point in the successful development of the Merlin at a critical time in the history of free Europe.

Few would dispute the Battle of Britain was won as a result of the Merlin II and III. Another significant development was the brilliant discovery by a Miss Shilling, a scientist at the Royal Aeronautical Establishment, who designed a most simple system – a small metal diaphragm in the float chamber of the carburettor – that enabled the engine to continue running in negative *g* situations in combat.

1938 saw Stanley Hooker join Rolls-Royce. It was Hooker who concentrated on the development of the Merlin's supercharger. Even modern-day Merlin rebuilders will tell you the engine's supercharger is the finest of its type ever produced. Why? Because it improves the power envelope from 12,000 to 40,000 feet. This unit is at the heart of the engine's remarkable performance over a significant altitude range.

At the beginning of World War Two and the beginning of the Battle of Britain, every RAF front-line fighter aircraft was fitted with the Merlin. One of the main Luftwaffe tactics was low flying and the sea-level power of the Merlin had to be enhanced as a result. Rolls-Royce achieved a 40% increase in power at sea level due to supercharger development, which forced the Luftwaffe to fly higher to combat British air superiority at low level. With the success of supercharger development the Merlin XX and Merlin 45

Early in 1933 Rolls-Royce decided to proceed with a conventional V-12 engine with cylinders 5.4 x 6 in (1,649 in³) which would start out at 750hp and be developed through 1,000hp. In a cruel twist of fate, Henry Royce died on 22 April 1933 – the day that the last P.V.12 drawing left the boards.

The early signs for the P.V.12 were disappointing after its first runs in mid-October 1933, and this did not bode well for the future. One of the major problems that plagued the new engine was the cracking of the then revolutionary aluminium monobloc casting that kept cracking through the water jackets. (In the early 1940s such cracks were being routinely repaired as engines were constantly run at full combat settings and generally abused in the heat of battle.)

Perhaps by sheer good luck a P.V.12 came through a test in July 1934 at almost 800hp and 2,500rpm, and by April 1935 one had been installed in a Hawker Hart and had flown.

The late John 'Jack' Sandberg gives the JRS Merlin in TF-51D-25NA 44-73458/N4151D a full-tilt engine run at Mesa, Arizona. Jack would often oversee the engine installation himself. Alan Gruening

The late Dave Zeuschel overhauled this Merlin using transport heads and banks. It was installed in Mustang G-PSID when with The Fighter Collection at Duxford. Mike Shreeve

Lee Lauderback of Stallion 51 puts the Merlin through its paces prior to a flight in P-51D-20NA 44-63810/N451BC Angels' Playmate. Author

were introduced into the Spitfire and Hurricane, thus enabling the Royal Air Force to maintain fighter supremacy.

During the war years over 150,000 Merlin engines were manufactured in the UK and USA. The Packard Motor Car Company undertook the latter and it was this version that was to power the legendary North American Mustang. However, unrecognised by many are the huge differences in the Packard-built version.

Packard manufactured some 57,000 Merlin engines, over one-third of all Merlin production. From its earliest version the Merlin was clearly a precision, hand-built work of engineering art constructed by some of the best British engineers. Even in its infancy the powerplant was built in small lots and had a string of design changes incorporated in an effort to squeeze performance and increase reliability in combat situations. The problem was that this was not an engine designed for mass production, so in 1940, when the British Government turned to Packard for help with production of the Merlin, some provisos had to be made.

In June 1940, Packard were requested to undertake the production of some 9,000 Merlin XX engines. It took just three days for the company to respond positively, but on the proviso that some modifications would be made to the powerplant to enable American accessories such as carburettors and fuel and vacuum pumps to be utilised. Packard then began the monumental task of organising an engineering group to handle drawings and redesign for American production. Packard also organised US sources for carburettors, magnetos, spark plugs and other accessories. Packard assigned some 200 personnel to the project, this figure including the draughtsmen who would undertake complete revisions of production drawings.

At the outset the Packard engineers ran into problems, generally due to the fact that the engine was not designed for mass production. That the project was completed at all is testament to the determination and skill of those assigned the task. At Rolls-Royce, engineers had been assigned to the project and many had stuck with it through stages of rapid development. Their experience and skill grew with this engine development as it progressed through various stages from 1935. Much of the detail required for Packard's mass production plans was missing because Rolls-Royce

worked very differently, depending on skilled craftsman and a depth of knowledge and experience built up as a result of working on the hardware itself.

Because British drawings were all in first angle projection as opposed to the American standard of third angle projection, they all had to be redrawn. To complicate matters still further, there were no sub-assembly drawings. Consequently, such details as stud lengths and overall dimensions of sub-assemblies were missing. It was necessary to utilise a finished engine and lay out sub-assemblies as the basis of the new drawings. The drawings did not specify fits or tolerances and the Packard engineers had great difficulty in obtaining complete information. However, the biggest problem was the necessity to duplicate British threads. The British system utilised four different standards: BSP (British Standard Pipe), BSW (British Standard Whitworth), BSF (British Standard Fine) and BA (British Association). Additionally, Rolls-Royce had also modified some of these threads. Throughout the Merlin engine there were 134 different external threads used.

Another relevant factor was the Rolls-Royce practice, at the time, of not utilising specific tolerances, practising instead the use of the engineer's own judgement based on 'assembly line' experience. This was not possible with mass-production procedures where less-experienced mechanics would be assembling engines. Packard devised a means of indicating tolerances by colouring

the head of the bolts yellow, black or blue for light, medium or heavy fits respectively. So, taps were made and holes marked in the blocks with the appropriate colour to indicate the degree of fit. This was particularly relevant where too tight a fit would destroy threads.

Drawings provided by Rolls-Royce indicated the position of oil lines and fire-suppressant lines but dimensions were conspicuous by their absence. However, Packard assumed that the drawings for the bent tubes were accurate, though o

Photographs on the opposite page:

You can almost hear the Merlin engine roar as P-51D-20NA 44-72035/F-AZMU *Jumpin'-Jacques climbs away from the Duxford runway and tucks up its undercarriage at the start of its display routine in concert with various other Mustangs.* Jim Winchester

A busy pit area at the Reno Air Races – where engine power really counts – as Dago Red *is prepared to race (to victory) in the Unlimited Gold, piloted by Bruce Lockwood.* Tom Smith

Below: *The moment of truth – a newly installed Merlin crackles into action for the first time in January 1985. This Merlin was overhauled by Jack Hovey of Hovey Machine Products, Ione, California and installed in P-51D-30NA 44-73149/N6175C, restored by Fort Wayne Air Service. The aircraft is now based in New Zealand as ZK-TAF.* RNZAF Photograph

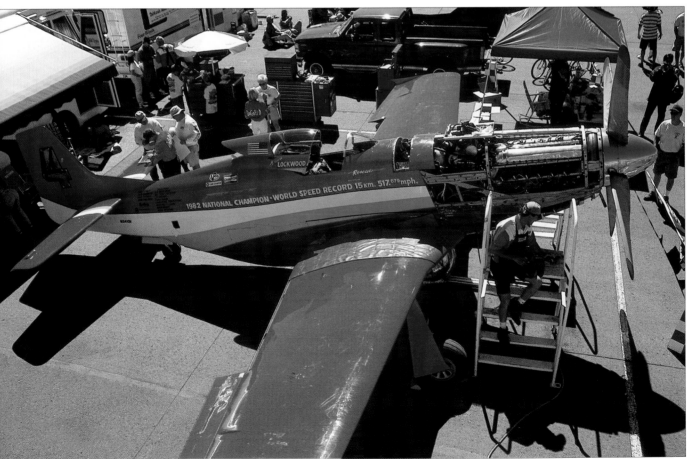

inspection it was soon discovered that the tubing on the sample engine did not match the drawings.

Drawing changes also caused problems. It was a British standard operating procedure to note changes to drawings by making a circle containing a number in the corner of a drawing. However, there was a lack of indication on the drawing itself as to when and why the change had been made. Apparently this information was circulated to the relevant departments in the form of memorandums. According to some sources, often changes were not recorded at all. An example of this was when Packard engineers discovered castings they had made from drawings did not match those on the sample engine. Investigations revealed the castings were thicker in parts than indicated on the drawings – Rolls-Royce engineers had simply beefed up the castings where they suspected they would be too weak to handle pressures. Rolls-Royce in England and Packard in the United States were undertaking some 400 alterations per month and so it became vital for both companies to liaise.

As in the case of the design drawings the material specifications submitted by Rolls-Royce were incomplete and not compatible with American standards. William Graves, Chief Metallurgist at Packard at that time was tasked with developing material specs for the American-manufactured Merlin. This involved considerable work and taking into account British manufacturing procedures. For example, Rolls-Royce specified nitrided steel for the Merlin crankshafts; this gave results superior to American steels then in use. Conversely, during the course of manufacturing the Merlin engine in the USA, improvements were made in the aluminium alloys used in the manufacturing of the engine which resulted in an alloy with considerably higher yield strength without a sacrifice in ductility.

After the end of hostilities, the Merlin saw extensive commercial service, particularly

in Great Britain and Canada, well into the late 1950s. The Merlin 600 and 700 series were the subject of most testing and modification. It is also relevant that the Merlin was still in service in military aircraft right up until the early 1980s.

In 1999 the Gathering of Mustangs & Legends, held at Kissimmee, Florida, saw some interesting seminars conducted for the benefit of all those Mustang owners and rebuilders present. Representatives from the world's leading Merlin shops in the United States were present. Vintage V-12's Mike Nixon, Jack Hovey of Hovey Machine Products, Paul Szendroi of Universal Airmotive, and Dwight Thorn of Mystery Aire Ltd faced some interesting questions about the state of Merlin rebuilding today.

Later, Dwight Thorn told me: 'I became involved with the Merlin in the early 1960s. Seattle was a hotbed of unlimited hydro racing, and most of the teams were based there. When Chuck Lyford got a Bardhal sponsorship for the 1964 Reno race it really put us on the fast track.

'Wear and corrosion are taking a heavy toll on the remaining Merlin parts. Some of the simple parts can be recreated. We have current test programmes for pistons, liners, camshafts, heads and skirt castings. These components are used in our racing engines. Mystery Aire shares its operational knowledge very freely with anyone, whether a customer or not. We encourage our customers to communicate any detail regardless how small regarding their engine as we feel that we are in partnership with them, sustaining the safe operation of their aircraft. Our website, www.mysteryaire.com is up to function as an information-clearing house.

'MAD was created when I left corporate aviation for the last time about 1975. A grizzled old associate of many aviation years carried a business card entitled SAM (Secret Air Motive), a fictional entity. So MAD was an easy reach.'

Mike Nixon of Vintage V-12's has also been building Merlins for many years for

both stock warbird applications and air racers, but has seen a reduction in air racing engines coming into his shop in Tehachapi, California. Most of the owners these days want stock-looking military-style engines the way they looked in the military.

Also in California is Jack Hovey of Hovey Machine Products based at Ione. Jack is the only Merlin builder that owns his own Mustang, 44-74602/N3580 which he has owned since 1967 – some kind of a record I'd guess. The founder of another Merlin shop, the late John R 'Jack' Sandberg of JRS Enterprises also owned a Mustang until his death in 1991 in *Tsunami*. Now Bill Moja and Sam Torvik run the shop which has also seen dozens of both stock and racing Merlins go through the rebuild process over the years. Last but not least is Universal Airmotive of Riverwoods, Illinois. This company have been overhauling Merlins for almost 40 years, for all sorts of aviation companies and some air forces.

At the time of writing I calculate there are in the region of 700 Merlin engines (not counting museum static aeroplanes) in circulation amongst warbird operators, either installed in aircraft or held as spares. Some parts are in short supply and there are a number of programmes being undertaken to manufacture these items to enable the Merlin to run for another 50 years, adding yet more achievements to what is already a remarkable history.

Of course in its earlier variants the Mustang was powered by the Allison V-1710 engine. This is a much-maligned power plant and in the areas it was designed to operate in it did a wonderful job. But as the majority of Mustangs were Merlin powered the Allison tends to get washed over. The numbers of early model, Allison-powered Mustangs are, however, on the increase with one restoration company tooling up to make P-51A model structures. I am confident we will see more early models airworthy in the not too distant future. Additionally there are some later H model Mustangs also being rebuilt and I believe the P-51H has yet to see its day. Bud Wheeler of Allison Competition Engines in Latrobe, Pennsylvania, has, over the last 25 years, overhauled a large number of Allisons, amongst them a pair of engines for James 'Pat' Harker's rare F-82E-NA Twin Mustang (46-256/N142AM) project in Minnesota. Because Bud specialises in Allisons, his workload is likely to increase as the earlier-model restorations come into their own.

F-82E-NA Twin Mustang 46-256/N142AM is seen in the Amjet facility in Minnesota while under restoration. Now owned by James 'Pat' Harker, its Allison V-1710 engines were overhauled by Allison Competition Engines as part of the programme to bring the Twin Mustang back to airworthiness. Dick Phillips

Chapter Five

Painting and Finishing

Though thousands of dollars can be lavished on restoring a Mustang, one of the most important aspects has to be the way the aircraft is painted and finished.

Throughout its distinguished history the North American P-51 has been a colourful aeroplane, due in most part to the military markings created by the 8th Air Force of the USAAF in the European Theater of Operations (ETO). Today, the majority of Mustangs appear painted in these markings, and though some modern interpretations are more garish than those they seek to represent, the trend today is towards authenticity. For today's owner there are many considerations when deciding how a Mustang should be painted. With air racing Mustangs the aircraft has to be brightly coloured and in many cases provide a canvas for the sponsor's advertising message. For the private owner who does not rely on sponsorship the possibilities are endless.

When the military Mustangs were rolled off the production line at North American they were finished in a very basic way. The forward 40% of the wing leading edge was filled, sanded and primered and then painted silver. The fuselage was left in a bare metal finish with just the national insignia (star and bars); the fiscal serial was applied on the rudder. A myriad of instructional and

guidance stencils and warnings were then applied to the aircraft, as was the data panel which showed contract number, aircraft designation in full and military fiscal serial number. (Interestingly, because this data panel was applied directly to the new alclad metal, it prevented oxidation of the surface and has been a great identifier of aircraft identities over the years.) The aircraft would then generally be painted in unit markings either at the receiving base or the Base Air Depot before delivery.

One of the most interesting aspects of paint schemes has been the way aircraft were named for loved ones. In some units it was traditional for the pilot to have his selected name painted on the port side while the crew chief was similarly allowed to adorn the starboard side.

Today, there is a trend to have the mainplane painted and the fuselage left in the bare metal finish; but rather than leave them untouched, these metal sections are buffed to a high polish. Though it is not an accurate representation of the way Mustangs were, it looks very attractive. In some cases the fuselage is also painted, but often in tough wearing and high gloss silver (Imron being the most common); a far more appealing prospect if the owner does not want to spend half his life polishing the metal sur-

Though photographed at dusk, effective lighting of CAC Mustang Mk.22 A68-198/N286JB's highly polished bare metal finish helps to reveal the subtle variations in tone and finish on different panels and sections. Thierry Thomassin

face. In some cases there is a mix of paint and polished metal.

Some owners chose to paint all the markings in a high gloss paint, which strictly speaking is not correct. The correct finish was a matt one, though some owners go for gloss paint with a matting agent which provides a very pleasing semi-matt finish which is also very durable when it comes to cleaning and staining. The Fighter Collection at Duxford in the UK appear to have been the first people to use this on a 357th Fighter Group marked P-51D. The result looks very attractive and authentic.

There are several companies worldwide specialising in the painting of warbird aircraft. In North America by far the most prolific is the award-winning Sky Harbour Aircraft Refinishing of Goderich, Ontario, Canada. They have refinished 45 Mustangs at the time of writing and have been in the business over 50 years. Their most recent news has been the acquisition of a cross draft paint booth that can accommodate aircraft up the size of a Gulfstream IV corpo-

rate jet. They have a computer design department and this coupled with very experienced staff make them one of the leading choices for warbird paint.

So, what happens to an aircraft when it goes in for repaint? First of all, existing paint is chemically stripped from the airframe that is then hand cleaned with all fairings, inspection plates and controls removed. If any corrosion is found it is removed before the surface is washed with a metal preparation solution. The metal is then treated with a corrosion-inhibiting conversion coating. Following any bodywork rectification, seams are aerodynamically sealed with a seam seal compound if required. Next an epoxy filoform primer is applied, followed by a polyurethane topcoat. Metallic colours are clear coated for extra protection and a better finish. The design department can produce details for individual paint schemes and Sky Harbour have an excellent reputation for accuracy and customer satisfaction, based on reports received by the author. John Edwards, the paint shop supervisor, recently completed his 45th Mustang job!

Also in the United States is warbird paint specialist Dan Caldarale of Caldarale Aircraft Refinishing in southern New Jersey. Dan has been painting warbirds for many years now. One of his favourite projects was Tom Patten's ex-Indonesian Air Force Mustang, 44-73543/N151TP. The aircraft's skin was polished to a high metal finish before Dan applied the blue nose and then went on to detail all the markings. (Dan obtained details of the military markings years ago for his first Mustang job and these have been applied to every Mustang to leave the shop since.) All the other detail markings like the aircraft name, kill markings, and minor details are added by hand. Detailing the nose art is Dan's favourite part of the job. Perhaps the most demanding in this respect was the application of all the artwork to James Beasley's P-51K 44-12852, painted in stunning olive drab as the 357th FG's *Frenesi* and appropriately registered N357FG.

In the UK another master of his art with dozens of difficult and challenging warbird paint schemes under his belt – including several Mustangs – is Clive Denney who, with his wife Linda, runs Vintage Fabrics in Essex. Clive has a vast library of paint scheme and technical drawings for most types of warbirds and years of experience to enable him to apply these paint schemes in an expert manner. One particular aircraft that was painted by Clive in the UK for a French customer was a fairly complex 9th Air Force paint scheme – that of Captain Richard E Turner's *Short Fuse Sallee* – which, uncharacteristically for Europe, was applied to a polished bare metal surface. The aircraft is now back in the United States.

In addition, many restoration shops undertake their own painting to very high standards. As a result, the Mustang is undoubtedly the most colourful of all warbirds on the aviation circuit today.

Tony Buechler's P-51D-25NA in full view on a photo sortie out of the Wings of the North airshow in 1999, showing how effective the artwork is in adding to the class lines of NAA's finest. Bob Luikens, Wings of the North 1999

The 352nd FG is one of the most famous and most represented 8th Air Force Fighter Groups on modern-day Mustangs. Here, Barbara Plaskett is seen applying intricate artwork based on full-size drawings supplied by the author. Gordon Plaskett

The artwork finished, with all 26 kill markings and codes applied to P-51D-25NA 44-72942/N5427V Petie 2nd. The Warbird Index

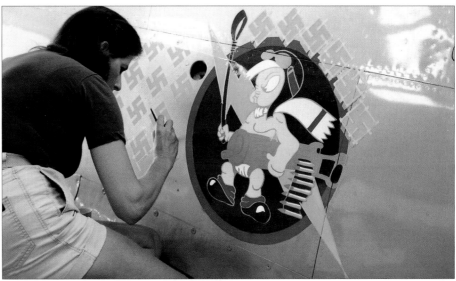

Photographs on the opposite page:

Before this F-6D fuselage was restored the owner carried out polishing trials to see what sort of finish was achievable! Author

Even the markings that will not normally be seen when the aircraft is on the ground are applied, like the sighting markings on the port wing of this F-6D. Author

The standard of painting and finishing has improved dramatically over the last 20 years. Some restorers paint after restoration of major structures, others paint prior to reassembly and some paint when the aircraft is complete. This port mainplane has had the internals painted and with all-new hardware fitted it already looks spectacular – if you know what you are looking at! Author

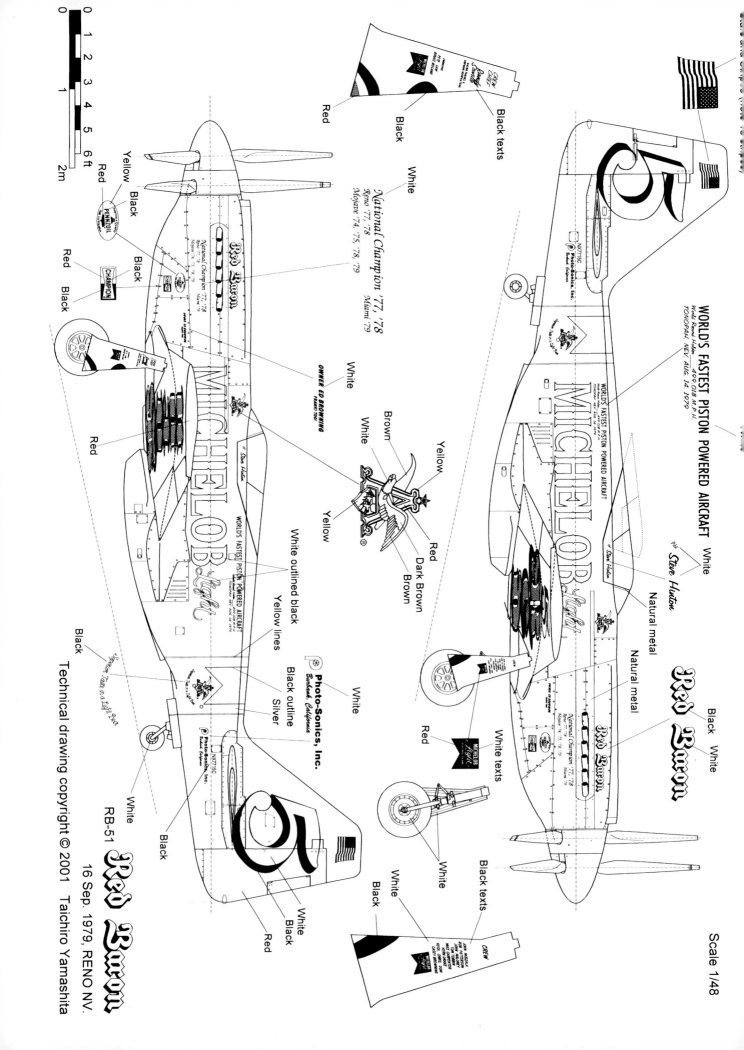

WORLD'S FASTEST PISTON POWERED AIRCRAFT

World Record Holder. 499.018 M.P.H.
TONOPAH, NEV. AUG. 14, 1979

plt Steve Hinton

White

Natural metal

Natural metal

Black   White

Red Baron

National Champion '77, '78
Reno 77, 78
Mojave 74, 75, 78, 79
Miami '79

MICHELOB Light

Red

White texts

White

Black texts

CREW
JOHN MUSCHALE
BOB PITTERSKY
DON WALLNEY
TOM TURNER
MIKE CARPENTER
KEVIN GANGE
KEVIN ORRES
DAVE BROWNLOW

White
Black

Photo-Sonics, Inc.

Scale 1/48

Black texts

Yellow
Red
Black

PENNZOIL

Red
Black

CHAMPION

Black

White
Black
Red

Red

5

Black

White

Photo-Sonics, Inc.
Burbank, California

Black

White outlined black
Yellow lines
Black outline
Silver

Superior Taste in a Light Beer

Technical drawing copyright © 2001   Taichiro Yamashita

RB-51   Red Baron

16 Sep. 1979, RENO NV.

Red

White

Brown
White

Yellow

Red
Dark Brown
Brown

Yellow

White

MICHELOB Light

National Champion '77, '78
Mojave 74, 75, 78, '79

Red Baron

White

WORLD'S FASTEST PISTON POWERED AIRCRAFT

OWNER   ED BROWNING
FRANK TROII

NX7115C

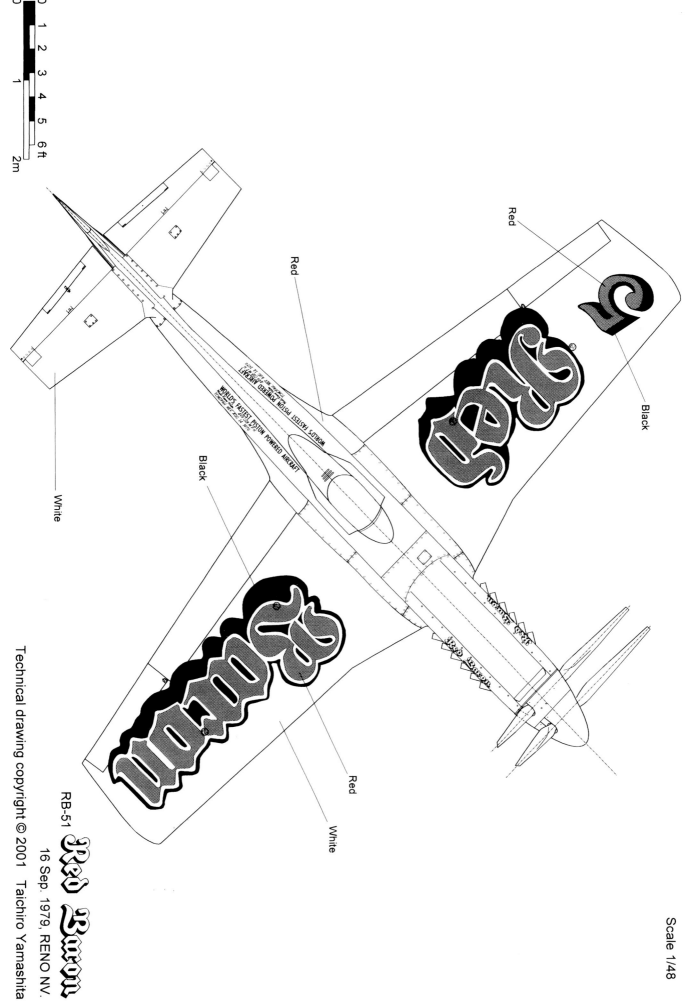

Red

Red

White

Black

Black

Red

White

WORLD'S FASTEST PISTON POWERED AIRCRAFT

WORLDS FASTEST PISTON POWERED AIRCRAFT

RB-51 Red Baron

16 Sep. 1979, RENO NV.

Scale 1/48

0 1 2 3 4 5 6 ft

0 1 2m

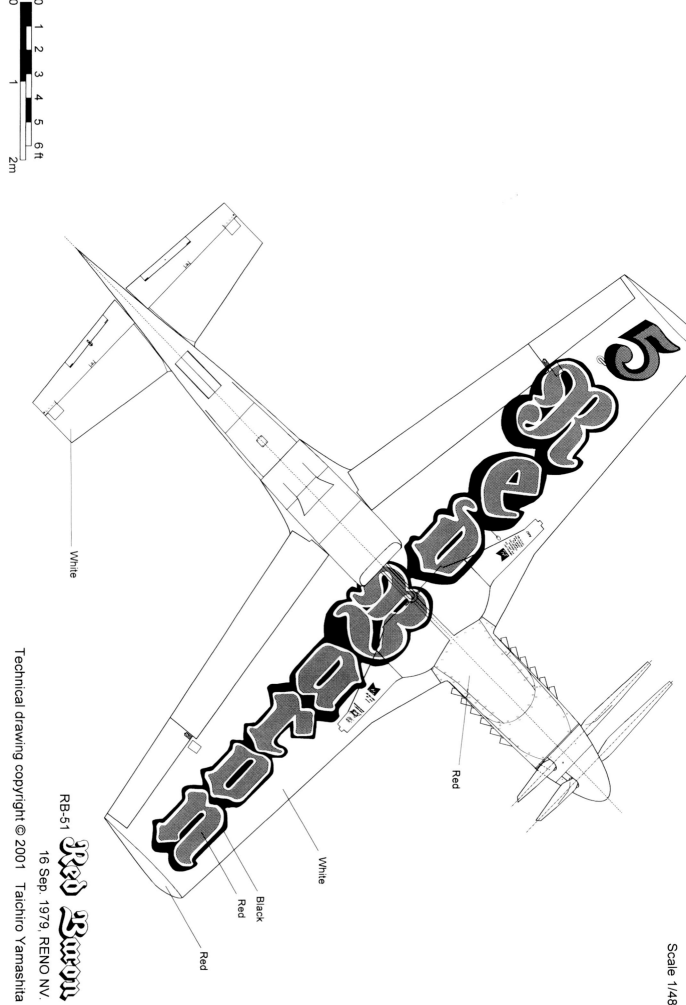

White

White

Red

Red
Black
Red

Red

RB-51 *Red Baron*

16 Sep. 1979, RENO NV.

Scale 1/48

5

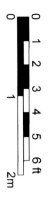

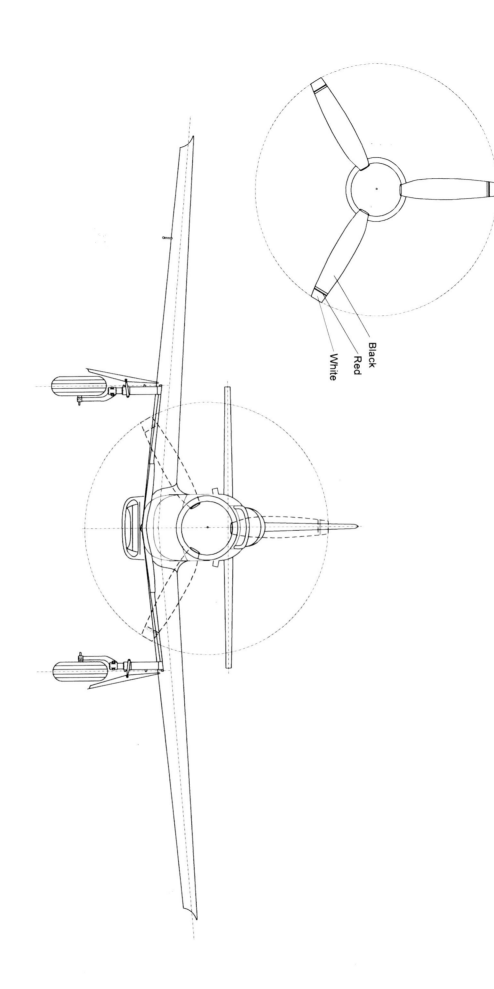

Black
Red
White

RB-51 Red Baron
16 Sep. 1979, RENO NV.

Scale 1/48

The Commemorative Air Force's P-51C-5NT 42-103645/N61429 nearing completion at Gerry Beck's Tri-State Aviation facility in Wahpeton, North Dakota. Note that the cowling's frames have all been painted prior to incorporation in the restoration. Some owners prefer to have the Rolls-Royce Merlin painted in standard military colours, others (as on this Mustang) simply go with the engine rebuilder's choice of paint.
James P Church

Another view of 42-103645/N61429 inside the Tri-State Aviation facility, and one which clearly explains why this was referred to as 'the red-tail project'. The aircraft was photographed in February 2001, just a few months before it took to the air once again.
James P Church

Principal at Vintage Fabrics is Clive Denney, seen here adding detail to a piece of Anglo-American artwork in his workshops.
via Vintage Fabrics

Photographs on the opposite page:

The paint scheme on P-51D-25NT 45-11391/ N51WT Nervous Energy V looks stunning against this dramatic but mundanely coloured backdrop. The late Jeff Ethell was flying the aircraft at the time. Joe Cupido

The same aircraft sitting outside Dan Caldarale's paint shop in New Jersey. The markings are a change from the usual 8th Air Force paint schemes that are prevalent and often repeated on P-51 survivors.
Bonnie Caldarale

P-51K-10NT 44-12852/N357FG in the paint shop of Caldarale Aircraft Refinishing – all masked up and with the first coat of paint going on over the primer. The aircraft was finished in the markings of the 364th FS, 357th FG as Frenesi. Bonnie Caldarale

An artist at work: Dan Caldarale carefully painting each of the kill markings on 44-12852/N357FG Frenesi. This is one of his favourite jobs when it comes to finishing the paint schemes and markings on historic warbirds. Bonnie Caldarale

Below, left: The quality and extent of the nose art are evident in this air-to-air study of Frenesi, which was decorated with mission markings, aircraft kills and a large-size name on either side of the nose. Robert S DeGroat

Photographs on the opposite page:

Square One Aviation rebuilt P-51D-20NA 44-63655/N5500S for Chuck Greenhill; it was then flown to Sky Harbour Aircraft Refinishing in Goderich, Ontario, Canada for painting and finishing as 414320/E2-B Geraldine, the personal markings of Major Chuck Cummins of the 375th FS, 361st FG. James P Church

John Edwards of Sky Harbour Aircraft Refinishing alongside his 45th P-51 paint job in the Spring of 2002. James P Church

Paul Sholdice, a local Goderich artist, painted the nose art for Geraldine. James P Church

Seeing if the paint sticks! Shortly after rollout from Sky Harbour Aircraft Refinishing, Tim McCarter brings Geraldine in for a low-level goodbye pass before delivering the aircraft to Chuck Greenhill. James P Church

Above left: *Photographed in 1944, this P-51D of the 487th FS, 352nd FG (coded HO-N and named* Sweetie Face*) is more representative of a Mustang in a combat unit. It sports flat paint, different shades of the famous blue and an unpolished natural metal fuselage, and is complete with mud caked tyres. However, present-day owners who choose to paint their aircraft in a gloss finish and highly polish that alclad skin can hardly be criticised – it looks so spectacular!* via Tom Patten

Above right: *Dan does a complete last-minute touch-up inspection on Tom Patten's P-51D-25NA 44-73543/N151TP* Sweetie Face, *to make sure the job is perfect.* Bonnie Caldarale

Left: Sweetie Face *artwork.* Uwe Glaser

Below left: *The Donald Duck character as applied to Robert Tullius' P-51D-30NA 44-74409/N51RT.* Robert S DeGroat

Below: Scat VII *artwork as applied to Jim Shuttleworth's TF-51D-25NA 44-72922/N93TF.* Robert S DeGroat

Some restoration shops do their paintwork in-house. Mike VadeBonCoeur's Midwest Aero Restorations painted Ken Wagnon's P-51D-20NA 44-74813/N151KW to represent Major George E Preddy's 44-14906 Cripes A'Mighty of the 328th FS, 352nd FG. This Mustang was awarded the coveted EAA Grand Champion Award at Oshkosh 2002. Mike is an expert at both rebuilding and detailing Mustangs and this aircraft is no exception. The former crew chief on the original Cripes A'Mighty, Art Snyder, provided a lot of help and advice on painting the newly restored Mustang. James P Church

The nose art was applied on the flat-painted nose of 44-74813/N151KW. There have been many different interpretations of the actual blue used on the Mustangs of the Bodney, Norfolk-based 352nd FG. Luckily, Mike VadeBonCoeur managed to locate some original paint chips from which the paint could be matched, rendering this beautiful powder blue colour. James P Church

487th FS, 352nd FG nose art as applied to Tom Blair's P-51D-30NA 44-74950/N51DT Slender, Tender & Tall. Uwe Glaser

Left: *Even the less colourful but original Mustang paint schemes can look better when accurately applied. Clive Denney of Vintage Fabrics applied the paintwork on CAC Mustang Mk.22 A68-198 which at the time was registered as F-AZIE* Short Fuse Sallee. *Richard Paver*

Below: *F-AZIE is now back in the United States where it is owned by William Bruggeman and registered N286JB.* The Warbird Index

Bottom: *Dan Martin's P-51D-20NT 44-13250/ N151DM wears the* Ridge Runner III *nose art of Major Pierce McKennon's 44-72308/WD-A when in service with the 335th FS, 4th FG.* The Warbird Index

Photographs on the opposite page:

Detail of the nose art applied to P-51D-25NA 44-72934/N513PA Shangrila. *Until a photograph appeared, it was disputed that Don Gentile ever flew a P-51D with this inscription.* Joe Cupido

After the author mentioned to David Arnold that one 4th FG paint scheme (that of Don Gentile's P-51D Shangrila, *painted post D-Day as a Fighter Group Victory Ship) had never been applied, he elected to paint 44-72934/N513PA in this scheme. Unfortunately, the only known photograph illustrated the nose of the aircraft, with Gentile posing by the aircraft, so the codes and aircraft serial were uncertain. But the rest made for a stunning-looking P-51D, as seen in this air-to-air with Elmer Ward at the controls.* Joe Cupido

Tom Cruise's F-6K-15NT 44-12840/N51EW Montana Miss *with artwork showing a scantily clad redneck girl toting a pair of six-shooters*. Author

P-51D-20NA 44-63663/N41749 as 1st Lieutenant E Robert Welch's Miss Marilyn II *of the 343rd FS, 55th FG.* Author

Chapter Six

Insurance

Robert Cannon, President and CEO,
Cannon Aviation Insurance Inc, Scottsdale, Arizona

Trying to buy insurance without knowing something about it yourself is like flying blind – you know for sure you'll fetch up somewhere, but that's about it.

You should be able to ask your agent or broker questions about your coverage and how it is placed and get answers that give you a better understanding of your protection and how it is obtained.

Most aircraft owned by individuals fall under the 'pleasure and business' class of insurance. The basic coverage available under this class are aircraft hull and liability.

Aircraft Hull
This insurance covers physical damage to the aircraft you own. This is different from the property damage covered under liability insurance; property damage covers your liability for damage to property of others that isn't in your care, custody or control.

Hull insurance can be written on a named perils or all risks basis (the latter is the most common). The basic difference between the two is that the first tells you what causes of damage (perils) are covered and the second tells you what causes of damage are not. In the first, you must prove that the peril was covered; in the second, the insurer must prove that it was not.

The type of insurance is subject to a deductible. Large aviation policies have only one deductible dollar amount that applies, but most pleasure and business policies provide for at least two deductibles: either in motion/not in motion or in flight/not in flight. Generally, the higher the deductible, the lower the cost of insurance. If you have a lien holder on your aircraft, they may specify maximum deductibles. Deductible amounts should represent the maximum out-of-pocket loss you can afford on an aircraft.

Policies differ as to what constitutes each type of deductible. For example, in some policies, an aircraft may be considered 'in motion' and therefore subject to a higher deductible unless it is at a complete stop. Others may consider an aircraft 'in motion' after it commences a take-off roll and until it completes a landing sequence.

When you are determining the amount of hull insurance to purchase, keep the market value in mind! If the insured value is lower than the market value and the aircraft is even slightly damaged, the insurer may decide to pay you the entire insured value. The insurer could then repair the damage, sell the aircraft

and make a tidy profit. They can do this because any aircraft declared a total loss belongs to the insurance company – and it is the insurance company's sole prerogative to decide if an aircraft is a total loss.

If the insured value is higher than the market value, your aircraft could probably be repaired at a lower cost than the value it is insured at, no matter how badly damaged it is. This would mean that, rather than paying you off for the tangle of metal in the meadow, the insurance company would repair it because to do so would be to save money.

This is not to say that you can never insure an aircraft for more than the 'blue book' value. If you have special equipment installed or the aircraft is in better than average condition, you may be able to push for a higher insured value. However, the insurance company will probably require you to substantiate your request.

One important thing to note about hull insurance is the function of the breach of warranty endorsement. A lien holder on an aircraft may require this in addition to the right to be paid directly in the event of a loss. Basically, the breach of warranty endorsement provides that if you perform an act, which voids the obligation of the insurance company to pay on your behalf (such as allowing non-approved pilots to operate it), the company will pay the amount of the lien to the lien holder, but the insurance company will require reimbursement from you.

Breach of warranty coverage is purchased in the amount of the lien, but this shouldn't necessarily equal the amount of hull insurance; otherwise, you are opening yourself up to underinsurance.

Liability insurance covers your legal liability to others. If you are held responsible for an act covered by the policy, the policy usually will pay on your behalf, although there may still be a few policy forms that will simply reimburse you. In its basic form, liability covers bodily injury and property damage arising from the use or ownership of the aircraft.

You can obtain liability insurance in a variety of different forms: Bodily Injury and Property Damage Excluding Passengers – Under this coverage, even if there were passengers aboard the aircraft who were injured, the insurance company would have no responsibility to pay for their injuries, leaving the burden of payment directly on your shoulders.

Bodily Injury and Property Damage Limited to $X per Passenger – Under this type of

coverage, any passengers who are injured or killed are limited to a maximum recovery under the policy. If the passengers and their estates do not feel the limit was adequate compensation, they then have the right to come after you for the rest. Common passenger liability limits are $100,000 or $300,000, due to high medical costs.

Combined Single Limit Bodily Injury and Property Damage – This can be written either including or excluding passenger liability. This is the best form of protection to buy because it allows the policy limit to be paid out as it may be needed rather than having limitations on how much can be paid to each passenger, how much can be paid for damage to property of others, etc. This is the most expensive option, but is the most flexible.

Because of the possibility of a high liability award, you should carry at least $1,000,000 in coverage. This may seem like a lot, but non-aviation types who suffer injury tend to figure that anyone who can afford an airplane can afford to pay out in a damages award.

Higher Limits of Liability
If you are very well off, fly in affluent areas of the country, or sometimes carry affluent people as passengers, you may want to carry higher limits because of the possibility of higher awards due to economic status. If you do carry higher limits, there are a couple of different types of quotes you should get.

First, ask your insurance professional to quote a higher limit within the same policy you have. This may sometimes be more expensive, but it does offer the convenience of only requiring one renewal each year. You may also be eligible for some discount on the higher limits because you have them with the same insurance company; and it also facilitates claims handling.

One of the tricks of the trade that insurance people use to get the best deal possible for higher limits is called 'layering', either with your primary carrier or another company. In this method you would purchase several layers of insurance that add up to the amount you feel you need. Each layer will cost less, based on the theory that smaller losses occur more frequently than larger losses. Insurance companies with higher layers figure they simply have less chance of being called on in the event of a loss.

If you are using the layering method however, *be careful*. If possible, get what is known as a 'following form'. Under this type of insurance policy, the excess policy raises your limits and follows the wording of your policy exactly.

If you don't get a following form, have your insurance professional make sure that there are no gaps or overlaps in coverage. This problem can arise when the excess policy doesn't cover something important in the primary policy, or when the excess policy requires a higher limit than you have in the primary policy. You will be responsible for the difference if this happens! Overlaps occur when the excess policy will operate above a lower limit of primary insurance, or when certain events are covered twice (you will only get paid once).

Medical Payments and
Personal Accident Insurance

As always, there are other types of protection you can buy. For example, Medical Payments coverage acts as a type of no-fault coverage. Regardless of whether your actions caused an injury or the other person's own carelessness led to injury, Medical Payments will pay up to a certain amount of first aid and medical treatment rendered to that person within a specified period of time (usually one or two years). Common limits range from $500 to $10,000 per person. Aircraft crew can be included or excluded from Medical Payments benefits. When selecting Medical Payments limits, remember to keep current health care costs in mind.

Personal Accident (PA) is a handy low-cost coverage to have on hand. Basically it is an accidental death and dismemberment coverage that will cover you while you're flying, unlike most life or health insurance policies. This coverage is extremely flexible and can be tailored to a wide variety of coverage limits and types of coverage. Unlike the other coverage detailed earlier, it is unavailable in a standard hull and liability policy, and must be purchased from an agent or broker who is licensed to obtain this type of insurance.

Policy Warranties

When you 'warrant' something in an insurance application, you are promising that it is true to the best of your knowledge – and if you go against your promise the insurance company doesn't have to pay. Your signature on the application warrants that you haven't misrepresented yourself to the insurance company, but the policy itself contains two warranties.

The pilot warranty and territorial limits are requirements to keep coverage in force rather than a statement of truth. Both impact your insurance rates. For example, it is more expensive to have a worldwide policy territory than one that is for the United States only because you are likely to be more knowledgeable about flying in your own country than in others.

There are two types of pilot warranties: Open Pilot Warranty or Named Pilot Warranty. Under an Open Pilot Warranty the underwriters state the minimum acceptable pilot qualifications (such as type of ticket, number of hours total time, etc) for anyone flying your aircraft. The higher the qualifications, the lower the price should be. A Named Pilot Warranty states the names of the people the insurance company has approved to fly the aircraft. All things being equal, a Named Pilot Warranty is less expensive than an Open Pilot Warranty because it is more restrictive.

The insurance company, contrary to popular belief, is not telling you who can fly your aircraft in a pilot warranty. They are telling you that, given the amount of premium you have paid, this is the most risk they are willing to take in terms of the pilot(s). Most insurance companies will be happy to charge you more for less-qualified pilots, but the cost may be more than you are willing to pay.

You should note that if the pilot in command at the time of the loss does not meet the pilot warranty, the insurance company has absolutely no obligation to pay, regardless of whether the pilot in command caused the loss or not.

The same goes for where the insurance company provides coverage. Many pleasure and business policies will pay for losses when the aircraft is operated in the United States (excluding Alaska), Canada and the Bahamas or while en route to those areas. If you are outside these territories when you go down, you are out of luck as far as getting any money from the insurance company. Check with your agent or broker if you plan to fly outside these areas, and purchase the appropriate insurance. Mexico and Canada both require liability insurance if you will be flying to a point in their respective countries.

Special Warbird and
Classic Jet Insurance Needs

Warbird and classic jet owners usually want to do more with their aircraft than it around for personal pleasure, so it is important to ensure that the so called 'special uses' are covered: fly-bys, static displays, aerobatics, air racing and even flight instruction.

Because each of these activities carries unusual risks that are not allowed for in normal aircraft insurance rating, they will probably have to be added by endorsement and will probably carry an additional charge. You should ask your agent, broker or insurance carrier to obtain a quotation for you, and you should add the coverage if you can afford it.

It is always advisable to carry all applicable insurance. Even though the cost of liability insurance, hull insurance and special endorsements may not have been something you counted on when you got your warbird or classic jet, they carry a benefit beyond paying out policy limits for covered events – they also pay for your defence costs if a suit is initiated against you. This may be of even more benefit than the liability payments, because the cost of defence is covered even if the suit is a frivolous one, or one in which you are ultimately determined to not be liable.

A word about non-standard airworthiness certificates; be sure your policy is endorsed to specifically cover the type of certificate you hold. The standard wording of most policies precludes coverage if the certificate is other than standard, so read your policy carefully, and have your insurance professional show you that coverage exists.

Other Considerations

Because of the technical nature of aviation, it is considered a specialty field within the insurance industry. The majority of the agents and brokers placing aviation insurance do so on a primary or even full-time basis. If your agent or broker is not a specialist, chances are that he or she may not know all the options available to you or have access to the insurance company that may be the best for your needs.

Even the most knowledgeable specialist may be unable to give you the service you deserve. Before you write next year's cheque, think for a moment. Were you given plenty of time to make your decision about renewal? Were you given several quotes or just told what the price would be? Were your questions answered in a useful way or did you just get more jargon? Were requested changes made promptly? Was everything in the policy right? Did you request certificates of insurance that never got to the people that required them? If you had a claim, was it settled fairly and promptly? Were there any unwelcome surprises lurking in your insurance policy?

You will want to know if your insurance company is financially stable so it can pay claims if they come up. You will also want to know what the policy form is, in terms of the broadness of its terms, definitions, conditions and exclusions. Admittedly, sitting down in the evening and reviewing your insurance policy has a much lower enjoyment factor than piercing holes in the sky, but if you find even one area that is unacceptably restrictive, the time is well spent.

As you read the policy, make sure that all the information about you and your aircraft is correct. If it is not, run – don't walk – to the phone and let your agent or broker know what changes are needed. As you review the policy, see if each section makes sense. If it does not, you should get some answers. It could be that the section you have a question about can be modified to better meet your needs.

Once you find an insurance company you like, stick with it! Believe it or not, most insurance companies repay loyalty with flexibility and consideration for their insureds.

The Final Analysis

Unfortunately, there is no instrument rating for insurance buying. If you cannot see it in the policy, it's not there. You should know what you want, what you need and how to tell if you have got it. A good policy can literally be worth more than its weight in gold when you really need it.

Chapter Seven

Flying and Owning the Mustang
The Views of Owners and Pilots

Ed and Connie Bowlin
Mustang pilots and former owners;
a unique husband-and-wife team

We have been very fortunate to share the experience of owning a couple of P-51s. Flying a Mustang was, and is, a dream come true. Having the opportunity to enjoy flying two P-51s together as much as we did is beyond dreaming!

Formation flying, 'rat racing', dogfighting and aerobatics in the P-51 is great. We're very lucky.

Paul asked me to relate a special, most memorable story. Here it is:

We arrived in Oshkosh the opening day of the Experimental Aircraft Association's annual convention, in July 1998. There were several hundred thousand people there to watch. The flight was uneventful until we came in over Oshkosh, and made our 360

overhead break for landing. I rolled out on downwind following Ed, put the gear down and got an unsafe indication on the gear. On final the tower confirmed that I had only one gear leg down. Ed had just touched down in his Mustang when I went around. The tower allowed him to take off again from his mid-field position. By the time he joined up with me again, I had completed all the emergency procedures without solving the problem. For the next hour we reviewed the options – there weren't many – and tried several ideas. The left gear leg was down, including the large 'clamshell' door that is normally closed after the gear sequence is completed. The right gear leg was up. This configuration eliminated the choice of landing with both gear legs up. The design of the Mustang is such that if the left gear door is open, the gear handle cannot be moved.

Looking back, there were several amus-

Mickey Rupp in P-51D-25NT 45-11450/N551MR Old Crow *leads* Glamorous Glen III *alias 45-11381/N551CB which was owned by Ed and Connie Bowlin and painted in Chuck Yeager's markings.* via Ed and Connie Bowlin

ing things that happened. The EAA Warbird area has a special frequency that we use when we taxi into the area for parking. That frequency is not normally very congested and we know all the guys who work that area, so Ed says to me: 'I think I'll call Tom Wise' (the Chairman of the Warbird Line Crew). I laughed and replied that I didn't think I really needed a parking spot yet! It was nice to be able to contact them and get the people in the loop that could be of the most assistance during the emergency. It was through this relatively discreet frequency that we co-ordinated our plan with the EAA officials, FAA and Fire Rescue.

I can't emphasise enough how nice it was to have a wingman to take a look at the airplane and to be there to discuss the best plan.

I did get one really wild suggestion from the ground. I think this guy had been watching too many movies. He asked Ed if he could use his wing tip to tap on my gear door with his wing tip to see if it would come loose. I didn't particularly like the idea of that huge Mustang prop chewing in to my wing! It was interesting to me that there was a very distinct time, when I transitioned from a maintenance (trouble-shooting, fix the problem) mind-set, to 'Okay, this is what I have now. How do I get on the ground safely?'

The wind was favouring Runway 27. In fact, the wind was 270° at 30 knots. I knew I would go off the right side of the runway after landing and there were aircraft parked along the edge of Runway 27. I could not use that runway because I would have hit a lot of airplanes and possibly hurt someone. Runway 36 is very wide and the right side is clear. So, the only problem is a 30-knot crosswind. We decided that the crosswind might actually be helpful. The airplane might try to weathervane into the wind, making it turn left, helping to keep it up on the left gear longer. Sounded good in theory.

When I was ready to land, we flew over the field once to take a look at the runway and then I came in for the approach on Runway 36, with Ed still on my wing. On short final, when the tower controller gave us the wind for the third time, and it was 270° at 18 gusting 27 knots, Ed asked him not to give us the wind anymore. I laughed. Ed knew that it didn't really matter and I didn't need to be reminded that I had a 30-knot crosswind. We knew that! I also ran out of rudder trim on short final, so if I had tried to go around, it would have been very interesting. I landed on the far left side of the runway, left wing low and held the right wing up as long as I could – until it was very slow. When the wing dropped, it turned the airplane around and I slid backwards for a short distance and came to a stop. When we hoisted the Mustang up, we had to pry the gear door open with screwdrivers. The cause of the jammed gear door was never determined for sure. The best guess is a malfunction of the linkage between the two gear doors. Since the left gear door was ripped off during the landing, we can't be sure. The aircraft was flying again within a month – so it could have been a lot worse. The owner of the Mustang, Jack Rousch, is a friend whom we have always admired a great deal. After I badly damaged his aircraft, his number one concern was for my welfare. He apologised for giving me a faulty piece of equipment. It is a very generous and gracious individual who will say that when I'm standing next to his aircraft, talking to him on the phone, describing how it looks and what is bent! Bud Anderson, who flew the original *Old Crow* during World War Two, commented that the aircraft committed suicide and I just happened to be along for the ride.

We have owned P-51s and other warbird aircraft for a long time. The longer we are around the aircraft, the more we appreciate the people involved with this type of aircraft and especially those who flew them during World War Two. None of these airplanes would have survived and all of our lives would be a lot different if it weren't for those who made the sacrifices in World War Two. The aircraft would not have survived the modern era without the dedication of the owners and operators who expend a lot of time, energy and money to keep them flying today.

Robert Converse
P-51D-25NA 44-72811/N215RC *Huntress III*

When I sit in the *Huntress* hangar and look at the most magnificent P-51 on Planet Earth, I hardly believe that it's mine.

I can sit there for hours, dreaming, gazing, staring in a lusty way at the sexiest machine to have flown the skies.

Even listening to *Huntress* being warmed up by my dear friend and caretaker of *Huntress*, Chuck Leonberg (who loves her as much if not more than me), drives a special passion and excitement in me. Soon it will be my turn to start her up, taxi, warm up, and FLY!

The thrill of mastering a Mustang is awesome to say the least. The opportunity to achieve this prominence is a serious endeavour yet breathtaking and humbling simultaneously. My love for aviation and the respect it deserves is ever-present in this form I can participate in, thankfully and with graciousness.

Stephen Grey
Principal, The Fighter Collection
P-51C-10NT 43-25147/G-PSIC *Princess Elizabeth*; P-51D-20NA 44-63864/G-CBNM *Twilight Tear*

These great Classic Fighters look able, aggressive, agile, speedy, smooth, sexy, sensational – compelling things, of dangerous beauty.

I have been fortunate to fly the P-51A, B/C and D models of the North American Mustang (fly but not fight – at least not for life or limb). Each scores highly as a legendary classic – compelling aircraft, of sensational beauty and slippery with the unwary. Each Mustang flight has fulfilled its promise, even those that finished not quite as intended.

Flight is the only way to capture and distil the very essence of this mythical Fighter. Nevertheless, the pages of this book excite the imagination – one can feel the bite of the harness, smell the exotic mix of avgas/coolant/hydraulics, feel the shuddering start of the magic motor, the thump of the retracting gear, the fluid sensation as wings first bite the air, the magnificent sound and thrust of the Merlin or Allison.

These histories are live with survival, the instincts of preservation – each an outstanding tribute to those who designed, built, maintained, flew and fought with these historic aircraft. Every page is a compliment to those who have preserved, restored, maintain and now fly the Mustang – for fun and for posterity.

May the Legend continue to excite the imagination – thank you, Paul.

'Age cannot wither her, nor custom stale her infinite variety.' William Shakespeare

Chris and Lorraine Gruys
P-51D-30NA 44-74977/N5448V

Needless to say, flying the Mustang is special. I cannot think of any plane more fun than a warbird, and the P-51 is probably the easiest to fly so long as it is done within the parameters of safe flight.

My favourite story about flying it was my first cross-country to Colorado Springs for a war memorial flight. On the way back, Lorraine was in the back seat, and we were passed off from Colorado Springs approach control to Pueblo. After contacting Pueblo they came back and asked if I wanted to take a picture of the Presidential Air Force One, as Clinton was making a re-election campaign speech there. I told them that my camera was in the gun bay, and I could not get out of the plane to get it.

After a minute, they came back on and asked if I wanted to come by, and look at Air Force One. Lorraine said, 'They want you to do a fly-by' and so I relayed Pueblo that would go ahead and fly by to see Air Force One.

They gave me a set-up on the east-west runway, heading in from the east. They advised that I must turn out south within one mile of the end of the runway so as not to overfly Clinton. So we came in at 350mph indicated, and I saw Air Force One next to the control tower with a number of guys in black suits around it. As they saw us in a shallow dive heading towards them, they all started running (I assume they were Secret Service agents). I passed over Air Force One at 400 indicated and pulled out with up elevator trim, and a slight left bank. The tower called me and said 'Well, what did you think of Air Force One?' I responded, 'Tell Clinton it needs a wash', and then departed to the south. Never did hear from anyone about this!

Chuck Hall
Cavalier Mustang Mk.2 67-22580/N2580

After a day of Mustang formation flying and rat racing with my friend Bill Anders, we parked our airplanes, shook hands and both agreed – it don't get any better than this. We are two very lucky men. This from a man who has been to the moon and back.

To me, owning and flying my Mustang is the ultimate aviation high. But one thing that really makes it special is having the opportunity to fly formation with other Mustangs and being able to experience the sight of that beautiful airplane, looking clean and mean, sitting a few feet away off your wing. After 50 years in aviation, nothing gives me a greater thrill. I've heard it said that 'flying Mustangs isn't a matter of life or death, it's more important than that.' I guess that says it all.

Bill Hane
P-51D-30NT 45-11628/N151X *Ho! Hun*

Humble. Yes, excellent. Call me humble! Humble Hane. Yes, I would like that on my tombstone.

First, being humble keeps you alive when you fly a Mustang. The second humble applies when you realise you don't own a Mustang, it owns you. You no longer get to ski, hunt, fish, go on exotic cruises. You are now a Slave, but alas a willing one. The third humble comes over time as you meet and

associate with some of the greatest pilots the world has ever produced. This to me is what the Mustang is all about. We all know that the Mustang is the greatest fighter ever made. This includes any war, any country, any time in history. But without the courageous pilots that flew them into battle, all would be for naught. Add the corresponding catalyst – the courageous enemy pilots who fought for their countries. You need both to prove the worth of a weapon. Practice doesn't count! When you are out there trying to kill something or somebody you want the finest equipment ever built to help you. In the violent world of the fighter pilot, the Mustang reigned supreme.

We have been privileged to fly many of these greats in *Ho! Hun*. To name a few: my old squadron commander and now one of my best friends, Larry Powell, Richard Turner, Subaro Saki (Japanese Ace), several US and Russian astronauts, a couple of Thunderbird pilots and one Blue Angel. All stated, in one form or another, it was the best damn ride they ever had – except for Mr Saki, but he did rate it equal to the Zero. His interpreter said that was quite an honour. Each and every encounter with people like them makes me feel very humble and honoured to ever be considered a small part of their lives, knowing what they have experienced, lived and fought for. The only reason

45-11628/N151X acquired the code letters of the 343rd FS, 55th FG in April 1984 when it was repainted for new owner John T Johnson. William T Larkins

44-73656 as N2151D during an airshow at Moffett Field in 1975. The aircraft went on to become Vlado Lenoch's Moonbeam McSwine. William T Larkins

44-84961/N7715C in July 1973 when named Miss R.J. and owned by Chuck Hall. At this point the aircraft remained pretty much stock externally, but was later radically modified in the quest for speed. The Warbird Index

am a small part of this? I own a Mustang. *Ho! Hun* has introduced me to a select group of very real, courageous people that I don't deserve to be in the same room with. But, it does keep me humble and probably alive.

One last incident. Back in the 1980s, Doug Champlin invited me to a dinner party given to World War Two Fighter Aces from the USA and Germany. I had flown *Ho! Hun* for them earlier in the day at Falcon Field, making several low passes down the runway at fairly high power settings. (I was later accused by the Airport Manager of damaging the asphalt with my prop – he lied!) As it turned out, Adolf Galland was one of the Aces in the audience. At the dinner that evening, I collected my meal and went to an unoccupied table to eat. I spotted Mr Galland and after he got his plate, lo and behold he comes right over to my table and sits right next to me; does not eat – just looks at me. I almost choked. He then said, 'You flew the Mustang today?' I choked out, 'Yes, I did.' He then retorted 'The Mustang was a very good airplane, but in an Me 109, if we got you under 15,000 feet, we had you.' Well, that pissed me off, and Humble Hane looked him right back in his black eyes and said, 'Maybe!' He didn't say anything more and I didn't say anything, knowing full well that this guy could eat my lunch any day flying anything with wings! So much for being humble.

Ho! Hun has enjoyed a perfect home at the Champlin Fighter Museum since I purchased her on 2 September 1981. Doug Champlin, owner of the Fighter Museum, has been most generous to us both in allowing us to be a part of one of the finest aircraft museums in the world. Doug has given me his friendship, which I very dearly appreciate. Right here starts that third humble!

Doug Champlin is Mr History. Through my association with him over the last 20-plus years, I have been privileged to meet with many of the people involved in the development of the P-51 such as Edgar Schumed, Ed Horkey, Dick Evans (Rolls-Royce); then to top it off, meet, talk and socialise with the greatest fighter pilots in history, the Aces.

Anyway, by now I think you get the drift of what I am trying to say. The Mustang has earned one of the highest combat honours in American history by courageous and daring pilots who fought and died in them. The men that came home are living symbols of that courage. The P-51 is no longer just a great fighter – it is part of the Great American Victory. It is History!

I feel very privileged to be able to fly the most superbly designed fighting machine ever built and so humble to have associated with these men of history. God take care of them all, they are truly Heroes.

Steve Hinton – fastest man in a Mustang
'RB-51' 44-84961/N7715C *Red Baron*

You ask why do I own a Mustang? In my thinking the Mustang is the most beautiful of the lot. It attracts people of all walks. In our museum environment it is the most popular, I think, because it appeals to people just on looks alone. The '51 isn't the best flyer of all. As a matter of fact, it can be one of the nastiest in certain situations. Most pilots never explore its dark side. On the historical side, the Mustang has a great story, from its 'built in 100 days' first manufacture to the 12,000th one built. The history books are full of stories of this great breakthrough fighter.

In the civilian world, the Mustang has a longer operating history then any other fighter I can think of. As you know, the Griffon-powered RB-51 *Red Baron* held the World's Speed Record for ten years at 499mph. There are a couple of racing Mustangs today that can recapture this record again, currently held by the Grumman F8F Bearcat at 526mph. In the racing field the Mustang is still being developed and improved – not bad for a 62-year-old fighter. The P-51 is a beautiful design, well built and very efficient for its time. There are a lot more stories about why the Mustang is attractive, but for me I guess I own one because I am lucky enough to be its keeper for now. It will long outlive me, and I hope the next group enjoys it as much as we do.

Ah, a flying story. I first flew the P-51 in December 1971. Through the course of my career I have had the opportunity to fly a lot of Mustangs on a lot of flights. I think the most memorable good one would be the record-setting flight in the RB-51. Working with our air race team, together trying to set the record. Running the big Griffon at 104 inches and 3,150rpm and seeing 450mph in level flight. To stay within the rules of the 3km course, you had to fly three consecutive opposite direction runs through a measured 3km run. During the turnarounds, you could not climb above 500 metres and you had to be level through the measured run below 50 metres. Flying the *Red Baron* through turbulence, running the engine hard, adjusting the water spray on the radiator, watching altitude and ground track, transferring fuel, talking on the radio as well as trying to keep an eye out for the unexpected and trying not to make a mistake and waste everybody's efforts was a lot of work but the result was very memorable. We had blown one engine earlier in the week, so the added drama of an engine change was there too. We were at Mud Lake, Nevada, near Tonopah. We did not know it at the time but we were right next door to the secret F-117 'Have Blue' flight-test facility. The USAF had given us permission to use this dry lake for the attempt, but we could only fly at certain times. We didn't know why at the time but we were grateful they even let us use the lake at all. Another part of the story: we actually could have gone faster but we were trying to set the record just at 500. We did not want to blow up our last engine. We thought we could find another sponsor, build a few spare engines, then return at a later date and set it as high as it would go, which we estimated to be around 515.

Vlado Lenoch
P-51D-25NA 44-73656/N2151D
Moonbeam McSwine

What powers me to want to own a Mustang? I can remember the day I first saw Bob Hoover just pirouetting in the sky in his *Yellow Bird*. The airplane was growling with power and seemed almost to be dancing in the blue, with little concern for gravity and the earth below. Ever since that day at a hot summer's airshow, I've always kept a solemn intent to own a Mustang. The first thing I decided to do to reach my goal, was to get a pilot's license!

Now that I have a Mustang, I am constantly thrilled and amazed by the aircraft's power, take-off acceleration and command of the skies. The Merlin engine that powers *Moonbeam* is a technical work of art; I am just in awe of the capabilities and precision of this motor that is the zenith, or nearly so, of piston engine development. How men (and women) were able to produce such a potent powerplant in such great numbers in such a short time is simply inspiring. Applying take-off power with the Merlin is a treat that is hard to duplicate. The sense of raw power in the cockpit and the acceleration is a visceral feeling that needs to be repeated often. In flight, the aircraft can be flown essentially wherever one wants to go. High, low, fast or slow, the speed range and altitude capabilities enable the P-51 to be positioned in the sky wherever one wants – and with beautiful aerobatics to be thrown in for good measure. I've found that only today's F-16 closely resembles the abandon with which one can fly.

With these joyful thoughts in mind, due respect must be shown to be able to safely perform demonstration flights in the Mustang time and time again. The maintenance of the engine and airframe components must be attended to and reviewed constantly. The airframe is not disposable as it may have once been during combat service in 1944. Thus regular study, inspection and overhaul of the airframe and powerplant are of prime concern as an owner and operator. In flight, careless disregard of the flight performance envelope can, and has been shown by others to lead to disaster. I love to fly the Mustang with exuberance yet within its limits. Seldom do I feel that during demonstration flights I am saying 'Look at Me!' but rather 'Look at what this machine can do.' This is a very fine line and difference. One may feel the need to display a specific energetic and possibly sparkling manoeuvre, but if the Mustang is not capable of doing so, one will not be able to fly such a manoeuvre let alone survive from an attempt.

Still, the Mustang is a joy to fly. Literally a thought away from the next manoeuvre. The history of free men is also preserved and presented to the watching public whenever the aircraft is demonstrated. I certainly feel blessed to continue to fly the Mustang for the public and in honour of all service personnel that heed the call of duty worldwide.

Ed Lindsay – son of David B Lindsay (founder of Trans Florida Aviation, later Cavalier Aircraft Corporation); owner of Cavalier Mustang II 44-13257/N51DL

Owning a Mustang is not something I often think on as I am fortunate to belong to a family for whom Mustangs were once a business. The aircraft that I fly has been in our family since 1959, a few years longer than I. However, I do think about it when writing the cheque for the annual inspection.

My earliest Mustang memory is sitting in the cockpit of a Cavalier F-51D (probably built for El Salvador) with my father standing on the wing. I remember him showing me the trigger on the stick and then pointing to the right gun bay, which, at the time, held six M2 Brownings!

Much later, my first Mustang solo flight would be in a similar F-51D – minus the Brownings.

First solo in a Mustang was my most memorable flight. Dad was not enthusiastic, having lost many Mustang pilot friends, so I waited. At long last, at age 27, with 2,000 hours in my logbook, I opened the throttle 'for the purpose of flight (FAR 1)' for the first time. She was magnificent; I was average.

Dan Martin
P-51D-20NT 44-13250/N151DM
Ridge Runner III

As far as what fuels me, it's my undying love for P-51s. It is, to me, the most beautiful wonder ever designed. I have been flying them since 1969, a little over 2,500 hours of Mustang time. It still humbles me from time to time, however. I love the way it flies, sounds, smells etc. As far as racing at Reno, I have always been competitive, and it's a rush that you can't describe. Like any competitive sport, you have butterflies and an adrenalin rush just before the race begins, but once it starts the fun begins.

Tom Patten
P-51D-25NA 44-73543/N151TP *Sweetie Face*

I do not ever remember not being intrigued with flying. As a child I played with airplanes, built models, read about Lindbergh and Doolittle, and was enthralled with the stories of those brave men who flew airplanes in defence of our liberty.

It took awhile to save enough money to learn to fly. The financial pressures of a young family and starting a business postponed the inevitable until I was almost 30. Flying was more wonderful than I imagined. Everything about it suited me. The required attention to detail and total concentration suited my personality perfectly.

Soon, very soon, I was in hot pursuit of additional ratings and was aggressively trying to fly other types. I was enamoured with everything that I flew, from the Pitts to the King Air. I always thought that 'some day, some day' I would like to own what I considered the ultimate airplane: the Mustang.

A few years ago a very good friend was diagnosed with a terminal cancer. As we sat around during his last months, I listened to him talk about the things that he wanted to do but never got around to doing. Something was always in Ted's way and at the end of his life we both realised that nothing should have come between him and his dreams. These conversations made me re-evaluate my relationships with my family, reprioritise the place of work in my life, and look at some of the dreams that I would really like to chase.

One of them was to own a Mustang. I had a serious conversation with my wife about the commitment that I felt was required to own one and she was supportive in every way.

I went to Stallion 51, flew with Lee Lauderback, and was completely smitten. With his help and that of other friends, Mark Clark, John Baugh and Roland Coles, began the search for a Mustang.

It was an exciting day when I flew my very own Mustang for the first time, and a more exciting day when I flew alongside my best friend, Bill Freeman, when he got one as well.

I had no idea when I was searching for the right airplane and getting the training that there was a rich part of ownership that would later unfold to me.

Since owning the airplane I have had the opportunity to meet veterans of all walks, men who have offered great sacrifices for our country. The greatness of these men cannot be adequately expressed in books or movies. From the men of the 352nd Fighter Group who I have become very close with, to the Legends that I met at the Gathering of Mustangs & Legends at Kissimmee in 1999, to the everyday infantrymen who come by the hangar with stories about how the Mustang somehow affected their lives – I have a much greater, reverential appreciation of what was given by so many to create the world and great country that I live in now.

I know now that I am only the keeper of this great symbol of our freedom.

The death of a close friend forced Dan Martin to re-evaluate the priorities in his life. One result was the decision to acquire P-51D-20NT 44-13250/N151DM Ridge Runner III. Bob Munro

Ed Shipley in P-51D-25NA 44-84634/N51ES Big Beautiful Doll (84th FS, 78th FG) leads Bob Tullius in P-51D-30NA 44-74409/N51RT. Robert S DeGroat

Excellent use of natural lighting by the cameraman reveals the outstanding finish of Tom Patten's P-51D-25NA 44-84634/N151TP Sweetie Face. The markings and colour scheme are those of the 487th FS, 352nd FG – the 'Blue-Nosed Bastards of Botney'. Uwe Glaser

Brian Reynolds
P-51D-25NA 44-73436/N51KD

My first flight in the Mustang wasn't that easy. After I had flown the T-6 for six months or so, I started sitting in the Mustang cockpit for hours, learning everything about every knob and switch and its location. Then I started memorising the flight manual; that's memorising it, not just reading it.

I wanted to know everything about the aeroplane I could, so when it came time I could concentrate on flying it and keeping my eyes outside. I had been listening to lots of stories about how dangerous the Mustang could be and about all the pilots that had been killed in them. All this put me on the defence, and made me realise that this is a very serious plane. So with a single-control aircraft I knew the first flight was going to be a solo flight. However, I also thought, 'Hey, 19-year-old kids were doing this in the war. So being that I'm almost twice their age with several thousand hours as a pilot, I should be able to handle it.'

After I had been listening to countless stories over several months on how to handle the first flight, I decided to contact a couple of very experienced Mustang pilots in order to get a cockpit checkout. First I contacted the most experienced warbird pilot in the northwest United States, Bud Granley. Bud has several thousand hours in the Mustang and is probably one of the best pilots I've had the pleasure to fly with.

We got airborne in a T-6 trainer and simulated that we were flying the Mustang as best we could; then we went on to aerobatics and confidence building. Mine. Bud did things in warbirds I didn't know could be done, and then he taught me how to do them. We did lots of aerobatics and he taught me what I should do in case I lost control. After several hours with me turning green and Bud having a great time, we called it a day and made arrangements for Bud to come down to Olympia and give me a cockpit checkout in the Mustang.

Well, this was October and the weather was not co-operating at all. On top of that, Bud and I were having schedule conflicts. Meantime I had been studying the flight manual and sitting in the Mustang every day, anticipating that first flight.

Finally it was a beautiful Saturday morning, but Bud was busy until Monday. The weather forecast for Monday did not look good. It was time.

I called another friend of mine in Ione, California. Dennis Sanders is another great warbird pilot. I told him I felt I was ready to take the Mustang up, and asked him if we could go through everything I was going to do on the flight over the phone. He said no problem and we began going through everything, from start through taxi to take-off and landing with all the potential warnings along the way. After about half an hour he said, 'There is a better way, Brian. Why don't I fly up there and help you?' I said, 'It's already

afternoon and the weather doesn't even look good for Sunday.' He responded by saying 'I'm on my way.' A little over two hours later he landed at Olympia, non-stop from Sacramento, California. He was flying this little homebuilt that looked like all engine with a set of wings attached. He called it a Lawn Dart.

By the time Dennis arrived I had started and taxied the Mustang around a little and it felt good. As a preliminary, Dennis climbed in the pilot seat and I climbed in the jump seat. We got airborne in the Mustang, Brian talking me through the flight. As I listened intently and looked over his shoulder, I felt overwhelmed.

We landed and shut the engine down. I transferred to the pilot seat and with Dennis on the wing we went through a very thorough cockpit checkout. Then he uttered something that scared me: 'Brian, you're ready; go have fun.' Suddenly I was very awake. Like Bud Granley, Dennis' confidence in my ability meant a lot to me and I didn't want to let them both down.

Dennis said he would be sitting in his Lawn Dart listening on the radio. If I had any problems or questions, he would be right there to help talk me through it.

I strapped on the parachute and the harness and started going through the pre-start checklist. I got the Merlin fired up and after going through everything twice I taxied out to the runway for take-off. By now the big thing going through my mind was the torque that everybody talks about from that giant engine and prop combination. I'd been warned it was going to take a lot of right rudder to keep the plane straight, so I kept that in the back of my mind the whole time.

Finally, with the run-up checks done, I rolled out onto the active runway and was cleared for take-off. I checked the whole cockpit over again from right to left, making sure I hadn't forgot anything. After what seemed like only a few seconds (it must have been a few minutes) the control tower asked me what my intentions were and asked if I had a problem. I told them no problem yet, just trying to slow the heart rate down.

On the brakes, I pushed the throttle forward to 2,000rpm, checked the oil pressure and coolant temp and then let her go. I moved the throttle up to 50 inches of manifold pressure, which is what we use for full power. Totally blind out the front from the big engine, at about 60mph I lifted the tail and was amazed that I was still in the centre of the runway.

At just over 100 I gave it a little backpressure and the Mustang flew off the runway. Airborne! The first thing I did was reach down and pull the landing gear handle to the up position as I was getting toward a best climb speed of 170.

It was then I felt a huge cramp in my right hip from pushing on the right rudder too hard. I tried to straighten up in my seat to dispel the cramp but I could hardly move. In the

meantime I was still holding on to the gear handle, which in the Mustang is very important until the gear cycle is complete because it could pop out of the up detent and mess up the gear door cycle. While I was doing this I noticed that the cloud ceiling had lowered down to 1,500 feet and I was climbing at full power in the Mustang. I had to push the nose down in order to stay out of the clouds. At the same time I got my hand off the gear handle and decreased the power also, still wondering if I was going to be able to move my legs with the cramp. (What actually happened is I was unknowingly pushing on both pedals hard at the same time due to my nervousness.)

At this time I was a very busy trimming up all three separate axis on the flight controls and putting the oil and coolant systems into auto positions.

My original plan was to take-off, go around the airport once and then land. I went around the airport but when I lined up on final approach where I was suppose to be landing, I still had the gear up and was still doing 220mph. And I was still 1,500 feet over the runway.

I radioed the tower: 'Think I'm going to go around one more time.' As you can see, I was way behind the Mustang at this point. The decision to go around gave me a chance to relax and get the landing checklist going. After relaxing, the cramp disappeared. As I came around again I put the landing gear back down, got the Mustang slowed down, and the flaps down. I came over the end of the runway at 120mph and made a decent landing.

I was pretty happy at this point as I was on the ground, but I noticed the plane was not slowing down and I was eating up a lot of runway very quickly. I immediately pulled the throttle back to idle, which I had forgotten to do, and the Mustang finally started losing speed.

When the tail came down, I went back to looking out of the sides so I could see, touched the brakes and turned off the runway. After leaving the runway I stopped to take a deep breath, get the flaps up, coolant doors open, then taxied to parking.

For two circuits around the airport I was tired. But it was over, and I survived, just like the 19-year-old kids did in World War Two.

Anders Saether
Principal, Scandinavian Historic Flight
P-51D-25NA 44-73877/N167F *Old Crow*

P-51D-25NA 44-73877 was built in Inglewood, California in July 1945. Her only military service was with the Royal Canadian Air Force in Calgary. She had two civil owners before I bought her in 1980. At the time she was parked in the open at Fort Collins, Colorado, there were 1,500 hours on the log and she had not flown for many, many years.

The restoration was done by Vintage Aircraft Ltd on the same field and took five years to complete. The engine was rebuilt

Anders Saether of The Scandinavian Historic Flight brings in P-51D-25NA 44-73877/N167F for a perfect landing soon after he ferried the aircraft to Norway. SHF

The filming of Enigma Productions' Memphis Belle *at Duxford in the summer of 1989 saw several Mustangs painted in a basic olive drab scheme, including Ander's Saether's N167F. Anders is seen here taxying out for a sortie during the filming.* The Warbird Index

by Jack Hovey of Hovey Machine Products and incorporates a balanced crankshaft, transport heads and banks, and Rolls-Royce pistons and connecting rods.

The cockpit is civilian. Full IFR instrumentation, a three-axis autopilot, oxygen and 300 US gallon internal fuel were installed. Choosing a paint scheme was not difficult; Col C E 'Bud' Anderson had been my World War Two all-time hero since I was a young boy. When I asked Colonel Anderson if he would mind if I painted my Mustang in his colours, he replied that he would be very pleased. Of course, I was honoured and happy with his reply.

Now I was the proud owner of an aircraft I had dreamed of owning for as long as I could remember. The fact that I did not know how to fly a Mustang had been pushed to the very back of my mind all this time. Now I had to face it.

My background was 1,000 hours on light aircraft, 500 hours T-6 time and knowing the flight manual by heart. In June of 1985, *Old Crow* and I survived our first flight together.

After local trial-and-error training in Fort Collins, I flew some long-range high-altitude flights in the United States. Fuel consumption and the moods of a Merlin were studied in detail. I did not understand much of the latter. Slowly, we got to understand each other while I stayed away from every corner of the envelope.

In the spring of 1986 I bought a one-way ticket from Oslo to Denver. From that time I knew there was no other way to get *Old Crow* home to Norway than to fly her myself. It was a matter of personal pride. I told myself a hundred times that Charles Blair flew the P-51B *Excalibur* across the Atlantic in 1952 so why couldn't I do it? Little did I know. We came across from Goose Bay via Narsarsuaq and Keflavik to Bergen at FL320. With a fresh IFR rating and no GPS, the trip was eventful to say the least.

A few weeks later I took her to Duxford, England, where I met the legendary Ray Hanna and his son Mark. They literally and physically took me under their wings and let me fly with them on the UK airshow circuit. Under Mark's leadership I practised aerobatics during the week and flew careful displays with my new professional friends on the weekends. It was a wonderful time.

In 1989 Ray and Mark were given the contract to be aerial directors for the Warner Brothers filming of *Memphis Belle*. Much to my surprise, they asked me to fly with them. Flying 58 hours in six weeks with experienced Royal Air Force pilots, all in formation, gave me a good step upwards on the learning ladder. *Old Crow* was painted olive drab and christened *Cisco* for the occasion.

Flying *Old Crow* on the European airshow circuit over the next ten years gave me nothing but good and sometimes exciting memories. The more time we spent together, the more we seemed to enjoy each other. Gradually, I truly looked forward to every flight – until we lost Mark Hanna in 1999.

Mark loved *Old Crow* as much as I, and I seriously thought of putting her in the hangar for good at that time. But remembering how Mark and I often spoke of how life should be if we lost one another, I decided to continue.

Since then I have had the pleasure of getting to know Colonel Anderson. He came to Europe in the summer of 2001 and flew *Old Crow* from Duxford, to his wartime base at Leiston in Suffolk. He is a most humble and sympathetic man. At 80 he flies tight formation as steadily as he did 60 years ago. It was a pleasure to hear my brave hero describe the flight as 'Mission Completed'.

I have flown the greater part of the 1,250 hours logged on *Old Crow* since 1985. Mostly, I have good memories. But we also have been through a series of miseries together, many of which were self-induced. Things started to go better when I understood her language. It took several years before I really learned how to treat the lady. I now know how she feels and what she likes and does not like.

We regularly go into 650-metre-long runways, and we both love it. Knowing I can slow-fly the Mustang safely gives me a tremendous degree of satisfaction.

My first flights were based on trial and error. I do not recommend this learning procedure. I was lucky. There is not a war going on and we cannot afford to lose more Mustangs. Proper instruction and a verdict on your abilities can now be bought from Stallion 51 in Florida. It is also the best life insurance you can buy. If I were to give some advice to new Mustang pilots, it would be:

1. Learn the flight manual down to the last detail and fly her by the book at all times. Put good margins on top of the listed stall and accelerated stall speeds.
2. Learn the language of a Merlin from somebody who knows and listen to what she tells you.
3. The single-control Mustang is not an aerobatic trainer for the novice.
4. Do not show off, even if she begs for it and you have your new girlfriend in the back.
5. Contrary to another well-known engine manufacturer, Rolls-Royce never described the Merlin engine as 'dependable'. Remember that and fly with this in mind.
6. Learn to fly a T-6 really well (ten successful 15-20 knot gusty 90° crosswind landings in succession on a paved runway) before you fly the Mustang.
7. Let Stallion 51 tell you when you are ready.

Old Crow has become well known on the European airshow circuit. In Scandinavian Historic Flight (www.shf.as), we feel it is important to remind the present generation that we would have lost World War Two to the Nazis if the Americans had not come to our rescue.

Everyone should be grateful to Colonel Anderson, his fellow surviving American pilots, and the 85,000 American airmen who lost their lives in Europe during World War Two. I am happy to have been able to participate in conveying this message by exhibiting *Old Crow* all over Europe.

I am very grateful to Paul Coggan, who helped me find 44-73877; to Ray and the late Mark Hanna, who took the time to tell me how to fly military aircraft; to Pete John, my brilliant RAF lead during filming of *Memphis Belle,* for his trust in his wingman; to Darrel Skurich; Lynn and Larry who built such a wonderful, straight and fast machine; and to Jack Hovey, who built my smooth engine which has always brought me home. Thank you all for making my dream come true.

Mike VadeBonCoeur
Owner and Chief Engineer, Midwest Aero Restorations Ltd

My first solo flight in the Mustang was quite exhilarating, needless to say. The thing I remember the most was taxying out and asking myself 'Am I really going to do this?' Well, I could always retard the throttle if needed to, and stop if it didn't feel right. Right? Wrong!

As I lined up for the departure from runway 21 at Danville Vermilion, I also remember thinking to myself 'I can do this and this is going to be very much like the back seat of *Crazy Horse*!' The only difference would be a much better line of sight. After the mandatory checks I brought the throttle up slowly while maintaining directional control; that was not a problem. Somewhere around 40 inches of manifold pressure, the noise level remained pretty much constant. About that time the tail came up slowly and soon after, I was airborne, still applying throttle to reach around 55 inches. Gear up, pitch to 150 knots climb and set throttle to 40 inches and prop to 2,700 turns, checking the oil temps and pressures and coolant temps and adjusting the doors as necessary. I remember being quite busy, with my head in the cockpit for probably too great a time. But this was my first solo! After I settled down I finally looked outside the airplane and to my most pleasant surprise I was now several miles from the field! Wow, this is way too cool! Settling into a nice cruise power setting and some local straight-and-level flying, I was ready to head back to the airport. One big difference between the Mustang and the T-6 is planning ahead. Stallion 51 taught me the overhead so that is what I did, albeit with a mild break, but the procedures were what I was after. The prop is a wonderful speed brake and it is amazingly effective in the Mustang. The landing was as perfect as I could ask for although I could use a little practice on not eating up runway! Sometimes the best part of a flight is the taxi back into the hangar and this is especially true in the Mustang.

Rolling back the canopy and hearing the Merlin 'panting' is a wonderful thing. I am very grateful to Butch Schroeder for giving me the opportunity to fly *North American Maid*. It is one experience I will not forget in a hurry!

Chapter Eight

Flying the TF-51 Mustang

As I strapped into the dual-control TF-51 in the winter sunshine at Kissimmee, Florida, several things flashed through my mind. My last affair with the Mustang began in 1970 and I've been lucky to fly in five P-51s since. However, here we are, in the early years of a new century and I was about to undergo the experience of a lifetime. Needless to say the beautiful form, the appropriate, purposeful, almost art deco design appeals as much to me now as it did back in 1970. The North American Mustang looks right from any angle. And I was about to fly one.

Nothing could have prepared me for this experience. I'm not a pilot. OK, engineering power and acceleration have always managed to get the adrenaline flowing – I've been amused by relatively powerful cars before but this was to be something else.

I'd already spent several hours with Lee Lauderback getting the feel of the operation at 3951 Merlin Drive, Kissimmee; very different to the modest, but effective operation on Hoagland Boulevard where Stallion 51 Corporation was born. Humble beginnings. The early years meant hard work for partners Lee Lauderback and Doug Schultz. Long

hours flying and building a reputation, not only with the close-knit warbird fraternity but with financial institutions as well. The hangar come office accommodation at Merlin Drive is impressive, custom designed by the Stallion team to facilitate and totally support the smooth operation of *Crazy Horse*, the money-earner sat on the immaculate hangar floor below. *Crazy Horse* is the most utilised, but carefully maintained Mustang on earth and fully deserves such lavish accommodation.

The concept was to make the Stallion 51 facility home for several Mustangs (up to nine in fact); a place where owners can house their Mustang and have it maintained by Stallion 51 Maintenance (Peter and Richard Lauderback have been involved in several Mustang projects over the years).

Stallion operates in four closely related spheres, with a fifth, that of high-quality corporate entertainment for companies such as Rolls-Royce and Cessna. The Stallion team get a buzz from flying people and from helping them to fly *Crazy Horse*; contributing (in very real terms) to flight safety in the warbird community; reacquainting a vet-

eran with his old steed and taking a young person for the trip of a lifetime. Stallion 51 is a very professional company with a corporate feel and a great deal of pride in demonstrating their abilities and passing on their expertise. *Crazy Horse* is 'hired out' at a flat rate, but even if you paid ten times that rate you would not come anywhere near the value of all that available knowledge and experience. It is a priceless commodity.

Lee Lauderback flies *Crazy Horse* regularly, often intensively, passing on his skills to a new Mustang owner or putting a checked-out P-51 qualified pilot through a refresher course. His wry grin indicates he wants more, and above all he is willing to teach more. Value for money for the customer is unrivalled; the clients come in all shapes and sizes, characters and degrees of ability.

To fly with Lee is an experience in itself. When he looked me straight in the eye and said 'You will fly *Crazy Horse* today', I began to get a little nervous. We walked around the

Lee Lauderback and Crazy Horse *make their entrance, very low and very fast.* Tom Smith

TF-51D which had been towed out of the hangar and onto the ramp. Once into the thorough pre-flight briefing (tailored no doubt to my non-pilot status but delivered in a friendly and non-patronising way), I was strapped in for a thorough cockpit and emergency egress procedure brief. Though bale-outs are rare, I felt at ease knowing what would happen if we ran into problems.

Having been suitably kitted out earlier (which made me feel the part and set the scene) and given a relaxed but serious tour of the cockpit – my cockpit, in this case – and shown what to press, switch, pull and monitor and what results to expect, I was issued with ear plugs to insert underneath the headset. I was then given a final check over to make sure I was properly secure and connected into the TF-51D systems. Lee grinned again, almost knowingly, before climbing into the front cockpit.

Lee involved me from the start, checking I was ready to go. Soon it became obvious that I was actually going to fly *Crazy Horse*. Though this was to be my second TF-51 trip (having flown with Darryl Bond in *Lady Joe* some six years previously in California), I had not spent so much time 'hands on'. Lee began his calm encouraging banter which is skillfully unobtrusive, a narrative throughout the flight; intelligent and delivered in a reassuring pitch. A quick lesson in how to taxi a Mustang was followed by a thorough but easy-to-understand brief on a high-power take-off and departure from Kissimmee.

Lee had briefed earlier by telephone with Eliot Cross, who was flying out of Bartow with a two-seat Spitfire. I leaned over to make sure my camera was secure and that I wasn't about to embarrass myself by scattering any loose items about the cockpit. I settled into the seat, ready for the forthcoming detail. Over the intercom and with meaningful looks outside the cockpit towards Richard on the ground, Lee began the pre take-off checks: '...flaps up, carb air controls cold and rudder trim six right, elevator zero, aileron zero, mixtures idle cut off, prop full forward, throttle cracked one inch.' On he continued until finishing the before start checks with 'All circuit breakers in.' Then a pause. This is the business!

'If you're clear of the canopy Paul, I'm going close it a little bit and we'll wake up the Merlin,' said Lee. 'CLEAR' was the cry from the front cockpit, duly acknowledged by Richard who was thumbs-up outside. Pulsing the aircraft into life, Lee enquired of my welfare. 'You all set?' came the question from the front. 'Sure am!' was the reply. I felt as relaxed as I'd ever been – little did I realise that this was to be about as much fun as you can have with your clothes on. The Merlin crackled, started without hesitation, and earned praise from Lee: '...she says "Let Me Run!"' Then into another banter of checks: '...radios on, nav lights on and nav mas on.' *Crazy Horse* was raring to gallop.

Following a brief conversation with the tower, clearance to taxi off the ramp was forthcoming and Lee lined her up, ready to let me attempt the famous weaving taxi to the runway at Kissimmee. 'OK Paul, taxi strictly with your feet. Give some pressure with the left foot and she comes left... then go with the right foot – as she swings to one side you look straight down the opposite side of the airplane.' We took a right turn and Lee demonstrated the maximum turn radius available on the TF-51. The next exercise was interesting. 'Now, Paul, I want you to find the brakes up on the toe pedal (Coggan envisages the headline: "Brit Noses over Mustang on First Flight"), and push the stick forward; push push, PUSH! Now give me right brake and we make a turn here. Hold it there. Stick back to central position, and advance the throttle forward to 1,500rpm, Paul...' I did so obediently and with pride. It was hard to imagine the gaggle of similarly coloured Mustangs assembling for a formation take-off at the 352nd FG base at Bodney in Norfolk, early on that famous day in June 1944. It may have been a long time ago but I didn't realise, until that moment, the sheer scale of it all.

But this was today. 'Canopy forward... good oil and pressures, everything's looking really good, so I'm going take the brakes and you can advance the throttle forward to 2,300rpm, Paul...' By now I was starting to feel a real part of what was going on rather than merely a passenger. 'OK Paul, with the small black round prop control, underhand with your finger tips pull it all the way back to you. Now quickly push it all the way forward – good, checks prop pitch is good and functional. Check left mag, 90 drop, right mag, 80 drop, back to the boost...good... 27.9 inches, boost induction carb air good, oil, engine pressures and temps good, hydraulic pressure thousand... Back to 1,500 to get the checklist stuff out of the way...flap handles verified up and visually checked (swift visual check), front and rear harnesses locked (thumbs up from me)...elevator trim zero, aileron trim zero and prop control full forward. Fuel boost pumps confirmed on. Fuel check full left, full right, no fuel venting left or right...set compass to 060 if you'd do that, Paul.' I fiddled a little... 'Parking brake in, transponder to ELT, Hydraulic T handles confirmed down. Fuel pressures good, mags are both...strobe lights coming on and circuit breakers rechecked.' By now the Mustang was throbbing. The vibration wracked my torso. The tempo increased... anticipation mounting. But I'd done this before. NO, I hadn't!

Ready to go?

I'd seen Lee's now famous high-power departure from the taxiway many times before, but to actually experience it from the cockpit was a thrill indeed. I did one last check of my harness and indicated to Lee verbally and physically (thumbs up) that I was ready to be 'Stallionised'. Last brief on the take-off and an instruction to follow Lee through on the controls. Lee visually checked finals and base legs to Runway and radioed '*Crazy Horse* departing'. Th aircraft was nicely lined up on the centre line with the tailwheel straight and locke Up on the brakes, one last check on th canopy.

I felt pretty hyped by this stage. Man things flashed through my mind. I imagine those ill-fated first hops by untrained civilia Mustang pilots in the early 1960s; the subje of those famous accident reports. Now could understand the lure of the Mustan and how the most sensible would-be fighte pilot could climb in and fly off to his death But again, this was today. Lee instructed m to push up the power to 2,300rpm, and h pushed the boost to 40 inches of manifol pressure. As the Mustang tanked down th runway on three points and with the pu pose of an express train, I felt the solid acce eration build, my heartbeat quicken. At 5 knots Lee flew the tail up with forward ele vator as it came up, and all was reveale ahead of the nose. Power was increased t 46 inches and the Merlin sang smooth through 100 knots. Let's hope Mike Nixo did a good job flashed through my mind. and more acceleration as Lee seemed t hold the aircraft down before flying *Craz Horse* very positively off the runway and int a steep angle skywards, as the gear came u and the nose rotated all the way up. I looke fighter pilot-like, left and right. Nothing lik seeing that famous laminar-flow wing doin its job oh so efficiently. Oh boy.

Power back to high cruise and as w gained height the power was pulled back little to reduce local noise nuisance. As th green Florida scenery fell away far belo and the airframe was buffeted in turb lence, I felt that silly grin spreading acros my face. I'm not so sure I would have felt s good had I been on my own! Even the mo experienced Mustang pilots of today pr vately admit to being in awe of the perfo mance – it's those that aren't in awe wh sometimes come unstuck. Respect is th name of the game in this business. In 200 the Mustang is still just as potent (but wort a lot, lot more money) than it was an age ag in 1944.

But this is today. My first lesson was ho to trim the Mustang. 'OK Paul, we're at 2,50 feet and I just want you to drive straig ahead.' Drive? Forge may have been a bette adjective. Lee gave me some basic instru tion and allowed me to feel the aircraft, to f it, sense its reactions to my inputs and co rections. It felt good. It felt better knowing had the best up front. Again, flashes throug my mind. Imagine having to do this AN keep an eye out for the enemy, watch th Big Friends head towards their target, know ing some would not return. Imagine th trauma of all that AND having to fly a pote fighter aircraft.

Lee Lauderback puts Crazy Horse *into a dive over the Florida countryside.*

After the first successful lesson (more grinning), Lee instructed a power increase and a climb up to 7,500 feet to await the arrival of the two-seat Spitfire out of Bartow '2,700rpm Paul, manifold up to 46 inches and raise the nose slightly. Go on little bit more… we're passing through 3,500 feet a 205 knots… that's great… OK, rotate the nose up more and slight right-hand turn a we pass 4,500 feet at 2,000 feet a minute climb and 180 knots…' I looked above and behind, often catching my reflection in the canopy. It was easy to see and appreciate how the D model's bubble canopy was a big improvement over the 'razorback' Mustang with its potential lack of blind spots.

In the distance the light grey and green Spitfire Tr.9 lumbered into view. Eliot Cross radioed in and joined up for the photographic sortie. What a unique experience The camera felt like a lump of gold as we did various manoeuvres to get some interesting photographs, pulling about 2.5-3 *g*. As Lee asked me how I felt, I was unable to reply with a handful of heavy camera and in deep concentration. The Mustang canopy is no an ideal layer to photograph through but much to my surprise, the pictures came out well. We dropped back in formation with the Spitfire for the wide-angle onboard video to get some footage of the formation and after a couple more manoeuvres Lee called it off and we parted company.

How good it must have felt to be headed home after an escort mission. But then, a an added complication, the World War Two fighter pilots were tasked with seeking 'targets of opportunity' if they had the gas to spare. Had it been me, I would have been keener to fell my feet on terra firma.

But no swift return to the air-conditioned crew room for me. Right. Back to training. obviously needed the practice! After passing the camera to Lee I was briefed on how was going to do a basic loop in the Mustang Now how on earth was Lee going to take the pictures and fly the TF-51 at the same time Simple. He was going to take the pictures and I was going to fly the Mustang!

'Right Paul, turn left 10 degrees, push to 3' inches of manifold pressure and roll wing level, put the nose down, little more… now pull really hard, come on, pull, pull, PULL LLL!!!' The nose came up into the vertical a I was instructed to feed in some right rudder I felt heavier in the seat as the Mustang pulled over, heavier still – hell's teeth! – and pulled my head back instinctively to see the horizon as Lee pointed the camera at me Poser's Paradise. Forget the fast women and expensive sportscars. Power coming back, throttle back. I repeated the experience, but, being the gentle person I am

really didn't get aggressive enough on the controls. It was later that Lee told me one of the best students he has ever had for rolling the Mustang aggressively was a female. Nevertheless, I looped *Crazy Horse*, and have the video to prove it.

After a few more manoeuvres, this time expertly performed by Captain Lauderback, we headed back towards the field. I relaxed, and began to savour the moment just as the intercom crackled into life: 'Paul, we're five minutes out of Kissimmee and I want you to do an overhead join and then land on Runway 6. I'll be here to help if you need me...' WHAT? If I *need* him? All right!

'Aircraft systems looking good. OK Paul, let's head for home for a nice overhead and full stop... little bumpy underneath the cloud deck here which is perfectly normal... use the stick more aggressively than you have been doing... raise the nose a little, and you're doing fine. Just relax – wooah! – right turn here, underneath the birds... the stationary birds are the problem!' Lee had spotted some buzzards, known in the past (this is not a joke) to mob the Mustang, then we were back on track after some fine adjustments. We were at 1,000 feet and six miles southwest of the airport. 'Boost pumps on... gentle right-hand turn, Paul... and we'll overfly the airport at 1,000 feet

and make a left turn for an overhead approach...' I listened intently and moved the controls. Flashback again. Hit by flak, venting valuable gas, my wounds hurt like hell and I can barely maintain consciousness.

No such misfortune, for this is today. Back to reality. 'Run the prop up to 2,700 rpm and throttle back to 26 inches manifold, now make a hard left turn... go on Paul, hard left... HARDER! Ease out of the turn, right stick and back, that's it, to 190 knots... drop off another 20 knots and we'll get the gear down here... level wings, nose up a little and aim for the threshold, Paul... nice... 170 knots, gear coming down, slight left turn, ease the nose up a little.' The gear ground down to a firm clunk and I felt the effect on the airstream immediately on the controls. Lee radioed Kissimmee: '*Crazy Horse*, three greens, finals for Runway 6'; then more instructions for me: 'After checking gear down and locked... 130 knots... line up with the centreline, make teeny corrections, and power back, relax... hey PAUL!!! Back pressure on stick; go on, pull some more, pull, pull... NICE JOB!' The aircraft kissed the runway. No fire tenders and ambulances rushed out to see if the wounded airman had made it home safely. This was today. We were on the deck, thanks more to Lee's

inputs than my good judgement I'm sure.

To give me a break, Lee taxied in with a few apologies for what he felt was a little bullying during the flight as he firmly instructed me what to do. Not the case – for me, Lee had struck the perfect balance with his instruction, and I hadn't even broke into a sweat it was so enjoyable. That was a day to remember. The debrief with the video was interesting, and I've almost worn it out playing it since. The certificate is a much-valued possession.

Since my last visit, the Stallion 51 facility – the result of many long and tedious hours of planning – is now well established. It is undoubtedly the Mustang Centre of the United States for training, maintenance and safety issues affecting the Mustang. It is a state-of-the-art information clearing house – ironic when you consider that the aircraft it supports is a 1940s fighter. Stallion 51 simply want to see owners operate the aircraft to their full potential and in the safest manner possible.

To date, Stallion 51 have worked with almost 100 people with the intention of them flying their own Mustang in the future, or building their experience to a more proficient level. The full training programme does not have a set number of hours – as you would expect, it all depends on pilot proficiency, the individual's background and talents and how each person reacts to different situations. On the other hand the company want to see a potential Mustang pilot progress through the process at his or her own speed. 'We are not here to try to extend the programme, but to do our very best to make the person a safe Mustang pilot,' explained Doug

Stallion 51 have seen some people, like Bill Anders (an astronaut), go through the course in less than ten hours. Bill was very impressed with the programme and found it extremely valuable. For the average trainee (a commercial multi-engined instrument pilot with 25 hours of T-6 time and perhaps 100 hours of total tailwheel time), approximately 15 hours are needed to go through the whole training syllabus. 'We consider that a student is the person working through the syllabus and a graduate is the person that has completed the syllabus,' said Doug. They make a major distinction, quite rightly, between the two. It would be easy, for instance, for someone to do five hours and profess to have completed the programme, but, as Lee pointed out '...the real heart of the Mustang is the last 20 per cent, where we go really deep into the envelope (such as loss of controlled flight), and deep into the emergency procedures, where the pilot has time spinning the aeroplane left and right and has learned the recovery techniques, in the high-performance role at least, that could cause some major grief.'

Consequently the insurance companies are also recognising the difference between the student and the graduate, to the point where they are saying '...if you are a gradu-

ate of the Stallion 51 programme we will insure you.' This is not, Lee is anxious to point out, a method of featherbedding their business or getting as many hours out of someone as possible.

Stallion 51 wants to see Mustang pilots who are proficient in every way. Additionally the custom-built facility allows the crew to present information in a much better environment with visual aids; Lee indicated that a lot of the programme covers the maintenance side, which is obviously key to the safe operation of the P-51. For example, the majority of pilots come in and will do a pilot's pre-flight with Lee and then Richard or Peter Lauderback (of Stallion 51 Maintenance) will do a maintenance pre-flight, providing a different focus. An entire day can be taken with the brothers covering dos and don'ts of maintenance, tips on what to watch for and how to accomplish various tasks. Undoubtedly this enhances the safety aspect.

Stallion 51 have been in the business since 1987 – the previous year had seen 12 accidents involving P-51s. Thankfully the trend is downward, due in no small measure to Stallion 51's input in the training role. The high-energy accelerated manoeuvre is something that is given great emphasis in the training programme.

What is the best preparation for entering the Stallion 51 training programme? Doug elaborates: 'We take each pilot on a one-on-one basis. We have people come to us that have as little as 300 hours total time and already own a Mustang, to the experienced commercial pilot we talked about earlier with 2,000 hours and taildragger experi-

ence. There really is no set experience level. We do recommend that people get some concentrated, high-quality T-6 time at checkout level for five or ten hours, which gives a better foundation to walk into the programme and makes sense on a cost basis.'

Stallion 51's philosophy is that the Mustang is a serious aeroplane, in a serious business and it needs to be treated with a professional approach. Such are the excellent maintenance levels at Stallion 51, administered by Richard and Pete, that rarely is *Crazy Horse* 'down' and unserviceable, apart from the planned inspections and checks. Having a second TF-51D (*Mad Max*) on line allows *Crazy Horse* to be taken offline for more than about two days at a time, so the aeroplane can be improved. (I found myself asking what could be improved, but Richard and Peter know best!). It also enables Stallion 51 to extend the training syllabus and incorporate high-quality formation training at a realistic cost.

Though I had been for a closely monitored and tightly controlled flight as a non-pilot, Stallion 51 had treated me courteously, seriously, and very professionally. With guys like this around, willing to impart their knowledge at a relatively reasonable cost and with such enthusiasm, the future of the Mustang is in safe hands. Finally, and for the record, the only thing crazy about all of this is the pilots who don't go through the full course!

Mad Max, *sistership of* Crazy Horse, *moves off the ramp at Stallion 51 at the start of another training flight.* Eric Quenardel

Chapter Nine

Surviving Aircraft

Potted Histories of Extant Mustangs

Mustang Survivors is an honest attempt at documenting surviving airframes based on information I have gathered during my long apprenticeship of researching the survivors.

Over the years many Mustangs have crashed and have been rebuilt. Identities have been swapped around and even the most ardent follower of modern Mustang history cannot claim to know it all. This is what makes it so interesting; not one week goes by without me picking up one snippet of information that adds to the big picture!

In the past 15 years huge leaps forward in the availability of major P-51 structures has meant that nothing is impossible to rebuild (or in some cases, more accurately resurrect). With an aircraft approaching its 60th birthday it is foolish to imagine that some of the parts from the airworthy original will not

have worn out. It is even more foolish to think that we can keep Mustangs safely airworthy without an ongoing programme of remanufacture and replacement.

So this list of Mustang survivors is presented in good faith and is, as far as this compiler is concerned, as accurate as possible. Not every historian will agree with my interpretation of the records and information presented to me. That is their prerogative. That said, a word about Mustang owners. For *Mustang Survivors* the registered owner is listed as the owner, ie, the name that appears on the public domain aircraft register. In some cases the names are companies or trusts. Some owners request privacy for various reasons and it is incumbent upon me to respect this request.

Though this work has been professionally

proofread, in presenting such a large number of military serial numbers, dates, construction numbers, foreign air force service histories etc, it is inevitable that gremlins will creep into the works. If you spot what you believe is an inaccuracy or you can add anything to what has been printed here, no matter how insignificant you believe it may be, I urge you to contact me.

The best way to do this is via email at pac@warbirdguru.com and I promise to do my best to answer you in the shortest possible time. If you do not have email the best way to get in touch is via the publisher, Midland Publishing, whose address details can be found at the front of this book.

Immediately below is an explanation of the various abbreviations that appear in the biographies on pages 74 to 173.

Aircraft Status

F	Flyable
GG	Gate guard
M	Museum exhibit
R	Under restoration
S	Stored
U	Unknown status

Aircraft History

acc	accident
adv	advertised
arr	arrived
boc	brought on charge
del	delivered
ff	first flight/flown
ffr	first flight following restoration
i/d	identification/identity
IA	Instructional Airframe
mod	modified
ntu	not taken up
recov	recovered
reg	registered
rep	reported
rereg	reregistered
rest	restored
ses	static exhibition status
soc	struck off charge
tfd	transferred
toc	taken on charge
wfu	withdrawn from use

Others

AB	Air Base
AFB	Air Force Base
ANGB	Air National Guard Base
ATC	Air Traffic Control
FA	Fuerza Aerea (Air Force)
F(AW)S	Fighter (All-Weather) Squadron

FG	Fighter Group
FS	Fighter Squadron
FW	Fighter Wing
Inc	Incorporated
LLC	Limited Liability Company
MDAP	Mutual Defense Assistance Program
NA	NAA production site (Inglewood, CA)
NAS	Naval Air Station
NT	NAA production site (Dallas, TX)
Pty	Proprietary (Aus/NZ)
RR	Rolls-Royce
UKCAR	United Kingdom Civil Aircraft Register
USCAR	United States Civil Aircraft Register

Military Operators

ANG	Air National Guard
CAF	Confederate/Commemorative Air Force
FA d'L GN	Fuerza Aerea de La Guardia Nacional (Nicaragua)
FAB	Fuerza Aerea Boliviana
FAC	Fuerza Aerea Colombiana/Costarricense
FAD	Fuerza Aerea Dominicana
FAG	Fuerza Aerea Guatemalteca
FAH	Fuerza Aerea Hondurena
FAN	Fuerza Aerea Nicaragua
FAS	Fuerza Aerea Salvadorena
FAU	Fuerza Aerea Uruguaya
Flygvapnet	Swedish Air Force
IDF	Israeli Defence Force
IDFAF	Israeli Defence Force/Air Force
RAAF	Royal Australian Air Force
RAF	Royal Air Force
RCAF	Royal Canadian Air Force

RNZAF	Royal New Zealand Air Force
TNI-AU	Tentara Nasional Indonesia-Angkatan Udara (Indonesian Armed Forces-Air Force)
USAAF	United States Army Air Force
USAF	United States Air Force
USN	United States Navy

Organisations / Companies

CAC	Commonwealth Aircraft Co
EAA	Experimental Aircraft Association
FAA	Federal Aviation Administration
NAA	North American Aviation
NACA	National Advisory Committee on Aeronautics
NASM	National Air and Space Museum
TFC	The Fighter Collection
USAFM	United States Air Force Museum

Locations

AK	Alaska
AL	Alabama
AR	Arkansas
AZ	Arizona
CA	California
CO	Colorado
CT	Connecticut
DC	District of Columbia
DE	Delaware
FL	Florida
GA	Georgia
HI	Hawaii
IA	Iowa
ID	Idaho
IL	Illinois
IN	Indiana
KS	Kansas

KY	Kentucky
LA	Louisiana
MA	Massachusetts
MD	Maryland
ME	Maine
MI	Michigan
MN	Minnesota
MO	Missouri
MS	Mississippi
MT	Montana
NB	Nebraska
NC	North Carolina
ND	North Dakota
NH	New Hampshire
NJ	New Jersey
NM	New Mexico
NV	Nevada
NY	New York
OH	Ohio
OK	Oklahoma
OR	Oregon
PA	Pennsylvania
SC	South Carolina
SD	South Dakota
TN	Tennessee
TX	Texas
UT	Utah
VA	Virginia
VT	Vermont
WA	Washington
WI	Wisconsin
WV	West Virginia
WY	Wyoming
ACT	Australian Capital Territory
NSW	New South Wales (Australia)
Qld	Queensland (Australia)
WA	Western Australia
UK	United Kingdom

XP-51 Mustang   73-3101   41-038   N51N
EAA Aviation Foundation, Oshkosh, WI

First flew 20May41 - assigned to RAF (AG348), not del - to NACA, Langley, VA, boc 27Dec41, soc 14Dec42 - tfd NASM, into storage Park Ridge, IL then Silver Hill, MD 1949-75 - reg N51NA to EAA Foundation, Hales Corner later Oshkosh, W 1975-96 - restored Vintage Aircraft Ltd, Fort Collins, CO, ff 1976 - retired to EAA Museum after last flight 1Aug82.

A-36A-1NA Invader   97-15883   42-83665   N3950
USAFM, Wright-Patterson AFB, Dayton, OH

Reg NX39502 to Essex Wire Corp; raced as No.44 and No.2 1946 - painted as racer No.15 *City of Lynchburg* 1947 - acc (crashed) during race, Cleveland, OH 1Sep47 - reg N39502 to Hanby Enterprises Harry McCandless and Ben Widfelt c.1950-52 - external storage Council Bluffs, IA 1949-52 - tfd Walter H Erickson, Minneapolis, MN c.53 - tfd Charles P Doyle, Rosemount, MN 1963-70 - recovered ex-trade school, Winona, MN - tfd USAFM, Wright-Patterson AFB, Dayton, OH 1971 - restored to ses by MN ANG 1973.

A-36A-1NA Invader   97-15949   42-83731   N251
Chino Warbirds Inc, Houston, TX

Tfd Jack P Hardwick, El Monte, CA 1950-75 (stored) - tfd Thomas L Camp, Livermore, CA for rebuild 1975 - rereg N50452 to Dick Martin, Carlsbad, CA Aug80 - rereg N251A to Tom Friedkin of Cinema Air Inc, Carlsbad, CA 1983-95 - tfd Champlin Fighter Museum, Mesa, AZ on loan 1991-93 - tfd Lone Star Flight Museum, Galveston, TX on loan 1994-96 - tfd Chino Warbirds Inc, Houston, TX 8May01 to current.

A-36A-1NA Invader   97-15956   42-83738   N4607
John R Paul, Hamilton, MT

Jack Hardwick, El Monte, CA 1962 - tfd Sidney Smith, Sheridan, IL later Bradenton, FL 1963-72 - tfd Wings of Yesterday Air Museum, Santa Fe, NM 1975-79 - tfd John R Paul, Hamilton, MT later Boise, ID Jun80-95 - reg to Warhawk Air Museum, Caldwell, ID 1990-96 - rebuilt Oakland, CA as 'P-51B' -

P-51A-1NA Mustang   99-22109   43-6006   N51
Gerald Gabe, Hollister, CA

Forced landing Fairbanks-Anchorage, AK 16Feb44 - wreck recovered by Waldon Spillers Oct77 - reg N51Z to Waldon D Spillers, Versailles, OH Feb78 - rebuilt Versailles with ex-Indonesian P-51D mainplane: fffr Jul85 - tfd Gerald Gabe, Hollister, CA 11Oct95 - named *Polar Bear*.

P-51A-5NA Mustang   99-22281   43-6178   N51KW
Kermit A Weeks, Polk City, FL

To Harry McCandless & Ben Widfelt c.1950-52 - external storage at Council Bluffs, IA 1949-52 - tfd Walter H Erickson, Minneapolis, MN 1953 - reg N8647E Walter H Erickson, Minneapolis, MN 1963-78 - tfd Kermit A Weeks, Tamiami, FL 1981-84 - rereg N51KW Weeks Air Museum, Tamiami, FL Dec84 to current - at Cal Pacific Airmotive, Salinas, CA awaiting rebuild.

P-51A-10NA Mustang   99-22354   43-6251   N4235
Planes of Fame Museum, Anchorage, AK

To Cal Aero Technical Institute, Glendale, CA 1946-53 - tfd Ed Maloney/The Air Museum, Claremont, CA 1953 - tfd The Air Museum, Ontario/Chino, CA 1965-81 - reg N4235Y to Planes of Fame Museum, Chino, CA Feb81 to current - restored by Fighter Rebuilders, Chino, CA, ff 19Aug81.

P-51A-10NA Mustang   99-22377   43-6274   N9035
Charles F Nichols, Baldwin Park, CA

Raced as NX73630 1948 - tfd N73630 to Harry McCandless & Ben Widfelt 1950-52 - external storage Council Bluffs, IA 1949-52 - tfd Walter H Erickson, Minneapolis, MN 1953-78 - rereg N90358 to Yanks Air Museum, Chino, CA 1978 to current - rebuilt Chino Dec93.

Right: *Darrell Skurich and his team at Vintage Aircraft Limited in Fort Collins, Colorado restored the world's rarest Mustang, the unique XP-51 41-038. The aircraft now belongs to the Experimental Aircraft Association (EAA) and is on display in the museum at their headquarters in Oshkosh, Wisconsin.* Author

Below: *First flown on 20 May 1941, XP-51 41-038/N51NA flew for a short time following its restoration before being grounded and put on display at the EAA Museum on 1st August 1982. It is seen here on display shortly after its ferry flight from Fort Collins to Oshkosh in 1976.* The Warbird Index

Bottom: *Affectionately called 'Pope Paul', EAA Founder Paul H Poberezny takes XP-51 41-038/N51NA for one of its last flights before it was put into the EAA Museum at Oshkosh.* courtesy EAA

Photographs on the opposite page:

A-36A-1NA Invader 42-83665/NX39502 was owned by the Essex Wire Corporation when this photograph was taken circa 1946. The aircraft crashed in 1947 during the air races at Cleveland, Ohio. William T Larkins collection

Hanby Enterprises owned 42-83665/NX39502 when this photograph was taken in 1951; 20 years later it was transferred to the USAFM at Wright-Patterson AFB, Dayton, Ohio. Dick Phillips collection

42-83665 Margie H *is one of only three known A-36A Invader survivors in the world, making it one of the rarest exhibits at the USAFM.* The Warbird Index

Chino Warbirds' A-36A-1NA 42-83731/N251A was containerised and shipped to Duxford for the 2002 Flying Legends event where it stole the show flown by Steve Hinton. Stephen Grey is seen at the controls in this air-to-air shot over the Cambridgeshire countryside. GHOSTS: Philip Makanna

The A-36A-1A just two days after its arrival at Duxford, almost complete and ready to be test flown. FAA Inspector and long-time Mustang pilot Frank Strickler flew over from the USA to sign the aircraft off. Author

Kent McMakin kindly pulled Kermit Weeks' P-51A-5NA 43-6178/N51KW out of storage at the Weeks Air Museum to be photographed by the author in 1983. The aircraft is now at Art Teeters' Cal Pacific Airmotive where it is slated for rebuild to fly. Author

Photographs on the opposite page:

Moon Spillers taxies in to the warbird ramp area at Oshkosh in August 1986 in his newly restored P-51A-1A 43-6006/N51Z, which was modified to use the D model cooling system. Though this was a valiant effort the warbird judges marked the aircraft down because of this non-standard fit. Author

Ownership of 43-6006/N51Z passed to Gerry Gabe in 1995. Duly named Polar Bear, it is seen getting airborne in February 1997 with Gerry at the controls. Wayne Gomes

P-51B-1NA   102-24560   43-12112
Pacific Fighters, Idaho Falls, ID   R

On build at Pacific Fighters - no further details.

P-51B-15NA Mustang   104-25789   43-24760
Michael Coutches, Hayward, CA   U

Reg NX28388 Jacqueline Cochran, Los Angeles, CA
1946-48, raced as No.13 - acc crashed Sep48, later crashed
Hayward, CA 1959 - tfd Michael Coutches, Hayward, CA,
believed parts only?

P-51C-5NT Mustang   103-26199   42-103645   N61429
American Airpower Flying Heritage Museum,
Midland, TX   F

On static exhibition Billings, MT then recovered by
Confederate Air Force c.1965 - to CAF, Mercedes, TX:
stored c.1965 - reg N9288 to CAF, Harlingen, TX; rebuild
began 1973 - rereg N215CA CAF, Harlingen (later Midland),
TX to current - rebuild commenced Omaha, NE 1973-80, to
Paul-Fleming Field, MN 1985 - aircraft transferred to
Odegaard Aviation, ND for completion 2000 - flew 2001 -
still on USCAR as N251CA.

P-51C-10NT Mustang   103-26385   42-103831   N1204
Kermit A Weeks, Polk City, FL   F

USAAF surplus ex-Stillwater AFB, OK - to Paul Mantz,
Glendale, CA 19Feb46 - reg NX1204 to Paul Mantz, Los
Angeles, CA 1946, raced as No.60 *Latin American* later
No.46 - rereg N1204 to Tallmantz Aviation at the Movieland
of the Air Museum, Orange County, CA 1948-84 - operated
by Frank G Tallman, Orange County, CA 1960-84 - tfd
Weeks Air Museum, Tamiami, FL; stored, then tfd Cal
Pacific Airmotive, Salinas, CA for rebuild - ffr 2000.

P-51C-10NT Mustang   103-26778   43-25147   G-PSIC
Patina Limited, St Helier, Jersey   R

Ex-Holtz Technical School, Tel Aviv, Israel 1960-75 - reg
N51PR Peter Regina, Van Nuys, CA Mar81-86; rebuilt Van
Nuys, CA using P-51B mainplane and unidentified fuselage
believed recovered from Israel, ffr 11Jun81 flown by Dave
Zeuschel - tfd Joseph Kasparoff, Montebello, CA Feb86-96
painted as 36913 *The Believer* - tfd World Jet Inc, Fort
Lauderdale, FL 1996 - tfd Patina as G-PSIC Nov96 - shipped
Pacific Fighters, Idaho Falls, ID for major structural work
Nov98 - reg G-PSIC to Patina Ltd, St Helier, Jersey 16Apr98
to current - operated by The Fighter Collection, Duxford,
Cambs, UK; restoration being undertaken by them.

TP-51C-10NT   103-2????   43-2????
Pacific Fighters, Idaho Falls, ID   R

On build at Pacific Fighters - no further details.

P-51D Mustang   '44-10753'   N405HC
Sale Reported, Oak Grove, LA   F

Built by Cavalier Aircraft Corporation, Sarasota, FL 23Oct68
as Cavalier Mk.2 - Project 'Peace Condor', to Fuerza Aerea
Salvadorena coded FAS 405 Dec68 - recov and reg N31FF to
Flaherty Factors Inc, Monterey, CA 1Nov74, adopting i/d
44-10753 on return to USA - tfd Wilson C Edwards, Big
Spring, TX 1978 - rereg N405HC to Heber Costello Apr99 -
sale reported 2Nov00.

P-51C-10NT Mustang   111-29080   44-10947
NASM, Washington, DC   M

Sold for scrap Stillwater AFB, OK 19Feb46 - to Paul Mantz,
Glendale, CA 19Feb46 - reg NX1202 Paul Mantz, Los
Angeles, CA 9Aug46-50 - mod as air racer No.46 *Excalibur*,
later No.60 *Houstonian* - tfd as N1202 to Charles F Blair,
New York, NY 27May50-52, named *Stormy Petrel* then
Excalibur III - record NY-London flight 31Jan51, returned
via North Pole to NY 29May51 - tfd Smithsonian
Institution/NASM, Silver Hill, MD 29May52-93 - tfd California
Museum of Science & Industry, Los Angeles, CA (on loan).

Photographs on the opposite page:

Planes of Fame P-51A-10NA 43-6251/N4235Y was raced at Reno in September 1981. The white titling visible on the nose is MGM Reno. William T Larkins

Still sporting its RAF camouflage in 1991, but now with the addition of crudely applied Luftwaffe insignia on the wings, fuselage and tail for a filming contract. Thierry Thomassin

P-51A-10NA 43-6274/N90358 is registered to Charles F Nichols of Baldwin Park, California. The aircraft is displayed at the Yanks Air Museum at nearby Chino. Thierry Thomassin

Kermit Weeks at the controls of his P-51C-10NT 42-103831/N1204 "Ina The Macon Belle". The immaculate rebuild and restoration work (see pages 26-27 for detail shots) was carried out by Art Teeters at Cal Pacific Airmotive. Tom Smith

Pete Regina (and passenger) flying P-51C-10NT 43-25147/N51PR Shangri-La which made its first post-rebuild flight on 11 June 1981. Today the aircraft is registered G-PSIC and forms part of The Fighter Collection at Duxford, England. It has been completely rebuilt, the work including the installation of a brand new wing spar. Philip Wallick

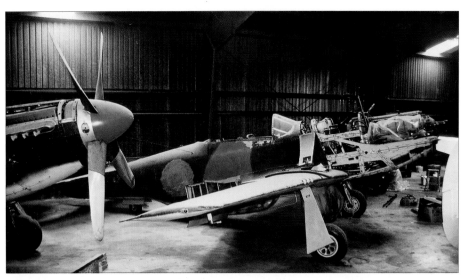

One of the Mustangs stored at Connie Edwards' ranch at Big Spring, Texas was this ex-Fuerza Aerea Guatemalteca Cavalier airframe, identified as '44-10753'/N31FF. In 1998 the aircraft was sold to Heber Costello who had it reregistered as N405HC and restored to flying condition by Ezell Aviation, complete with a Cavalier Mustang tall fin. Dick Phillips

P-51D-5NT 44-11153/N34FF 'Ge Ge' with Scott Smith circa 1978. It was later registered N51WE with the Clark Motor Company of State College, Pennsylvania. The markings are those of the 20th Fighter Group, which has been virtually unrepresented in Mustang paint schemes since. Bill Clark lost his life in the crash of N51WE on 7 March 1988. The Warbird Index

Ed Lindsay gets raises the tail of his Cavalier F-51 Mustang Mk.2 44-13257/N51DL which first flew as a Cavalier Aircraft Corporation company demonstrator in 1967. The aircraft was photographed in April 2000 by Tom Smith.

P-51D-5NT Mustang   111-29286   44-11153   N451TI
Banta Aviation Corporation, Dover, DE

Assigned to FAS coded FAS 409 Sep68 - recovered from Salvador by Jack Flaherty 1974 - reg as N34FF to Flaherty Factors Inc, Monterey, CA 1Nov74 - tfd Scott Smith, Orlando, FL - tfd Clark Motor Co, State College, PA; raced as No.3 *Doll* 1979 - tfd as N51WE to Clark Motor Co, State College, PA Sep85-88 - acc (crashed) near State College, PA (Clark killed) 7Mar88 - i/d tfd Peter Regina, Granada Hills, CA 29Oct98 to 18May00 - tfd Anthony J Banta, Union City, CA 17May00 - rereg N451TB to Anthony J Banta 18May00 to current - tfd Banta Aviation Corporation 21Feb01 to current.

P-51D-5NA Mustang   109-26890   44-13257   N51DI
Lindair Inc, Sarasota, FL

Assigned to NACA coded NACA 108, boc 22Dec44, soc 12Jul57 - mod to EF-51D - reg N4222A to Charles Snydor 1957 - sold surplus ex-NAS Norfolk, VA 1957 - tfd Trans Florida Aviation, Sarasota, FL 1959-67 - mod to Cavalier II by Cavalier Aircraft Corporation, Sarasota, FL 1967 - allocated Cavalier c/n 11 - later modified to Cavalier Mk.2 with underwing hardpoints, ff Dec67, company demonstrator in camouflage paint - military demonstration tour El Salvador Dec68 - tfd Lindsay Newspapers Inc, Sarasota, FL 1970 - rereg N51DL to Lindair Inc, Sarasota, FL 1972 to current.

P-51D-5NA Mustang   109-26911   44-13278
Yugoslav Aviation Museum, Belgrade

Yugoslav Aviation Museum, Belgrade; source unknown, believed fuselage only.

P-51D-5NA Mustang   109-27024   44-13571
USAFM, Armament Museum, Eglin AFB, FL

To Cavalier Aircraft Corporation, Sarasota, FL 1967 - mod to Cavalier T Mk.2 as 68-15796 - assigned US Army 1967 as 68-15796 - to US Army Museum, Fort Rucker, AL then USAFM, Armament Museum, Eglin AFB, FL 1979 to current.

P-51D-5NA Mustang   109-27587   44-13954
Dave Kingshott, Coventry, Warwickshire, UK

Crashed (forced landing on beach) and abandoned Cap Ferrett near Bordeaux, France 26Aug44 - recovered Ailes Anciennes ile de France, Paris 1981 - excavated from beach Cap Ferrett 3May81, damaged further during recovery - tfd Musée de l'Air, Paris-Le Bourget 1984-96 as crashed aircraft exhibit - to Phil Earthey, Norfolk, UK as wreck 1998 - tfd Dave Kingshott, Coventry, Warwickshire Jul01 for rebuild.

P-51D-10NA Mustang   109-27767   44-14134
Private owner, Lincolnshire, UK

Aircraft scrapped in USA post WW2; some structure and identity stored in Lincs, UK for intended rebuild project.

P-51D-10NA Mustang   109-28207   44-14574
East Essex Aviation Museum, Clacton, Essex, UK

Assigned 436th FS/479th FG, Wattisham, Suffolk as 9B-J *Little Zippie* (Capt. Hans J Grasshoff) - ditched off Clacton Pier, Essex 13Jan45 - recovered by East Essex Aviation Museum, Clacton 16Aug87, wreck displayed in crash scenario.

P-51D-10NA Mustang   109-28459   44-14826   N551D
Erickson Group Ltd, Beaverton, OR

Sold to Trottner Iron & Metal Co, San Antonio, TX 1949 - said to be destined for RNZAF (still in original packing case) 1951 reg N1740B to Dal-Air, Dallas-Love Field, TX 1951 - tfd Aircraft Sales Ltd, Dallas, TX 1951 - sold to FAH as 14826, later coded 826, delivered 10Jul51 - sold to FAD for disposal c.1973 - tfd Cavalier Aircraft Corporation, Sarasota, FL c.1973 - tfd Gordon Plaskett, King City, CA - tfd Bruce Morehouse, San Antonio, TX (fuselage only) 1978 - rereg N551D to Bruce Morehouse, San Antonio, TX - registration tfd to Commonwealth CA-17 Mustang c/n 1364 - reg J Erickson, OR.

The late Heber Costello draws in close to the camera-ship of Uwe Glaser. Cavalier Mustang II N405HC was stored for many years at Big Spring, Texas with Connie Edwards before being sold to Heber. It made its first appearance at The Gathering of Mustangs & Legends at Kissimmee in April 1999.

This magnificent cloudscape shows off the sleek lines of Heber Costello's Cavalier Mustang II N405HC in 2000. Both Uwe Glaser

Dr Clifford Cummins raced the heavily modified P-51D-15NA 44-15651/N79111 No.69 Miss Candace *between 1963 and 1979. Other race names it has worn include* Galloping Ghost, Jeannie, Spectre *and* Cloud Dancer. The Warbird Index

On 4 September 1980, N79111 suffered an engine failure on take-off from Van Nuys Airport in California but was repaired quickly enough to compete at Reno that year. William T Larkins

Jimmy Leeward 'hugging the contours' in Bahia Oaks Inc's natural metal N79111. Tom Smith

P-51D-15NA Mustang   109-28618   44-14985   N350R
Robert J Odegaard, Kindred, ND

Reg N350RJ to Robert J Odegaard, Kindred, ND 1May01 to current.

P-51D-15NA Mustang   109-35934   44-15651   N7911
Bahia Oaks Inc, Ocala, FL

Sold for scrap ex-Walnut Ridge AFB, AR 1946 - reg NX7911 to Steve Beville and Bruce Raymond, IL Jul46-49 - mod as air racer No.77 *The Galloping Ghost* 1947-49 - frustrated export to Israel - tfd as N79111 to Dr Clifford D Cummins, Riverside, CA 1963-79; stripped fuselage rebuilt Chino, CA 1964, flown painted as 413366, air racer No.69 *Miss Candace* - acc (damaged, forced landing) Reno, NV Sep70 repaired Long Beach, CA 1971 - tfd Dave Zeuschel of Zeuschel Racing Engines and Wiley Sanders, Van Nuys, CA 1978-80 - acc (engine failure) on take-off Van Nuys, CA, repaired 1980, ff 4Sep80 - tfd Wiley Sanders Truck Lines,Troy, AL 1980-81, raced as No.69 *Jeannie* - to Bahia Oaks Inc, Ocala, FL 1981 to current; raced as No.10 *Spectre* later No.9 *Cloud Dancer*.

P-51D-20NT Mustang   111-36292   44-13009
Richard E Knowlton, Portland, ME

Assigned to RAAF as A68-687, boc 21Jul45, soc 22Dec47 - to Indonesian AF/TNI-AU - recovered from Indonesia by Stephen Johnson/Vanpac Carriers, Oakland, CA 1978 - reg N31RK (ntu) Richard E Knowlton, Portland, ME 1985-96.

P-51D-20NT Mustang   111-36299   44-13016   N5551
Spirit Wing Aviation Limited, Edmond, OK

Assigned RAAF as A68-674, boc 4Jul45, soc Dec48 - recovered from farm Benalla, Victoria, Australia 1966 - tfd Pearce Dunn/Warbirds Aviation Museum, Mildura, Victoria 1966-82 - to Vincent Thomas, Geoff Milne and Alan Lane, Albury, NSW, Australia; parts stored 1982-84 - reg VH-CVA to Vincent Thomas, Albury, NSW - containerised and shipped to Shafter, CA 1984; rebuilt 1984-87 - rereg as N9002N to King City Aviation Dec87 - rebuilt King City, CA 1990-92, fffr 1992 -

P-51D-20NT Mustang   111-36388   44-13105   N71F
Bill G Destefani, Sisters, OR

Assigned to RAAF as A68-679, boc Jul45, soc Dec48 - recovered from farm Benalla, Victoria, Australia 1966 - tfd Pearce Dunn/Warbirds Aviation Museum, Mildura, Victoria 1966-80; rebuilt to ses, exhibited as A68-679 - sold and tfd to David Zeuschel, Van Nuys, CA c.1980; shipped to USA, rebuilt and heavily modified as air racer No.7 *Strega* - reg N71FT to Bill Destefani of Shafter, CA and Sisters, OR to current - acc (engine failure, force landed) Reno 10Sep02.

P-51D-20NT Mustang   111-36389   44-13106
Australian War Memorial, Canberra, ACT, Australia

Assigned RAAF as A68-648, boc Jun45, soc 1950 - tfd as instructional airframe to Royal Melbourne Institute of Technology 30Jun50-83 - tfd Australian War Memorial, Canberra, Australian Capital Territory 1983 to current.

P-51D-20NA Mustang   122-31076   44-63350   N51T
Charles Greenhill, Mettawa, IL

Reg N2870D to Clarence A Head, Elgin, IL 1963-64 - tfd Marl R Foutch, Champaign, IL 1966-84 - tfd Fort Wayne Air Service, Fort Wayne, IN 1984-86; rebuilt 1984-85 as a TP-51D - rereg as N51TK (2nd allocation) to Fort Wayne Air Service, Fort Wayne, IN May86-88 - acc (take-off) Fort Wayne, IN 11Apr89 - tfd International Aircraft Ltd, Hockessin, DE Apr89-92 - rereg N151RR (ntu) International Aircraft, Balliston Spa, NY Oct89 - N51TK to International Aircraft Ltd, Hockessin, DE Oct89-92 - tfd Charles Greenhill Mettawa, IL Sep93-95 - acc (forced landing) Round Lake, IL 29Dec94 - rebuilt Tri-State Aviation, Wahpeton, ND 1996.

nteresting rear view of P-51D-15NA 44-15651/N79111. This Mustang was flown for many years as Dr Clifford Cummins' No.69 Miss Candace *but is een her as No.9* Cloud Dancer *at Reno in 1998.* Tom Smith

4-15651/N79111 No.9 Cloud Dancer *with the Leeward Air Ranch (note the black titling on the nose) of Ocala, Florida at Reno in 1999.* Alan Gruening

The shade of blue used on P-51D-20NA 44-63350/N51TK Lou IV – seen here in March 1988 – and on several other Mustangs over the years, has long been the subject of heated debate. Most historians now agree the colour was actually olive drab, and the legend came about due to the bluish tinge on a World War Two colour photograph. The Warbird Index

P-51D-20NA 44-63476/N63476 was pulled from a lake in Uruguay and is being restored by Gerry Beck at Tri-State Aviation. The aircraft was photographed in February 2001 painted in 402 Sqn, RCAF markings. James P Church

P-51D-20NA Mustang   122-31302   44-63576   N51D
Evergreen Ventures Inc, McMinnville, OR

Reg as NX37492 to Ron Freeman, raced as No.37 *Wraith* and *Jay Dee* 1946-49 - disassembled and stored 1950-70 - rereg N37492 to Edward G Fisher, Kansas City, KS 1963-66 tfd John E Dilley, Muncie, IN 1969-72 - tfd Max I Ramsay, Johnson, KS 1977-83 - rereg N51DH to Consolidated Airways, Fort Wayne, IN Feb81-84 - rebuilt Chino, CA 1977-85 with Bruce Goessling - tfd Fox 51 Ltd, Denton, TX Jan 85-86 - tfd Lewis Shaw, Dallas, TX 1986 - tfd Evergreen Heritage Collection, Marana, AZ 1986 to current.

P-51D-20NA Mustang   122-31303   44-63577   N151J
John R Turgyan, New Egypt, NJ

Assigned FAU coded FAU 265 4Apr49 - Museo de Aeronautica, Montevideo, Uruguay 1960-85; exhibited as FAU 285 - tfd Dante Heredia, Montevideo Jan85 - shipped t USA aboard cargo ship - rereg N51TE to Tyrone Elias, Tulsa OK for rebuild Feb85-94 - to Ezell Aviation, Breckenridge, TX - tfd and rereg N151JT to John R Turgyan, New Egypt, NJ Jul94 to current.

P-51D-20NA Mustang   122-31341   44-63615
ILOC Corp

Assigned FAU coded FAU 270 1950 - to Carrasco AB, Montevideo, Uruguay, exhibited 1965-84 - recovered and tfd Joseph Kasparoff, Montebello, CA 1984-90 - rebuilt to ses at Van Nuys, CA 1986-87 - exhibited Tuskegee Foundation, Tuskegee, AL 1989 - tfd Ascher Ward, Sepulveda, CA; adv for sale 1993 - tfd ILOC Corp 2May94.

P-51D-20NA Mustang   122-31202   44-63476   N63476
Dakota Mustang Inc, Wahpeton, ND   R

Ex-FAU, recovered from lake in Uruguay - tfd Dakota Mustang Inc, Wahpeton, ND 8Mar00 to current.

P-51D-20NA Mustang   122-31233   44-63507   N51EA
Swiss Warbirds Inc, Stratford, CT   F

Assigned RCAF as 9554, boc 7Jun47, soc 20Sep60 - reg N6345T to James H Defuria and Fred J Ritts of Intercontinental Airways, Canastota, NY 25Feb57-60; stored complete Carberry, Manitoba, Canada 1957-61 - tfd Aero Enterprises, Elkhart, IN 10May60-63 - tfd Harold R Hacker, Noblesville, IN Dec63/64 - acc (minor damage) La Porte, IN 22Feb64 - Aero Enterprises, La Porte, IN 7Mar64 - tfd Hammonton Investment Co, Hammonton, NJ 1Sep64 - tfd John Dilley, Elkhart, IN Oct64-65 - tfd Gardner Flyers Inc, Brownwood, TX 16Sep65-72 - acc (badly damaged) Brownwood, TX c.1968 - rereg N12073 (ntu) - rereg N38FF (ntu) - tfd Marvin L Gardner, Brownwood, TX - rereg N13410 to Ray Stutsman, Elkhart, IN 1978-81; Stutsman

rebuilt the aircraft using i/d of 44-72483 and painted as 414303/SX-B *Double Trouble two* - rereg N51EA to Don C Davidson, Nashua, NH; raced as No.27 Apr82-90 - tfd Swiss Warbirds Inc, Basle; ferried, arriving 26Aug90 -

P-51D-20NA Mustang   122-31233   44-63507   N6345T
Patrick J Peters, Saline, MI   R?

Reg N6345T to Paul J Peters, Saline, MI Jan99 - Registration Pending 23Jul01 to current - reregistered to Patrick J Peters, Saline, MI 31Dec01 to current.

P-51D-20NA Mustang   122-31268   44-63542   N51HR
Contri Family LP, Yuba City, CA   F

Sold for scrap McClellan AFB, CA 11Dec57 - reg N5450V to David L (Homer) Rountree, Marysville, CA 18Feb58-79; external storage becoming derelict at Marysville, CA to 1981 - rereg N51HR toTed E Contri and Homer Rountree, Reno, NV Jun82-91 - tfd Contri Construction Co, Yuba City, CA Jan91-Mar01 - Registration Pending Yuba City, CA 8Mar01 - tfd Contri Family LP, Yuba City, CA 9May01 to current.

Bill 'Tiger' Destefani sold his interest in Dago Red to Frank Taylor Racing in 1983 to take on his own air racer, P-51D-20NT 44-13105/N71FT Strega, seen here on early flight tests minus registration and sponsor logos. Dick Phillips

Assigned to the RAAF in July 1945 as A68-679, 44-13105 was sold to Dave Zeuschel of Sylmar, California in the early 1980s. It later passed to Bill Destefani who modified the aircraft, which has evolved into Strega – Italian for witch! The Warbird Index

Strega awaits her turn to qualify at Reno. Note the wing-to-fuselage fairing mods, the special canopy and the wingtip modifications. What you cannot see is the explosive Merlin engine hidden from view beneath the cowlings. The Warbird Index

Above: *Don C Davidson of Nashua, New Hampshire is seen taxying out in P-51D-20NA 44-63507/N51EA* Double Trouble two *for a display in Texas in March 1987. The aircraft has been based in Switzerland with Swiss Warbirds since 1990*. Dick Phillips

Opposite: *44-63507/N51EA* Double Trouble two *in October 1990, high over the Swiss Alps. The aircraft had been ferried from the USA to Switzerland the previous month*. Erich Gandet

Below: *A longer canopy and full dual controls mark out 44-63507/N6345T, seen here at Pioneer Aero Service's Chino base in April 1995, from the standard P-51D Mustang. Some Mustangs have been modified with skeleton dual controls but lack the space and canopy modifications*. The Warbird Index

Ted Contri's P-51D-20NA 44-63542/N51HR Sizzlin Liz, *from an unusual angle.* The Warbird Index

44-63542 at Madera in 1987 as N51HR with Robb Satterfield in the cockpit. Previously it was registered N5450V to Homer Rountree of Marysville, California and spent over 20 years 'stored' outside before being acquired by Ted Contri of Yuba City, California in January 1991. Alan Gruening

Fox 51 Ltd of Denton, Texas operated two Mustangs for some time: P-51D-20NA 44-63576/N51DH is seen being escorted by CAC-built Mustang Mk.22 A68-198/N286JB in the late 1980s. Frank Strickler

P-51D-20NA Mustang   122-31381   44-63655   N5500S
Amphib Inc, Wheeling, IL

Assigned Flygvapnet (type designation J 26 in Swedish service) as Fv26152 - tfd to FA d'L GN Nicaragua coded GN 84 17Jan55 - reg N6153U to MACO Sales Financial Corp, Chicago, IL 2Sep63 - acc (damaged, forced landing) Nicaragua, on delivery flight 1May65 - reg N5500S to Wings & Wheels Inc, Palos Park, IL Jan85-98 - tfd Amphib Inc, Wheeling, IL 24Aug1998 to current - rebuilt by Square One Aviation, Chino, CA 2000; fffr Apr02.

P-51D-20NA Mustang   122-31389   44-63663   N41749
Richard Hansen, Batavia, IL

To Trans Florida Aviation, Sarasota, FL c.1958 for Cavalier programme - assigned to FA Guatemalteca as FAG 354 in 1962 - reg N41749 to Don Hull, Sugarland, TX Aug72 - tfd Wilson C Edwards, Big Spring, TX 1978-96 - tfd Richard Hansen, Batavia, IL May96 to current; rebuilt by Ezell Aviation, Breckenridge, TX.

P-51D-20NA Mustang   122-31401   44-63675   N1751D
Roger A Christgau, Edina, MN

Combat veteran assigned to 9th Air Force as 463675/E6-D *Sierra Sue II* - tfd Flygvapnet (type designation J 26 in Swedish service) as Fv26152 - assigned to FA d'L GN Nicaragua as GN 91; put on display at Officers' Mess, FAN base - tfd MACO Sales Financial Corp, Chicago, IL 2Sep63 - reg N5452V (2nd allocation) to Dave Allender 1973; rebuilt, ff 11Sep73, air raced as No.19 - tfd Roger A Christgau, Edina, MN Apr77-78 - rereg N1751D to Roger A Christgau, Edina, MN 23Feb78 to current.

P-51D-20NA Mustang   122-31427   44-63701   N26PW
Almanor Aviation Inc, San Jose, CA

Assigned Flygvapnet (type designation J 26 in Swedish service) as Fv26015 23Apr45-52 - sold to Fuerza Aerea Dominicana coded FAD 1904 Dec52-84 - Cavalier field modification - tfd Johnson Aviation, Miami, FL 19May84-87 - tfd Vincent Tirado, Miami, FL; rebuilt 1987-91, reg N51VT - tfd Brian O'Farrell - tfd Plane Works, Rockford, IL 27Jan99 to current - rereg N26PW 9Nov99 - Registration Pending San Jose, CA - tfd Almanor Aviation, San Jose, CA 20Mar00 to current.

P-51D-20NA Mustang   122-31533   44-63807   N20MS
Jon S Vesely, Inverness, IL

Assigned FAU as FAU 272 4Dec50-60 - Cavalier programme - assigned FAB as FAB 506 under Project 'Peace Condor' 19Mar60-77 - sold to Arny Carnegie, Edmonton, Alberta, Canada Dec77 - reg C-GXUO to Bill Bailey Aviation Service, Calgary, Alberta Jul78-84 - rereg N20MS and tfd Ed L Stringfellow of Mid South Lumber Company, Birmingham, AL Jun85-Mar01 - tfd Jon S Vesely, Inverness, IL 9Mar01 to current; on rebuild at Midwest Aero Restorations Ltd, Danville, IL.

P-51D-20NA Mustang   122-31536   44-63810   N451BC
Joseph K Newsome, Cheraw, SC

To Norton AFB, CA 1963; exhibited as 463810 - tfd The Air Museum, Ontario, CA 1965-72 - rebuilt to fly Chino, CA 1972 with identity 45-11367 - reg N63810 to The Air Museum, Buena Park, CA 1972 - tfd Robin Collard, Merced, CA and Weslaco, TX 1973-78 - transported by road to Fullerton, CA for rebuild in 1973; flown painted as 463810/B6-C *Stump Jumper* - tfd Jerry Hayes, Henderson, CO 1982-88 - acc (damaged, belly landing) Denver, CO Jun84 - tfd Bernard H Raouls, Zephyr Cove, NV 1988-92 - tfd Joseph K Newsome, Cheraw, SC Sep92-93 - rereg N451BC to Joseph K Newsome, Cheraw, SC Aug93 to current.

Roger Christgau has owned P-51D-20NA 44-63675/N1751D Sierra Sue II *(a genuine 9th Air Force and Flygvapnet veteran) since April 1977 when he rescued it from a life as an air racer. It is seen in the air in May 1986.* Dick Phillips

Built for Dick Hansen, P-51D-20NA 44-63663/N41749 Miss Marylin II *(an ex-FAG Mustang) was in store with Connie Edwards at Big Spring, Texas for over 20 years before being sold and subsequently beautifully restored by Ezell Aviation.* Chad Ezell

P-51D-20NA Mustang   122-31590   44-63864   G-CBNM
The Fighter Collection, Duxford, Cambs, UK   F

Assigned Flygvapnet (type designation J 26 in Swedish service) as Fv26158 17Jun49 - to IDFAF coded 2338 - Israeli Air Force Museum, Herzlia; stored 1978 - to Israel Yitzhaki, Sde-Dov, Israel Mar78-84; rebuilt Herzlia 1978-84 using parts ex-USA; adopted i/d 44-63864, ff Herzlia 5Feb84 - reg 4X-AIM to Israel Yitzhaki, Herzlia Feb84-86 - reg SE-BKG to Novida AB/Flygexpo Vasteras, Vasteras 24Mar87-94; flown from Israel via Cyprus and Frankfurt Dec86, arrived Malmo, Sweden 23Dec86; painted as Fv26158 coded 16K - leased to Duke of Brabant Air Force, Eindhoven, Holland Sep94 - tfd The Fighter Collection, Duxford Apr02 to current; reg G-CBNM to Patina, operated by The Fighter Collection.

P-51D-20NA Mustang listed i/d 44-63864   N42805
Kenneth Hake, Tipton, KS   U

Assigned Flygvapnet (type designation J 26 in Swedish service) as Fv26158 17Jun49 - sold to IDFAF coded 3506 9Feb53-58 - sold to Israeli Aircraft Industries, Tel Aviv 1958 - reg N251L to William P Lear/Lear Inc, Los Angeles, CA 18Jul60 - tfd William R Pearce, Fullerton, CA Dec62-70 - acc (crashed) Keflavik, Iceland on ferry flight from Israel to the United States, via Paris 6Jun63 - mangled wreckage reportedly moved from fire dump in Iceland to USA 1989 by Cham S Gill of Canada - rereg N42805 to Cham S Gill, Central Point, OR May91 - to Kenneth A Hake, Tipton, KS Mar92-95.

P-51D-20NA Mustang   122-31591   44-63865   N151T
Classic American Aircraft Inc, Poland, OH

Ex-9th AF - assigned Flygvapnet (type designation J 26) as Fv26018 Apr45-54 - to FA d'L GN Nicaragua coded GN 90 17Jan55-63 - reg N6163U and sold to MACO Sales Financial Corp, Chicago, IL 23Sep63 - tfd PAAL Inc, East Point, GA 1966 - tfd O J Kistler, Long Valley, NJ 1969 - reg N51JK to O J Kistler, Long Valley, NJ; racer No.47 1973-96 - tfd Classic American Aircraft Inc, Poland, OH and rereg N1251D 28Dec1998 - rereg N151TF to same owner 25May00 to current.

P-51D-20NA Mustang   122-31597   44-63871
Musée de l'Air, Paris, France   N

Assigned Flygvapnet (type designation J 26 in Swedish service) as Fv26039 - sold to IDFAF - reg N9772F to Robert I Turner/Marom Air Services Ltd, Tel Aviv, Israel 1963-70 - reported at Cannes, France Sep65 - tfd Musée de l'Air, Le Bourget, Paris, France 1975 to current.

P-51D-20NA Mustang   122-31615   44-63889   C-FFU
Reported Sold May 2002

Sold Harry E Padley, Hamilton, OH 1963-64 - tfd Harold Reavis, Fayetteville, NC 1966-69 - tfd Dan Furtrell, Nashville TN Aug69 - tfd W R Rodgers, Rolling Fork, MS 1970-72 - reg CF-FUZ to Gary D McCann, Stratford, Ontario, Canada Dec73-83 - rereg C-FFUZ to same owner 1984 to May02 - rereg to John D Anderson, Alpena, MI to current.

P-51D-20NA Mustang   122-31619   44-63893   N3333
Wayne Rudd, Basalt, CO

Assigned RCAF as 9560, boc 7Jun47, soc Sep60 - external storage Carberry, Manitoba, Canada 1957-60 - tfd Aero Enterprises, Elkhart, IN 1960-62 - to RCAF Lincoln Park, Alberta as gate guard 1960-62 - sold to Ed Fleming, Calgary, Alberta; rebuilt 1963 - reg CF-PIO to Helmsworth Construction, Wetaskiwin, Alberta 1965-66 - tfd Keir Air Transport, Edmonton Alberta - rereg N3333E Specialty Restaurants, Long Beach, CA 1969-75 - tfd MARC, Chino, CA 1975 to current - USAFM, March AFB, CA - tfd Wayne Rudd, Basalt, CO 10May01 to current.

Colonel Bruce Carr flying Joseph K Newsome's P-51D-20NA 44-63810/N63810 Angels' Playmate, *named after Carr's original Mustang. On 2 April 1945 Colonel Carr became an 'Ace in a day' when, during a fighter sweep over Nuremberg, Germany, he downed three Fw 190s and two Bf 109s. Bruce Carr passed away in April 1998.* Brad Lauderback

44-63810 was exhibited at Norton Air Force Base, California in 1963. The aircraft is seen here in spurious markings and an unlikely sharkmouth paint scheme. It is now N451BC with Dr Joseph Newsome as Angels' Playmate. R F Besecker

The original Angels' Playmate – *which is NOT a Mustang survivor! This photo shows how accurate the representation of the name artwork is on N451BC.* Norm Avery collection

Photographs on the opposite page:

The history of P-51D-20NA 44-63807/N20MS Tiger Lily *includes service with the Bolivian and Uruguayan air forces before it was recovered by Arnie Carnegie and registered C-GXUO. Now owned by Jon Vesey of Inverness, Illinois, it is currently being rebuilt and restored to flying condition.* The Warbird Index

The restoration of 44-63807 is being undertaken at Midwest Aero Restorations' facility in Danville, Illinois. Mike VadeBonCoeur of MAR told the author it was one of the most original Mustangs he has ever seen. James P Church

P-51D-20NA 44-63865 served with the 9th AF before being passed to Sweden and Nicaragua. It was registered to Jack Kistler in 1973; nearly 30 years later it was rebuilt (in TF-51D configuration) by Square One Aviation and was about to fly, as N151TF, at the time of writing. Thierry Thomassin

Jack Kistler's cowling-stripped N51JK getting some attention at Reno in September 1980. William T Larkins

Leif Jaraker's P-51D-20NA SE-BKG at Duxford in 1994. This Mustang's identity has since been confirmed as 44-63864 which served with the 78th FG as Twilight Tear. Author

Photographs on the opposite page:

P-51D-20NA 44-63864 was rebuilt in Israel in the early 1980s and registered 4X-AIM. Seen here in primer on an early post restoration flight, it was seldom flown before being acquired by Flygexpo of Sweden and registered SE-BKG in 1987. The Warbird Index

The same aircraft painted in the colours of 122 Squadron, Netherlands East Indies Air Force (1947) in September 1994. Duke of Brabant Air Force

P-51D-20NA Mustang 122-31718 44-63992
Flygvapenmuseum Malmen, Linkoping, Sweden   **M**

Assigned Flygvapnet (type designation J 26) as Fv26020 -
to IDFAF coded 2353 - tfd Flygvapenmuseum Malmen,
Linkoping, Sweden Dec65 to current.

P-51D-20NA Mustang 122-31731 44-64005   N51CK
Charles S Kemp, Hazlehurst, MS   **F**

Combat veteran: originally assigned to 8th Air Force as
464005/E9-Z *Mary Mine* (mount of George Vanden Heuval) -
surplussed and assigned RCAF as 9561, boc 7Jun47, soc
20Sep60 - reg N6339T to James H Defuria and Fred J Ritts of
Intercontinental Airways, Canastota, NY Dec58-60; external
storage Carberry, Manitoba, Canada 1957-61 - tfd Aero
Enterprises, Elkhart, IN 10May60-62 - Carberry-Winnipeg-
Elkhart 1962 - tfd Lewis C Buell, Springfield, OH 27Sep62-65
- Sherman Aircraft Sales, Baer Field, IN 8May65 - tfd G S
Vincent, Winchester, MA 30Jul65 - tfd Robert Bleeg, Seattle,
WA Oct67-73 - reg N51WB (1st allocation) to Wayne
Brown, Port Gibson, MS 1973 - tfd Joe Arnold,
Eudora/Mulberry, AR 4Oct75 - rereg N51CK to Charles S
Kemp, Jackson/Hazlehurst, MS 20Jul78 to current.

P-51D-20NA Mustang 122-31848 44-64122   N339TH
Ozark Management Inc, Jefferson City, MO   **F**

Assigned Flygvapnet (J 26 and S 26 in Swedish service) as
Fv26130 - sold to FA d'L GN Nicaragua as GN 80 17Jan55 to
1963 - reg N6151U to MACO Sales Financial Corp, Chicago,
IL 23Sep63 - rereg N150U to John Lowe, Chicago, IL -
Gardner Flyers Inc, Brownwood, TX 1966 - tfd Wilson C
Edwards, Big Spring, TX May67 - rereg N339TH 23May97.

P-51D-20NA Mustang 122-31887 44-72028   N51JY
Jeremy Porter, Chicago, IL   **R**

Reg N22B 1948 - exported to IDFAF coded 41 18Jul48 -
wreck recovered from Palmahim kibbutz playground,
Israel by Robert J Lamplough, Duxford, UK - containerised
and shipped to UK Dec76 - tfd Noel Robinson and David
Laight, North Yorks 1980-95 - reg G-LYNE to E Noel
Robinson & Partner 5Dec95 - sold USA Dec01 - reg N51JY
28Nov01, no owner listed.

P-51D-20NA Mustang 122-31894 44-72035   F-AZMU
Jacques Bourret, Brunieux St Desirat, France   **F**

Reg N5411V to Whiteman Enterprises, Pacoima, CA
1963-78 - rereg HK-2812P to H Escobar, Bogota, Colombia

*Charles Kemp, the owner, taxies P-51D-20NA
44-64005/N51CK Mary Mine at Harlingen, Texas
some years ago. This genuine ex-8th Air Force
combat veteran of the 361st FG was the
personal mount of Lt George Vanden Heuval
who is in the back seat of the aircraft. The nine
kill markings are genuine. Richard Paver*

*Though published many times before, this
evocative shot of P-51D-20NA 44-72028/'41' in
Israel in the late 1970s says it all. The aircraft
saw combat with the IDF and like many other
IDF aircraft following retirement, was put out to
grass in a children's playground on a kibbutz. It
was discovered by Robert J Lamplough and
bought back to the UK. After languishing stored
in the UK for many years it was sold to Jeremy
Porter of Chicago in 2001 and registered N51JY.
Harry Holmes*

*P-51D-20NA 44-72035/N5411V when owned by
Marvin Whiteman of San Fernando, California
in 1959. Norm Avery*

May82-87 - rereg HK-2812X - reg N5306M (ntu) Dec88 - reg F-AZMU to Jacques Bourret of Aero Retro, St Rambert d'Albon, France Sep89 to current.

P-51D-20NA Mustang   122-31910   44-72051   N68JR
Roland J Fegen, Granite Falls, MN   F

Assigned Flygvapnet (designated J 26 in Swedish service) as Fv26026 21May45-52 - sold FAD coded FAD 1912 Oct52-84 - Cavalier field modification - Johnson Aviation, Miami, FL 19May84-85 - tfd John R Sandberg, Minneapolis, MN 1985 - reg N68JR John R Sandberg, Minneapolis, MN Apr88-91 - rebuilt Fighter Rebuilders, Chino, CA; fffr 21Mar91 coded 28 *Platinum Plus* - tfd Janet S Bjornstad, Scottsdale, AZ Oct91-95 - tfd Ron Fegen 30Aug95 to current.

P-51D-20NA Mustang   122-31918   44-72059   N951HB
Vintage Aero Inc, Wilmington, DE   R

Assigned Flygvapnet (type designation J 26 in Swedish service) as Fv26142 - sold FA d'L GN Nicaragua coded GN?? 17Jan55-63 - reg N6150U to MACO Sales Financial Corp, Chicago, IL 2Sep63-66 - tfd Aviacion Sanford, Gardena, CA 1966 - sold to FA Boliviana coded FAB 513 Jun66 - rereg N711WJ to World Jet Inc, Fort Lauderdale, FL Jan 95 - rereg N951HB to Vintage Aero, Wilmington, DE Jun97 to current - on rebuild with Glen Wegmann, Fort Lauderdale, FL.

P-51D-20NA Mustang   122-31945   44-72086   N510JS
Vintage Air Ltd, Yardley, PA   F

Assigned Flygvapnet (type designation J 26 in Swedish service) as Fv26009 21Apr46-52 - sold to FA Dominicana coded FAD 1936 20May53-84 - Cavalier field modification - to Johnson Aviation, Miami, FL 19May84 - mod to TP-51 (dual controls) by FAD 1984 - reg N789DH to Johnson Aviation Miami, FL Apr86 - tfd Joseph E Scogna of Vintage Air Ltd, Yardley, PA 1987 - rereg N510JS to Vintage Air Ltd, Yardley, PA 1994 to current.

P-51D-20NA Mustang   122-31982   44-72123
Museo de Fuerzas Armadas, Dominican Republic   M

Combat veteran: assigned Flygvapnet (type designation J 26 in Swedish service) as Fv26092 21Aug47-52 - sold FA Dominicana coded FAD 1914 31Oct52 - rebuilt by FAD at San Isidro AB, Dominican Republic; displayed (pole-mounted) 1984-95 - tfd Museo de Fuerzas Armadas, Santo Domingo, Dominican Republic 1995 to current.

P-51D-20NA Mustang   122-38604   44-72145   N51PT
Castlewood Air Motive Inc, Towson, MD   F

Reg N6169C - rereg N311G to John C Seidel, Sugar Grove, IL 1963-70 - tfd Waldo (Clay) Klabo, Pleasanton, CA 1978-83; raced as No.85 *Fat Cat* - tfd Don Whittington, Fort Lauderdale, FL 1984 - tfd Peter McManus, Fort Lauderdale, FL 1984 - tfd and rereg N51PT to Peter McManus of Castlewood Realty, Miami, FL Jan85-86 - tfd Castlewood Air Motive, Baltimore, MD Aug86 to current.

Just imported to France and wearing a small registration, P-51D-20NA 44-72035/F-AZMU was registered N5306M in December 1988 but it was not taken up. Thierry Thomassin

Acquired by Frenchman Jacques Bourret in 1989, 44-72035/F-AZMU Jumpin'-Jacques wears the unit markings of the Pacific-based 3rd Fighter Squadron, 3rd Fighter Group. The aircraft was photographed at La Ferté Alais in France. Thierry Thomassin

P-51D-20NA 44-72086/N510JS, previously in service with the Fuerza Aerea Dominicana and the Flygvapnet, during an engine run at Baer Field, Indiana. Fort Wayne Air Service

P-51D-20NA 44-72086/N789DH Baby-Duck *was acquired by Joe Scogna of Vintage Air in 1987 from Brian O'Farrell of Hialeah, Florida. The late Jeff Ethell is seen flying the aircraft out of Oshkosh in 1988.* Robert S DeGroat

When Brian O'Farrell recovered the remaining Fuerza Aerea Dominicana Mustangs in 1983, one airframe (FAD 1914) was left behind. Originally 44-72123, it is documented as Edwin Giller's The Millie G *when it served with the 55th FG, 8th AF. It was mounted on a pylon at the gate of San Isidro AB but was recently removed and refurbished and will be installed in the Museo de Fuerzas Armadas once the buildings are completed.* Brian O'Farrell

P-51D-20NA 44-72145/N311G was raced as No.85 Fat Cat *by Waldo (Clay) Klabo from 1978-83. Ownership then passed to Pete McManus in January 1985.* William T Larkins

That's about as close as you can get! Telephoto foreshortening aside, long-time Mustang owner Pete MacManus holds formation to the rear of the B-25 Mitchell camera-ship in P-51D-20NA 44-72145/N51PT Petie 3rd. He has owned this aircraft since 1984. Uwe Glaser

Registered to Castlewood Air Motive of Towson, Maryland, 44-72145/N51PT is painted as Lt Col John Meyer's Petie 3rd of the 487th FS, 352nd FG. Tim Bivens

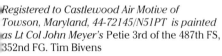

The late Mark Hanna taxies in at Duxford in Robs Lamplough's newly restored P-51D-20NA 44-72216/G-BIXL shortly after the first flight in May 1987. Michael Shreeve

The same aircraft in an earlier guise while serving with the Israeli Defence Force. Robs Lamplough's restoration used a Netherlands-sourced mainplane. via Robs Lamplough

FAD 1916 Dec52-84 - Cavalier field conversion - Johnson Aviation, Miami, FL 19May84-87 - Brian O'Farrell, Miami, FL - rereg N723FH to Flying Heritage Collection, Bellevue, WA 5Jan99 - tfd Flying Heritage Inc 5Apr01 to current.

P-51D-20NA Mustang   122-38859 44-72400
New England Air Museum, Bradley, CT   R

Reg NX69406 to Woody Edmondson, Lynchburg, VA and raced as No.42 *City of Lynchburg* 1Jul46 - rereg NX13Y to Woody Edmondson, Lynchburg, VA 5Dec46 - tfd DiPonti Aviation, Minneapolis, MN 21Dec46 - tfd Anson Johnson, Miami, FL and raced as No.45 21Jul47-59 - attempted piston airspeed record 1952 - rereg N502 to Robert Bean, Danville, IL 28Sep59 - tfd John Juneau and George Nesmith, Opa Locka, FL May62 - tfd John Juneau, Opa Locka, FL Nov62 - tfd Robert D'Orsay, Opa Locka, FL Dec62 - tfd Frank W Lloyd, Miami, FL 1963-64 - tfd Walter E Ohlrich, Tulsa, OK Feb65 - rereg N913Y to Richard Vartanian, Pasedena, CA Mar66-72 - tfd Leonard Tanner, Granby, CT 19Jul72 - rereg N13Y to the Bradley Air Museum, Windsor Locks, CT 16Aug72-88 - rebuilt Skaneateles, NY 1984 - tfd New England Air Museum, Bradley, CT 1988 - on rebuild to ses.

P-51D-20NA Mustang   122-38897 44-72438   N7551
Lady Alice Corporation, Wilmington, DE   F

Assigned Flygvapnet (type designation J 26 in Swedish service) as Fv26131, del 24Apr48 - sold to FA Dominicana as FAD 1920 Dec52-84 - Cavalier field conversion - Johnson Aviation, Hialeah, FL 19May84-87 - tfd Selby R Burch, Kissimmee, FL 1987 to current - reg N7551T to Selby R Burch Sep95 to 16Feb99 - tfd Lady Alice Corporation, Dover, DE 16Feb99 to current.

P-51D-20NA Mustang   122-38651 44-72192   N5460V
California Warbirds, Cupertino, CA

Reg N5460V to James H Bohlander, Roselle, IL 1963-64 - tfd William S Cochran III, Houston, TX 1966 - tfd John V Crocker, San Mateo, CA 1969-72 - tfd California Warbirds, San Jose, CA Jun78 to current.

P-51D-20NA Mustang   122-38661 44-72202
SAAF Museum, Swartkop AB, South Africa   F

Assigned Flygvapnet (type designation J 26 in Swedish service) as Fv26112, del 13Jun47 - sold FA Dominicana as FAD 1917 Dec52-84 - Cavalier field conversion - to Johnson Aviation, Miami, FL 19May84- 87 - to SAAF Historic Flight, Lanseria 19Nov87 - rebuilt as SAAF 325, to SAAF Museum, Swartkop AB; ff after rebuild in South Africa 13Oct1998.

P-51D-20NA Mustang   122-38675 44-72216   G-BIXL
Robert J Lamplough, Hungerford, Berks, UK   F

Combat veteran 352nd FG, 8th AF: sold Flygvapnet (type designation J 26 in Swedish service) as Fv26116 25Feb48 - sold IDFAF coded 2343 19Mar53 - recovered from Ein Gedi kibbutz, Israel by Robs Lamplough; to Duxford, UK 1976 -

reg G-BIXL to Robs Lamplough, Duxford/North Weald, UK 3Jul81 - restored at Duxford, later North Weald using mainplane from 44-72770 from Dutch tech. school; ff North Weald 5May87 - painted as 472216/HO-L, later HO-M; appeared in film *Memphis Belle* Jun89 painted as AJ-L

P-51D-20NA Mustang   122-38798 44-72339   N51JC
James A Cavanaugh Jr, Addison, TX   F

Sold Flygvapnet (type designation J 26 in Swedish service) as Fv26115 13Jun47 - sold FA Dominicana coded FAD 1918 Oct52-84 - Cavalier field conversion - Johnson Aviation, Miami, FL 19May84 - tfd Elmo Hahn, Muskegon, MI 1984 - reg N51EH to Hahn Inc, Muskegon, MI Nov85-90 - ff Fort Wayne, IN 15Oct85 - tfd James A Cavanaugh, Dallas, TX 1990-91 - rereg N251JC to Jani-King International Inc, c/o Cavanaugh Flight Museum, Dallas-Addison, TX Dec91 - rereg N51JC (to same owner) 20Jan01 to current .

P-51D-20NA Mustang   122-38823 44-72364   N723FH
Flying Heritage Inc, Seattle, WA   R

Sold Flygvapnet (type designation J 26 in Swedish service) as Fv26061, del 25Apr47 - sold FA Dominicana coded

P-51D-20NA 44-72438/N7551T appropriately named Lady Alice to reflect its ownership by the Lady Alice Corporation of Dover, Delaware. The aircraft has since been repainted by Sky Harbour Aircraft Refinishing as the 486th FS, 352nd FG's Hell-er-Bust, the mount of Edwin Heller. Dick Phillips

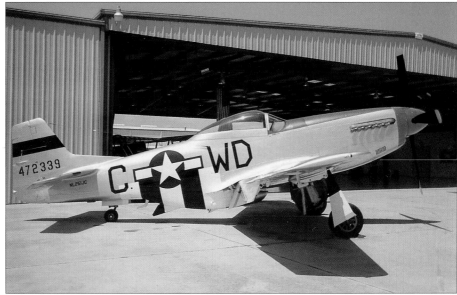

Photographed in November 1996 wearing the 'WD' code of the 335th FS, 4th FG, N7551T served with the air forces of Dominica and Sweden before returning to the USA in 1984. Tom Smith.

A 1991 shot of James Cavanaugh's P-51D-20NA 44-72339/N251JC at Dallas, Texas. It has since been reregistered N51JC to the same owner in Addison, Texas. Author

P-51D-25NA 44-72773/G-SUSY was registered to Charles Church (Spitfires) Ltd after arrival from the United States (where it had been N12066). With the death of Charles Church in July 1989 led to the aircraft being sold to Paul Morgan in May 1990. Sadly, Paul was killed in Sea Fury WH588/G-EEMV in May 2001. G-SUSY is pictured here at Duxford in 1988. Michael Shreeve

Cavalier II Mustang 44-72777 is one of the most historic Mustangs extant today, with significant 15th Air Force history. Modification by Cavalier in 1972 led to it being reserialled 72-1537. Seen at Mojave in 1981 as Singapore Sally prior to its first flight following restoration by Al Letcher, it was later sold to Steve Seghetti who painted it in its wartime markings and reregistered it N151D. The Warbird Index

Steve Seghetti fast-taxies P-51D-25NA 44-72777/N151D at Reno in 1998. It was recovered from Indonesia in 1978, having served with the TNI-AU as F-344. Kevin Grantham

P-51D-25NA Mustang   122-39198   44-72739   N44727
Elmer F Ward, Santa Ana, CA

Recovered from Universal Studios, Hollywood, CA by Ascher Ward, Van Nuys, CA Aug70 - reg N44727 to Ascher Ward, Van Nuys, CA 1971-73 - tfd Elmer F Ward, Chino, CA Aug75 to current; painted 414292/QP-A *Man O'War*.

P-51D-25NA Mustang   122-39226   44-72767

Reg N6836C to Walter Oaks, Ida Grove, IA 1963-64 - tfd Cavalier - tfd O K Airways Inc, Chicago, IL 1966 - tfd Cavalier Aircraft Corp, Sarasota, FL 1969-70 - tfd Lindsay Newspapers Inc, Sarasota, FL 1972-85 - tfd David B Lindsay King City, CA for storage 1984-87- fate unknown, believed to have been absorbed by Pioneer Aero Service, Chino, CA

P-51D-25NA Mustang   122-39232   44-72773   G-SUS'
Paul J Morgan, Brixworth, Northants, UK

Sold to FA d'L GN Nicaragua as GN 120 31May58-63 - reg N12066 to MACO Sales Financial Corp, Chicago, IL 8Jul63 - tfd I N Burchinall Jr, Paris, TX 1966-84 - tfd Robert L Ferguson, Wellesley, MA 1985-86 - rereg G-SUSY 23Jul87 and tfd Charles Church (Spitfires) Ltd, Winchester, UK; ferried ex-USA, arrived UK 26Jun87 - tfd Paul Morgan, Sywell, UK 1May90 to current.

P-51D-25NA Mustang   122-39236   44-72777   N151
Steve Seghetti, Klamath Falls, OR

Combat veteran: to Trans Florida Aviation, Sarasota, FL 28Aug59-67 - mod as Cavalier Mk.2 serial 72-1537 - sold TNI-AU coded F-344 1967-78 - recovered by Stephen Johnson of Vanpac Carriers, Oakland, CA - tfd Al Letcher, Mojave, CA 16Jul79-81 - reg N8064V to Al Letcher, Mojave, CA Apr81-84 - rebuilt Mojave; ff 22Apr81 - sold and rereg N151D to Steve Seghetti, Vacaville, CA 14Apr84 to current.

P-51D-25NA Mustang   122-39270   44-72811   N471
Cascade Warbirds Co, Forest Grove, OR

Sold to IDFAF coded 13 - Holtz Technical School, Israel 10Jan80 - recovered by Angelo Regina and Ascher Ward, Van Nuys, CA 1980-82 - rebuilt Van Nuys 1982 as TP-51D using ex-CA ANG airframe recovered from film studios; ff 1983 painted as 472218/WZ-I *Big Beautiful Doll* - reg N268BD to Phil Dear, Terry, MS 1983-85 - tfd Bob Byrne, Bloomfield, MI 1987-88 - rereg N215RC to Robert Converse Sisters, OR 1988 - rereg N471R to Cascade Warbirds Co, Sisters, OR Apr89 to current.

P-51D-25NA Mustang   122-39285   44-72826   N51Y
Mikoyan LLC, Paducah, KY

Assigned RCAF as 9563, boc 7Jun47, soc 20Sep60 - reg N6344T to James H Defuria and Fred J Ritts of Intercontinental Airways, Canastota, NY 25Feb57-60 - in storage Carberry, Manitoba, Canada 1957-62 - tfd Aero Enterprises, Elkhart, IN 10May60-62 - tfd John Milton, Edwardsville, IL 4May64-73 - tfd Max and Danny Ramsay, Johnson, KS 31Mar73-78 - tfd Thomas J Watson, Stowe, VT 4Jan78-85 - rereg C-FBAU (2nd issue) to Canadian Warplane Heritage, Hamilton, Ontario 3 Mar85-91 - tfd and rereg N51YS to Steve C Collins, Dunwoody, GA 4Nov91-02 - tfd Mikoyan LLC, Paducah, KY 1May02 to current.

P-51D-25NA Mustang   122-39361   44-72902   N33
Violet M Bonzer, Los Angeles, CA

Assigned RCAF as 9564, boc 7Jun47, soc 20Sep60 - reg N6343T to James H Defuria and Fred J Ritts of Intercontinental Airways, Canastota, NY 25Feb57-60 - open storage Carberry, Manitoba, Canada - tfd Aero Enterprises, Elkhart, IN 10May60-64 - reg N335 to E D Weiner, Long Beach CA and raced as No.14 17Apr64-73 - tfd Violet M Bonzer, Los Angeles, CA 8May73 to current - exhibited EAA Museum, Hales Corner, WI 1973-80 - to GossHawk Unlimited, Mesa, AZ for rebuild 1996 -

Photographed at Breckenridge, Texas in May 1987 wearing an adaptation of an already inaccurate 361st FG paint scheme, P-51D-25NA 44-72826/C-FBAU Old Boy was at the time operated by the Canadian Warplane Heritage. Dick Phillips

Once a tour attraction at Universal Studios, P-51D-25NA 44-72739/N44727 was restored at Van Nuys, rebuilt by Aero Sport at Chino and finished as 44-14292/QP-A Man O'War, the mount of Lt Col C H Kinnard of the 334th FS, 4th FG. Note the Spitfire rear-view mirror (one of two on the windshield frame), as featured on Kinnard's original aircraft. Bob Munro

Ready to race – P-51D-25NA 44-72902/N335 No.14 when registered to the famous E D Weiner. This Mustang was regularly raced from 1963 through 1974 before being transferred to Violet Bonzer in May 1973. William T Larkins

Ray Hanna in P-51D-25NA 44-72917/G-HAEC dressed as Missy Wong from Hong Kong *(appropriate as the aircraft had been rebuilt in Hong Kong by Mal Rose and crew) for the Spielberg film* Empire of the Sun *which saw the Mustangs dropping 'bombs' on film sets!* The Warbird Index

Rob Davies in 44-72917/G-HAEC Big Beautiful Doll *(nearest the camera, 78th FG markings) and the late Paul Morgan in P-51D-25NA 44-72773/G-SUSY* Susy *(4th FG markings) make a pairs fly-by at Duxford's Flying Legends 1999 airshow.* Eric Quenardel

P-51D-25NA Mustang   122-39366   44-72907   N334FS
Duane S Doyle Trustee, Castro Valley, CA   F

Assigned FA Guatemalteca coded FAG 357 1958 - reg
N41748 to Don Hull, Sugarland, TX Aug72 - tfd Wilson C
Edwards, Big Spring, TX 1978-Jan00 - tfd Duane Doyle,
Castro Valley, CA 7Jan00-Feb02 - rereg N334FS to same
owner 14Mar02 to current; painted as QP-O/*Red Dog XII*.

P-51D-25NA Mustang   122-39376   44-72917   G-HAEC
Robert W Davies, Ashford, Kent, UK   F

This aircraft carried identity of A68-192 until 2002 (A68-192:
assigned RAAF, boc 8Mar51, soc Apr58 - reg VH-FCB to
F Chris Braund, Tamworth, NSW, Australia Apr58-61 - tfd
Jack McDonald, Moorabbin, Victoria 1961-66 - tfd Ed
Fleming of Skyservice Aviation, Camden, NSW Oct66-69 -
rereg PI-C651 to George Scholey of Prontino Inc, Manila,
Philippines 27Feb69-75 - acc (landing) Manila Airport
18Oct73 - rebuild began Manila, using centre-section/parts
of ex-Philippine AF P-51D-25NA 44-72917) - tfd Ray Hanna
and Mal Rose, Hong Kong Aeronautical Engineering Co, Kai
Tak Airport, Hong Kong 1975-85 - rebuilt Kai Tak 1976-85,
fffr Feb85 painted in RAAF markings coded CV-H - rereg
VR-HIU to D E Baker & Partners, Hong Kong 1981 - rereg
G-HAEC to The Old Flying Machine Company, Duxford, UK
- airfreighted to London-Gatwick Airport 28Feb85 - tfd Rob
Davies, Woodchurch, Kent 1997 to current.

TF-51D-25NA Mustang   122-39381   44-72922   N93TF
Carol L Shuttleworth, Huntington, IN   F

Reg N7718C (1st issue) to Robert H Fee, San Antonio, TX
17Feb58 - rereg N18Y to Larry Sheerin, San Antonio, TX
May58 - tfd Robin Eschauzier, Lackland AFB, TX Nov58-61 -
rereg N6803T to Robin Eschauzier, Lackland AFB, TX
3Feb61-62 - tfd William D Owens, Hondo, TX Oct62-63 -
rereg N577WD William D Ownes, Hondo, TX 28Jan63 - tfd
Space Systems Laboratory Inc, Melbourne, FL 1963-66 - tfd
Trans Florida Aviation, Sarasota, FL 24Mar67-71 - tfd
Lindsay Newspapers Inc, Sarasota, FL 10Sep71-84 - in
storage at King City, CA 1971-85 - tfd Gordon W Plaskett,
King City, CA 1984-85 - tfd James Shuttleworth, Huntington,
IN 1991- to Fort Wayne Air Service, Fort Wayne, IN 1985-90
for rebuild as TF-51D - rereg N93TF to James Shuttleworth,
Kenney, TX May93 to current - ff Fort Wayne IN 6Jun93.

P-51D-25NA Mustang   122-39393   44-72934   XB-HVL
Humberto de la Gaza, Mexico   F

To Merlin Aire Ltd - reg N513PA to Pioneer Aero Service,
Chino, CA Feb91 - Warbirds of Great Britain Ltd, Biggin Hill,
UK 1991-92 (rebuilt by Pioneer Aero Service at Chino,
shipped to UK); ff Biggin Hill 3Mar92 - tfd Humberto de la
Gaza, Mexico 1994.

P-51D-25NA Mustang   122-39395   44-72936   N7711C
Marvin L Crouch, Encino, CA   F

Reg N7711C to Arthur J Stasney, Altadena, CA 1963-66 -
rebuilt Van Nuys, CA 1968 - tfd Solomon J Pasey,
Coatesville, PA Jun69 - tfd Flight Lease Inc, Columbus, OH
1970 - tfd Warren G Schulden, Elizabeth, NJ 1972-78 - acc
(crashed) Eufala, AL 16Dec79 - i/d tfd Marvin L Crouch,
Encino, CA Mar83 to current.

P-51D-25NA Mustang   122-39401   44-72942   N5427V
Anthony A Buechler, Elm Grove, WI   F

Reg N5427V to Robert Fulton Co, Newtown, CT 1963-83 - tfd
Gordon W Plaskett, King City, CA 1983-85 - rebuilt King City,
CA; ff 1985 painted as 414151/HO *Petie 2nd* - tfd Anthony A
Buechler, Elm Grove, WI Sep85 to current.

P-51D-25NA Mustang   122-39407   44-72948
USAFM Collection, WV   M

Assigned USAFM, ex-Charleston ANGB, WV 1957-94.

P-51D-25NA Mustang   122-39448   44-72989
Volk Field ANGB, Madison, WI   M

USAFM Collection, Volk Field ANGB, WI 1984 to current.

*The first engine runs of Jim Shuttleworth's
TF-51D-25NA 44-72922/N93TF at Fort Wayne Air
Service, Baer Field, Indiana on 23 April 1993.*
Jim Shuttleworth

*Rob Davies in P-51D-25NT 44-72917/G-HAEC
Big Beautiful Doll breaks away from Uwe
Glaser in the Harvard camera-ship in June
2000. Registered as a CAC-built Mustang, its
paperwork was later corrected by the owner
after looking into the history of the aircraft with
assistance from the author.* Uwe Glaser

P-51D-25NA 44-72934/N513PA Shangrila *after its rollout by Pioneer Aero Service in October 1991 following a full restoration. The author supplied details for the markings to David Arnold prior to its rebuild.* Joe Cupido

Jim Shuttleworth's dual-control TF-51D-25NA 44-72922/N93TF Scat VII *bears the markings of the 434th FS, 479th FG and was flown by Major Robin Olds who went on to fly in the Korean War and Vietnam War.* The Warbird Index

44-72934 Shangrila *is now with Humberto Lobo de la Gaza in Mexico as XB-HVL. It was photographed at Kissimmee in April 1999. While the 336th FS, 4th FG markings and individual artwork remain, the colour of the rudder has been changed.* Author

Seen in an unusual paint scheme in 1977, P-51D-25NA 44-72942/N5427V was first registered to Robert Fulton in 1963. It still wears this registration today but is now in authentic 352nd FG markings with Tony Buechler as Petie 2nd. The Warbird Index

Two colourful Mustangs formate on the B-25 camera-ship flown by former Mustang owners Ed and Connie Bowlin for the camera of Tom Smith. In the lead is Tony Buechler's P-51D-25NA 44-72942/N5427V Petie 2nd (352nd FG markings), while holding formation is Jeff Michael's tall-tailed Cavalier-modified P-51D-30NA 44-74976/N98582 (since re-registered N651JM).

P-51D-25NA 44-72989 at Volk Field Air National Guard Base, Madison, Wisconsin. There are still a handful of Mustangs in use as gate guards, much to the chagrin of some of us. Dick Phillips

P-51D-25NA 44-73079/N576GF Bernies Bo in trademark white. Above the exhaust stack is the inscription 'Illegitamus Non Carborundum' (Don't Let the Bastards Grind You Down). Bob Munro

P-51D-25NA 44-73129/N51SL No.22 Merlin's Magic in August 1983. Stu Eberhardt of Danville, California has owned this Mustang since 1986 and it has appeared regularly at Reno's Unlimited Air Races with mixed results. It is now registered N151SE. Thierry Thomassin

P-51D-25NA Mustang   122-39449   44-72990
US Army Aviation Museum, Fort Rucker, AL

Assigned RCAF as 9283, boc 23Jan51, soc 29Apr58 - reg N6322T to James H Defuria and Fred J Ritts of Intercontinental Airways, Canastota, NY 25Feb58-60 - tfd Aero Enterprises, Elkhart, IN 10May60-62 - tfd Eastern Truck Rentals, Lowell, MA 17Apr62-63 - tfd James W Vandeveer, Dallas, TX 24Jan64-65 - tfd John Peters, Norwood, CO 5May65-66 - acc (crashed) Grand Junction, CO 21Aug65 - tfd Stanley W Kurzet, Covina, CA 2Feb66-67 - tfd US Army, Edwards AFB, CA 27Apr67-78; chase a/c 0-72990 - tfd US Army Aviation Museum, Fort Rucker, AL 7Feb78 to current.

P-51D-25NA Mustang   122-39488   44-73029   N51JI
James E Beasley, Philadelphia, PA

Assigned FA d'L GN Nicaragua coded GN122 31May58-63 - reg N7999A to MACO Sales Financial Corp, Chicago, IL 13Jul63 - tfd James R Almand, Grand Prairie, TX 1963-64 - tfd Jerald L Baker, Angleton, TX 1966 - rereg N51JB to Jessie A Baker, Houston, TX and raced as No.51 Jun69-78 - tfd James E Beasley, Philadelphia, PA Oct79 to current.

P-51D-25NA Mustang   122-39538   44-73079   N151BI
Bill Dause, Wellington, UT

Reg N7716C, ex-surplus sale from McClellan AFB, CA Feb5: - tfd Joseph P Dangelo, Campbell, CA 1963 - rereg N576GF to Growers Frozen Foods, Salinas, CA 1963-66 - tfd Jerry G Brassfield, San Jose, CA Jun69-71 - tfd Robert Love, Oakland, CA 1973 - tfd Experimental Aircraft Association (EAA), Franklin, WI 1978 - tfd Robert J Love, Oakland, CA 1982-85 - tfd Russell R Francis, San Francisco, CA 1987-88 - rereg N151BL to Russell R Francis, South Lake Tahoe, CA Jul89-90 - tfd Bill Dause, Wellington, UT Apr91 to current.

P-51D-25NA Mustang   122-39540   44-73081   N5074I
Michael E Coutches, Hayward, CA

Reg N5074K to Michael E Coutches of American Aircraft, Hayward, CA Jul63 to current.

P-51D-25NA Mustang   122-39557   44-73098
Cougar Helicopters, Daytona Beach, FL

Assigned Italian AF coded MM4292, boc 26Feb45, soc 7Feb49 - to Rome-Ciampino as IA for fire drills - external storage (fuselage and wings) Cappenelli, Italy coded SM-6: - recovered by Robert J Lamplough, Duxford, UK 1981 - tfd Paul Raymond, Whitehall Theatre of War 1982-85 - reg G-BMBA to Robert J Lamplough, North Weald, UK - sold at auction 5Jun85 to Aces High Ltd, Duxford, UK - sold in USA struck off UKCAR 2Aug85 - tfd Steve Dill, Orlando, FL c.198: - to Cougar Helicopters, Daytona Beach, FL 1987.

P-51D-25NA Mustang   122-39576 44-73117   N251S(
Square One Aviation, Chino, CA

Registered by Square One Aviation, Chino, CA 26Nov96.

P-51D-25NA Mustang   122-39588   44-73129   N151SI
C S Eberhardt Trustee, Danville, CA

Reg to Tony Randozza, Oakland, CA 1958 - reg N5480V to J M Jackson, Long Beach, CA 1963 - to Thomas W Winship Corona Del Mar, CA 1963-64 - tfd Stan's Aircraft Sales, Fresno, CA 1966 - tfd Frank A Barrena, San Luis Obispo, CA 1969 - sold FA Haiti coded FAH 15650, ferried Jul69 - mac c.1970 - recov ex-Haiti, stored Miami, FL 1972 - tfd and rereg N51SL to Dixon J Smith, Seattle, WA 1972 - tfd Rodne Barnes, Oconomowoc, WI 1978-86 - rebuilt Chino, CA 1982 85 for Stuart Eberhardt, Danville, CA as racer No.22 Jul86-9 - rereg N151SE to Stuart Eberhardt, Danville, CA Sep94 - tfd Eberhardt C S Trustee, Danville, CA 11Oct00 to current.

A beautiful study of Jim Beasley's P-51D-25NA 44-73029/N51JB Bald Eagle *as it dances with the clouds in 1999. The aircraft was in fact registered with the 'JB' suffix for its previous owner, Jesse Baker of Houston, Texas.* Tom Smith

P-51D-25NA Mustang   122-39599 44-73140   N314BG
Ice Strike Corporation, Dover, DE   S

To RCAF as 9567, boc 7Jun47, soc 20Sep60 - reg N6337T to
James H Defuria and Fred J Ritts, Intercontinental Airways,
Canastota, NY 25Feb57-60 - external storage Carberry,
Manitoba, Canada 1957-62 - tfd Aero Enterprises, Elkhart, IN
10May60-64 - tfd J D Kent, Des Moines, IN13Apr64-67 - rereg
N169MD (2nd issue) to Dr Burns M Byram, Marengo, IA and
raced as No.71 8Nov67-78 - rereg N51N to Charles Ventors
of Aerodyne Sales, El Reno, OK Oct78-82 - rereg C-FBAU
(1st issue) to Dennis J Bradley, Burlington, Ontario, Canada
Jan82-84 - forced landed and burned at Massey, Ontairo
7Jul84 - i/d tfd to C-GZQX (ntu): Fill-R-Up Ltd, Edmonton,
Alberta, Canada Jul85 - tfd Trans America Helicopters,
Edmonton, Alberta 1986 - tfd Marvin L Gardner, Mercedes,
TX Apr86 - rereg N314BG to Gordon Plaskett of BG Aero,
King City, CA Sep86 - tfd Pioneer Aero Service, Chino, CA
Jan87-88; rebuilt Chino, ff 25Jul88 - ferried to UK, operated
by Warbirds of Great Britain Ltd, Biggin Hill 1988-92 - tfd
Eastwind Inc, Wilmington, DE Feb93-Nov95 - tfd registered
to Ice Strike Corporation, Dover, DE 29Nov95 to current.

P-51D-25NA Mustang   122-39601 44-73142   N51BK
Banta Aviation Corporation, Dover, DE   R

Reg N6173C to Michael T Loening, Salmon, ID 1963-64 - tfd
Westair Co, Westminster, CO 1966 - tfd Vernon S Peterson,
Valley View, TX 1968-78 - rereg N51PW to Vernon S
Peterson, Valley View, TX Apr78 - rereg N51VP to Vernon S
Peterson, Valley View, TX - tfd Universal Life Church, TX
1983-84 - tfd J Bradford Enterprises, Prescott, AZ 1987-89 -
acc Denton, TX (Peterson killed) 6Sep89 - i/d tfd to N51BK
Bruce C Morehouse, Jefferson, TX Apr91-May01 - tfd Banta
Aviation Corporation, Dover, DE 18May01 to current.

P-51D-25NA Mustang   122-39608 44-73149   G-BTCD
Pelham Ltd / The Old Flying Machine Company,
Duxford, Cambs, UK   F

To RCAF as 9568, boc 7Jun47, soc 20Sep60 - reg N6340T to
James H Defuria and Fred J Ritts, Intercontinental Airways,
Canastota, NY 25Feb57-60 - external storage Carberry,
Manitoba, Canada 1957-61 - tfd Aero Enterprises, Elkhart, IN
10May60-62 - by road Carberry-Elkhart Jun62 - tfd Ernest W
Beehler, West Covina, CA 30Jul62-74 - tfd Charles E Beck
and Edward J Modes, Burbank, CA and raced as No.7
Candy Man 19Aug74-76 - tfd Robert E MacFarlane,
Placerville, CA 4Aug76-80 - tfd Patina, c/o The Fighter
Collection, Duxford, UK May80-86 - ferried via Reykjavik,
Iceland to Geneva, Switzerland 23Aug80 - arrived Biggin
Hill 2May81 - rereg N51JJ to John V Crocker, San Mateo, CA
May 1986 - op by The Fighter Collection, Duxford 1986-91 -
acc Stapleford, UK 9Aug90 (repaired) - rereg G-BTCD to
Patina, c/o The Fighter Collection, Duxford 11Jan91-Apr99 -
tfd Old Flying Machine Company, Duxford Apr99 to current.

P-51D-25NA Mustang   122-39622 44-73163   N51MR
Jackson McGoon Aircraft Corp, Los Angeles, CA   R

To RCAF as 9285, boc 8Feb51, soc 29Apr58 - reg N6300T to
James H Defuria and Fred J Ritts, Intercontinental Airways,
Canastota, NY 5Feb57-60 - tfd Aero Enterprises, Elkhart, IN
10May60-61 - tfd Suncoast Aviation, St Petersburg, FL 8Jul61
- tfd Valair Aircraft Inc, Cincinnati, OH 28Sep61-63 - tfd
Farnum Brown, Michigan City, MI 4Mar64 - tfd Robert A
Mitchem, Broomfield, CO 12Mar64 - tfd James D Morton,
Aero Enterprises, Elkhart, IN 14Apr64 - tfd D K Fesenmyer,
Mount Pleasant, MI 25Apr64 - tfd Robert H Pollock,
Abbotstown, PA 21May65-66 - rereg N5151M to Herbert E
Rupp, Mansfield, OH 17Nov66 - rereg N5151R to Rupp
Industries Inc, Mansfield, OH 1969 - rereg N51MR to same
company 1972-74 - tfd Edward O Messick, San Antonio, TX
2Mar74-79; painted as 473656 *Minute Man* - tfd Charles
Knapp, Los Angeles, CA 1983-89 - acc (take-off) Santa
Monica, CA 2Sep89 - tfd Jackson McGoon Aircraft,
Los Angeles, CA 89 -95 - tfd Randall Kempf 1996 to current.

Coming in low and fast in a striking red and white paint scheme, 44-73149/N6340T arrives at Bex in Switzerland. The arrival of this aircraft heralded a long-overdue influx of airworthy Mustangs to the UK and continental Europe. Erich Gandet

Photographed at Oakland Airport, California on 15 August 1981, N6340T is prepared (with spectacular long-range auxiliary fuel tanks) for the ferry flight to Europe. William T Larkins

Clive Denney of Vintage Fabrics painted the Old Flying Machine Company's 44-73149/G-BTCD with a yellow nose for the Breitling Fighters. The Mustang was photographed at La Ferté Alais, Cerny aerodrome near Paris in May 1999. It has since been repainted as Lt Col Wallace Hopkins' 413704/B7-H Ferocious Frankie of the 374th FS, 361st FG. Thierry Thomassin

P-51D-25NA 44-73163/N51MR Danny Boy at an airshow in 1976. Some 25 years earlier it was in service with the Royal Canadian Air Force as RCAF 9285. William T Larkins

Photographs on the opposite page:

Seen in the Warbirds of Great Britain hangar at Biggin Hill in 1989, Pioneer Aero Service rebuilt P-51D-25NA 44-73140/N314BG Petie 2nd which flew for the first time after restoration in July 1988. It is now thought to be in storage at North Weald, England though it is registered to the Ice Strike Corporation of Dover, Delaware at the time of writing. Author

P-51D-20NA 44-73149 served in Canada as RCAF 9568 but was struck off charge on 20 September 1960 and sold to James H Defuria and Fred J Ritts of Intercontinental Airways. It is seen here at Carberry in 1962 as N6340T and was imported to the UK by Stephen Grey in 1981. First displayed by Ray Hanna at Biggin Hill on 16 May 1981, it is now G-BTCD operated by The Old Flying Machine Company based at Duxford. Jerry E Vernon collection

44-73149 in the hangar at La Ferté Alais, France for some engine work. Registered as N51JJ and operated by The Fighter Collection, the aircraft was painted as 463221/G4-S Moose, as flown by 357th FG pilot Myron Becraft. Author

P-51D-25NA Mustang   122-39665   44-73206   N3751D
Blue Sky Aviation Inc, Sellersburg, IN   F

Reg N7724C, sold surplus McClellan AFB, CA 1958 -
tfd Trans Florida Aviation, Sarasota, FL 1963-64; modified
as Cavalier Mustang 2000 - reg N3751D to Henry B Faulkner,
Stoddard, NH 1966-70 - rereg F-AZAG to Jean-Francois
Lejeune, Faaa, Tahiti 1975-83 - shipped to Tahiti ex-Chino,
CA 1976 - rereg N3751D to Jean-Francois Lejeune, Chino,
CA Apr83 - tfd Clyde Logan Neill, Indian Wells, CA Apr83
(shipped Tahiti-CA as deck cargo aboard *Polynesia* 1983)
- rebuilt Chino, CA; ff Feb84 coded JF-L and named *Hurry
Home Honey* - tfd Al Ashbourne, Chino, CA 1985 - tfd Blue
Sky Aviation, Louisville, KY and Sellersburg, IN 1985 to
current.

P-51D-25NA Mustang   122-39669   44-73210   CF-IKE
Manitoba Ltd, Manitoba, Canada   F

Reg N5461V to Flying W Inc, Medford, NJ 1963 - tfd Rusk
Aviation, Kankakee, IL 1963-64 - tfd Edward G Fisher,
Kansas City, KS 1966-69 - tfd Gardner Flyers Inc,
Brownwood, TX 1970-72 - tfd Kenneth Boomhower, KS
1973 - acc (crashed) Valley Airpark, CO (Boomhower
killed) 17May73 - i/d tfd Angelo and Peter Regina, Van
Nuys, CA 1978-80; rebuilt Van Nuys based on IDFAF
airframe - Long Beach, CA 13Jan78 - ff Van Nuys, CA
30Jan80 as 473210/WD-B *Widowmaker* - rereg N1040N to
Angelo Regina, Van Nuys, CA Jan80-87 - tfd Joseph
Kasparoff, Van Nuys, CA 1988-92 - rereg CF-IKE to Manitoba
Ltd, Manitoba, Canada 11Jul95 to current.

P-51D-25NA Mustang   122-39713   44-73254   N6328T
Donald R Weber, Baton Rouge, LA   F

Assigned RCAF as 9571, boc 7Jun47, soc 20Sep60 - reg
N6328T to James H Defuria and Fred J Ritts of
Intercontinental Airways, Canastota, NY 27Feb57-60 -
external storage Carberry, Manitoba, Canada 1957-61 - tfd
Aero Enterprises, Elkhart, IN 10May60-61 - tfd Clifford C
Pettit, Ligonier, IN 3Oct61-70 - acc (crashed) Crumstown, IN
31May63 - tfd A C Lofgren, Battle Creek, MI 6Jun72 - tfd
Donald R Weber, Baton Rouge, LA 15Aug74-96; fffr Jan78.

P-51D-25NA Mustang   122-39719   44-73260   N83KD
David O'Malley, OH   R

Reg N5075K - rereg N451D to Joseph E Anzelon, Whitestone,
NY 1963-64 - tfd Howard Olsen, Midland, TX 1966 - tfd Trans
Florida Aviation, Sarasota, FL 1969 - tfd Cavalier Aircraft
Corp, Sarasota, FL Aug69-70 - sold to Indonesian AF/TNI-AU
coded F-360 - acc in service (crashed) Java 24Jun75 -
recovered by Stephen Johnson, Oakland, CA 1979 - tfd
Steve Wilmans, CA, 1999 to current - rebuilt Aero Trader,
Chino, CA - tfd David O'Malley, Ohio, May02 to current.

P-51D-25NA Mustang   122-39723   44-73264   N5428V
American Airpower Flying Heritage Museum,
Midland, TX   F

Reg N5428V to Mathew P Kibler, Luray, VA 1963 - tfd
Charles B Schalebaum, Ridgewood, NJ 1963-64 - tfd John M
Sliker, Wadley, GA 1966 - tfd William Ross Enterprises Inc,
Chicago, IL 1969 - tfd Confederate Air Force, Harlingen, TX
1970 - tfd George F Williams, Hobbs, NM 1972 - tfd
Confederate Air Force, Harlingen (later Midland), TX
3Nov77 - acc (crashed) Omaha, NE 17Jun81 - rebuilt as
airworthy to current.

P-51D-25NA Mustang   122-39732   44-73273   N200DD
John G Deahl, Denver, CO   F

Sold FAS Jul69 - reg N34DD reserved 1976 - rereg N200DD
to Donald R Anderson, Saugus, CA 1978 - tfd John G Deahl,
Denver, CO May80-81 - tfd J G Deahl Estate, Denver, CO -
rereg N210DD (ntu) - tfd Charles Mothon, Gallway, NY 1989.

P-51D-25NA 44-73254/N6328T Buster *seen at Breckenridge, Texas on 26 May 1985, painted in pseudo 361st FG colours.* Dick Phillips

Colonel Regis Urschler regularly flies the Commemorative Air Force's P-51D-25NA 44-73264/N5428V Gunfighter II *to airshows in the United States. His CAF 'rank' actually demotes him somewhat as in the RAF ('real air force') he reached Brigadier General status (USAF Ret'd). The Mustang is seen here in July 1988.* The Warbird Index

P-51D-25NA 44-73273/N200DD in a relatively subdued colour scheme at Reno in 1981. This Mustang was last known to be with Charles Mothon of Gallway, New York but is seldom seen in public. William T Larkins

Photographs on the opposite page:

Modified by Cavalier in the 1960s, P-51D-25NA 44-73206/N3751D Hurry Home Honey *was operated in Tahiti for a number of years wearing a bright yellow colour scheme and registered F-AZAG. Photographed out of Oshkosh in 1991, its accurate presentation of Pete Peterson's 364th FS, 347th FG colours more than compensates for its time dressed as a civilian.* Robert S DeGroat

Ike Innes of Manitoba Limited gets airborne in P-51D-25NA 44-73210/CF-IKE The Miracle Maker *in April 2000.* Tom Smith

P-51D-25NA Mustang   122-39734 44-73275   N119H
James D Elkins, Salem, OR   F

Sold surplus McClellan AFB, CA 16Sep57 - reg N2868D to Richard E Blakemore, Tonopah, NV 1963-64 - rereg N119H to Vernon E Thorpe, Oklahoma City, OK 1966 - tfd Paul D Finefrock, Hobart, OK 1969 - tfd Richard L Wood, Houston and Refugio, TX Jun69-72 - tfd Jack W Flaherty, Monterey, CA and raced as No.9 1973 - tfd Wilson C Edwards, Big Spring, TX 1978-83 - tfd Foy Midkiff, Houston, TX 1984-85 - tfd Alan S Kelly, Middlebury, CT 1988 - tfd Kelco Aircraft, Wilmington, DE 1989-90 - tfd John Mills 1991 - tfd Aviation Sales Inc, Englewood, CO Mar92-Feb97 - tfd James Elkins, Salem, OR 12Feb97 to current.

P-51D-25NA Mustang   122-39746 44-73287   N951M
Michael J George, Springfield, IL   F

Sold surplus ex-McClellan AFB, CA for $957.58 - reg N5445V to William Kelbaugh, Chico, CA Mar58-64 - tfd William S Cooper, Merced, CA 1964-72 - tfd James Francis, Medina, OH 1974 - Courtesy Aircraft, Rockford, IL 1977-78 - tfd James S Francis, Medina, OH 24Jan78-80 - rereg N51DF to James S Francis, Medina, OH Aug80 - tfd Jack A Rose, Spangle, WA Jun82-87 - acc (damaged, landing) Reno-Cannon NV 9Sep86 (repaired) - rereg N751JC to C & C

Vintage Aircraft, Rockford, IL Oct88 - rereg N5445V to John J Castrogiovanni, Rockford, IL 1988 - tfd Michael J George/Air Combat Museum, Springfield, IL 1989 to current.

P-51D-25NA Mustang   122-39782 44-73323   N151MD
Marvin L Crouch, Encino, CA   R

Reg N6167C to Aero Service Inc, Nogales, AZ 1963-64 - tfd Darryl G Greenamyer, Van Nuys, CA 1966 - tfd Michael A Geren, Kansas City, MO 1969-70 - rereg N4270P to Marvin L Crouch, Encino, CA Jan81 - rereg N151MD to Marvin L Crouch, Encino, CA 11Feb81 to current.

P-51D-25NA Mustang   122-39798 44-73339   G-SIRR
David J Gilmour/Intrepid Aviation, London, UK   F

Assigned FAC coded 2, del 16Jan55, crashed 19Jan55 - via Cavalier to Indonesian AF/TNI-AU as F-3?? - recovered by Stephen Johnson, Vanpac Carriers, Oakland, CA 1979 - tfd Ronald M Runyan, Fairfield, OH 1982-84 - rebuilt Chino, CA 1982-84; adopted i/d 44-74008 *Dallas Doll*, ff Chino 1984 - rereg N151MC (ntu): Ronald M Runyan, Fairfield, OH Feb84 - rereg N51RR to same Dec84-95 - tfd Robs Lamplough, North Weald, Essex, UK 1989 - tfd Intrepid Aviation, North Weald 1991-96; arrived UK 14Feb91 - reg G-SIRR to David J Gilmour/ Intrepid Aviation Co, London 3Feb97 to current.

P-51D-25NA Mustang   122-39802 44-73343   N5482
Bruce C Morehouse, Celeste, TX

Reg N5482V to Ben W Hall, Seattle, WA 1963-67 and raced as No.2 *Seattle Miss* - tfd Chance Enterprises Inc, Half Moon Bay, CA 1969 - tfd Michael T Loening, Boise, ID and raced as No.2 Jun69-72 - acc (badly damaged) Reno, NV Sep71 - rebuilt Chino 1974 - tfd Bruce Morehouse, San Antonio TX 1983 to current.

P-51D-25NA Mustang   122-39806 44-73347
National Aviation Museum, Rockcliffe, Ottawa, Canada

Assigned RCAF as 9298, boc 16Mar51 - to Canadian War Museum, Ottawa 9Aug61-64 - tfd Canadian National Aeronautical Collection, Rockcliffe AB, Ontario and exhibited as 9298/Y2-E 1964-82 - tfd National Aviation Museum, Rockcliffe, Ontario, Canada Sep82 to current.

P-51D-25NA Mustang   122-39808 44-73349
Swiss Transport Museum, Lucerne, Switzerland

Assigned Swiss AF coded J-2113, boc 6Nov48, soc 11Apr58 tfd Swiss Air Force Museum, Dubendorf AB 1960-93 - tfd Swiss Transport Museum, Lucerne (loan) 1977-90 -

P-51D-25NA 44-73287 was sold surplus at McClellan AFB, California and registered N5445V to William Kelbaugh of Chico, California in March 1958. Boardman C Reed

A pristine P-51D-25NA 44-73275/N119H Never Miss on 28 February 1990 after rollout from the paint shops of Business Air Services, Goderich, Ontario, Canada. The Warbird Index

Photographs on the opposite page:

P-51D-25NA 44-73287 was originally rebuilt by Jack Rose as N51DF and is seen here in a later guise as N951DM Worry Bird with Mike George at the controls. Joe Cupido

David Gilmour of Intrepid Aviation now owns 44-74008/G-SIRR, photographed in September 1988 as N51RR. It was rebuilt by Ron Runyan and Fighter Rebuilders. Thierry Thomassin

P-51D-25NA Mustang   122-39809   44-73350   N33FF
Lee O Maples, Vichy, MO   F

Reg N6176C to Donald F Baldocchi, San Francisco, CA 1963-64 - mod to Cavalier Mustang - rereg YS-210P to Archie A Baldocchi, Illopango, El Salvador 1965-69 - sold FA Salvadorena coded FAS 402 Jul69-74 - rereg N33FF to Jack W Flaherty of Flaherty Factors Inc, Monterey, CA 1Nov74 - tfd Wilson C Edwards, Big Spring, TX 1978-88 - tfd Robert H Nottke, Barrington Hills, IL 1988-92 - tfd Lee O Maples, Vichy, MO Feb95 to current.

P-51D-25NA Mustang   122-39874   44-73415   N551VC
Button Transportation Inc, Dixon, CA   F

Assigned RCAF as 9289, toc 8Feb51, soc 14Aug59 - reg N6526D to James H Defuria of Intercontinental Airways, Canastota, NY 21Jul58-60 - tfd R Ferrer, Patchoque, NY 21Mar60-66 - crashed (badly damaged) Richmond, VA 15Feb62 - tfd Frederick W Wild, Averne, NY 6Jan66 - tfd Airlease Inc, Chicago, IL 10Jan66 - tfd Frank Guzman, Massapequa, PA 10Jan66-68 - tfd Don Bateman, Las Vegas, NV 9Mar68 - tfd Michael E Coutches, Hayward, CA 17Jun69-74 - tfd H Matteri, Stateline, NV 15Jan74-75 - tfd

William Veatch, Olympia, WA 1Sep75-77 - crashed on take-off, Olympia, WA 19Mar77 - tfd William A Speer, La Mesa, CA 1980-94 - rebuilt Chino, CA; ff 1988 as No.45, later No.55 *Pegasus* and No.5 *Voodoo*; components also used for P-51D static restoration for RAF Museum - sold at auction, San Diego-Montgomery Field, CA 10Dec94 - tfd Delbert Williams 1996 - tfd Button Transportation Inc, Dixon, CA 23Oct98 to current.

P-51D-25NA Mustang   122-39879   44-73420   ZK-PLI
Alpine Deer Group Ltd/B L Hore, Wanaka, New Zealand   F

Sold surplus McClellan AFB, CA 1958 - reg N7722C to Michael E Coutches of American Aircraft Sales Co, Hayward, CA 17Feb58 - tfd West Foods Inc, Soquel, CA 1958 - tfd Richard B McFarlane 21Jul58 - tfd Donald G Bell, Livermore, CA 25Aug58-64 - tfd Robert G Bixler, San Jose, CA Oct65-71 - tfd Robert H Phillips, Phoenix, AZ Mar71-78 - tfd Robb Satterfield, Aaron F Giebel and Dallas L Smith, Harlingen, TX 9Sep78-89, named *Miss Torque* - tfd Dallas L Smith, Midland, TX 1990-92 - tfd Brian Hore/Alpine Fighter Collection, Wanaka, New Zealand Dec93 - rereg ZK-PLI to Brian Hore & Tim Wallis, Alpine Fighter Collection, Wanaka, NZ 28Mar94 -

P-51D-25NA Mustang   122-39894   44-73435

Assigned RCAF as 9290, boc 8Feb51, soc 1Nov60 - reg CF-MWN to James H Defuria of Intercontinental Airways, Canastota, NY Dec58-60 - rereg N6311T Aero Enterprises, Elkhart, IN 10May60-61 - tfd Suncoast Aviation, St Petersburg, FL Oct61-62 - tfd James G Shaw, Columbia, SC 27Feb62-63 - tfd Angels Aviation, Zephyrhills, FL 3May63 - tfd Selby R Burch, Winter Garden, FL 3May63-69 - acc Daytona Beach, FL 6Jul68 - tfd Marvin L Gardner/Gardner Flyers, Mercedes, TX as wreck 1984 - tfd Pioneer Aero Service, Chino, CA 1987 to current.

P-51D-25NA Mustang   122-39895   44-73436   N51K
Olympic Jet Inc, Olympia, WA

Assigned RCAF as 9300, boc 16Mar51, soc 1Nov60 - reg N6313T to James H Defuria of Intercontinental Airways, Canastota, NY Dec58-60 - tfd Aero Enterprises, Elkhart, IN 1960-62 - tfd Ralph Rensink, Lewiston, ID 10Jan62 - tfd Walter D Peterson, Manson, WA 26Jun62-77 - rereg N51TK (1st issue) to Tom Kelly and John Dilley of Consolidated Airways, Fort Wayne, IN; raced as No.19 *Lou IV* 17Jul77-86 - rereg N51KD to American Horizons Inc, Fort Wayne, IN Mar86-92; raced as No.91, painted as 413926/E2-S *Cutters Capers* - tfd Amjet Aircraft Corp, St Paul, MN Aug93-96 - tfd Northwest Helicopters, White City, OR Nov97-Mar01 - tfd Olympic Jet Inc, Olympia, WA 15Mar01 to current.

Modified by Cavalier in the 1960s, P-51D-25NA 44-73350 spent time in El Salvador as YS-210P and then FAS 402 with the Fuerza Aerea Salvadorena. The aircraft returned to the USA and is seen in August 1999 when owned by Lee Maples of Vichy, Missouri and registered N33FF, with the name Archie. *Tim Bivens*

The beautiful lines of 44-73415/N551VC No.5 Voodoo *at Reno in September 1998. Note the wing-to-fuselage fairings and the modifications to the turtle decking. Tom Smith*

A flamboyantly coloured and much-modified racing Mustang which started life as a P-51D-25NA, Voodoo's appearance is in sharp contrast to its more stock condition as No.55 Pegasus when owned by the late Bill Speer of La Mesa, California. Kevin Grantham

The scene in the pits at Reno 1999, with Voodoo having just had its propeller removed prior to an engine change between races. Alan Gruening

Bill Speer rebuilt P-51D-25NA 44-73415/N6526D, which was raced as No.55 Pegasus. *It went on to become Bob Button's* Voodoo. The Warbird Index

A dramatic pairs take-off by Robb Satterfield in P-51D-25NA 44-73420/N7722C Miss Torque *(nearest the camera) and Jimmie Hunt in P-51D-25NA 44-73683/N5551D* Jumpin-Jacques. Alan Gruening

Formerly owned by Robb Satterfield of Midland, Texas, P-51D-25NA 44-73420/ZK-PLI Isabel III *is seen taking off at Wanaka in New Zealand where it is based as part of the Alpine Fighter Collection.* Dave McDonald

P-51D-25NA 44-73436/N51KD, seen here in November 1987, was rebuilt by John Dilley and the team at Fort Wayne Air Service and regularly raced as Lou IV *at Reno. It is now owned by Brian Reynolds at Olympic Jet, Olympia, Washington.* Thierry Thomassin

P-51D-25NA Mustang   122-39910   44-73451
Italian Air Force Museum, Vigna di Valle AB, Italy   M

Assigned to Italian Air Force as MM4323, boc 22Mar45, soc 10Sep50 - tfd Italian Air Force Museum, Vigna di Valle AB 1984 to current.

P-51D-25NA Mustang   122-39913   44-73454   N2051D
Richard A Bjelland, Dairy, OR   F

Reg N6172C to Ligonier Flying Service Inc, Ligonier, IN 1963 - tfd Cavalier Champion Developers Inc, Jacksonville, FL 1966 - mod to Cavalier 2000 - acc Jacksonville, FL 14May67 - rereg N2051D to Cavalier Aircraft Corp, Sarasota, FL 1968 - tfd Rufus A Applegarth, Plymouth Meeting, PA 1968-72 - tfd John J Schafhausen, Spokane, WA May72-73 - tfd Richard Bach 1973 - acc (landing) Midland, TX 24Sep73 - tfd Gordon Plaskett, King City, CA; rebuilt back to stock configuration - tfd John Herlihy, Montara, CA 1976-84 - tfd Richard A Bjelland, Dairy, OR Apr84 to current.

TF-51D-25NA Mustang 122-39917 44-73458 N4151D
William L. Hane, Mesa, AZ   F

Assigned RCAF as 9294, boc 16Mar51, soc 14Aug59 - reg N6525D to James H Defuria of Intercontinental Airways, Canastota, NY 21Jul58 - rereg N6347T to James H Defuria, Canastota, NY 1960 - rereg N554T to Ray A Alexander, Memphis, TN 1963-64 - tfd W R Rodgers, Rolling Fork, MS 1966-69 - mod by Cavalier as Mustang II - sold to FA Salvadorena coded FAS 404 1969-74; field modification to TF-51D by FAS - acc (crashed) in FAS service - reg N36FF to Flaherty Factors Inc, Monterey, CA (fuselage) 28Oct74 - tfd John Herlihy, C-Vu Airmotive, Half Moon Bay, CA 12Mar75 - rereg N4151D to Gordon W Plaskett, King City, CA 24Jun75-78; rebuilt Chino, CA using wing from 44-74012 in Temco TF-51D configuration - fffr 22Nov77 painted as 484662/ TF-662 - tfd Ben R Bradley, Fort Lauderdale, FL 1981 - tfd Basil C Deuschle, Pompano Beach, FL 1981-83 - tfd World Jet Inc, Fort Lauderdale, FL 1983-85 - tfd Lone Star Flight Museum, Houston, TX 1987-88 - tfd Warbirds of Great Britain Ltd 1988 - c/o William L Hane, Mesa, AZ Oct91-96, painted as 484660/TF-660; exhibited at Champlin Fighter Museum, Mesa, AZ.

P-51D-25NA Mustang   122-39922   44-73463   N351D
Robert S Baker, Alva, OK   F

Assigned RCAF as 9575, boc 7Jun47, soc 20Sep60 - tfd James H Defuria and Fred J Ritts of Intercontinental Airways, Canastota, NY 27Feb57-60 - open storage

Carberry, Manitoba, Canada - tfd Aero Enterprises, Elkhart, IN 1960-62 - sold as scrap metal to Leonard Tanner, North Granby, CT - tfd Duane Egli, Fabens, TX - tfd Richard Ransopher, Grapevine, TX; rebuild project 1977-82 - moved Richard Ransopher, Kernersville, NC then Tampa, FL 1982-89 - tfd Bob Baker 8Jun99 - rereg N351D to Robert S Baker, Alva, OK 18Apr00 to current.

P-51D-25NA Mustang   122-39953   44-73494
Yongdungpo AB, Seoul, South Korea   G

Assigned Republic of Korea AF coded 205 - tfd Yongdungpo AB, Seoul, South Korea and exhibited 1967 to current.

P-51D-25NA Mustang   122-39977   44-73518   N5483
Whittington Brothers Inc, Fort Lauderdale, FL

Reg N5483V to Edward G Fisher, Kansas City, KS 1963-72 - tfd Don Whittington, Fort Lauderdale, FL 1978-83 - mod as racer No.09 *Precious Metal* - tfd EAA Aviation Foundation, Oshkosh, WI 1985 - tfd Don Whittington/World Jet Inc, Fort Lauderdale, FL 1988-92; rebuilt and mod to take RR Griffon with contra-rotating props 1988 - accident Reno, NV during racing 17Sep88 - acc (ditched in sea) off Galveston, TX 24Jan90 - recovered for parts.

P-51D-25NA MM4323 in the Italian Air Force Museum at Vigna Di Valle Air Base. For many years it was thought that this aircraft was 44-73443, but Gregory Alegi has recently confirmed that it is in fact 44-73451. Gregory Alegi

Located at the War Memorial Museum in the Yongsan-ku district of Seoul, South Korea, P-51D-25NA 44-73494 had recently been repainted when this photograph was taken in 2000. Dave McDonald

Don Whittington in the Griffon-engined, World Jet Inc sponsored N5483V No.09 Precious Metal during its bid for victory at Reno in 1988. *The Warbird Index*

It all went very wrong when the loss of the propeller governor gear caused all six blades of the contra-rotating props to go flat and the engine literally became a dead weight. *Philip Wallick*

Using the tailcone from N5483V, the new Griffon-powered P-51XR N6WJ returned to Reno in 1995. In 2000 it was sold to Lake Air's Ron Buccarelli but hopes of doing well at Reno in 2001 were dashed when the races were cancelled following the tragic events of 11 September 2001. *Alan Gruening*

P-51D-25NA 44-73656/N2151D Moonbeam McSwine *is raced at Reno in the Unlimited Class by owner Vlado Lenoch. 1997 saw the aircraft appropriately carrying race number 51.* The Warbird Index

P-51D-25NA 44-73683/N5551D Jumpin-Jacques, *wearing the markings of the Pacific-based 3rd FS, 3rd FG, prepares to move off at Oshkosh in the late 1980s. The cartoon artwork beneath the cockpit is Bugs Bunny with a gun and the command "Halt".* The Warbird Index

P-51D-25NA Mustang   122-40002   44-73543   N151TP
Patten Aviation Inc, Wilmington, DE   F

Reg N5458V to Trans Florida Aviation, Sarasota, FL 1958 - to Indonesian AF/TNI-AU as F-3?? date unknown - recovered ex-Indonesia 1978 by Stephen Johnson of Vanpac Carriers, Oakland, CA - tfd Chris Warrilow, Woburn Green, Bucks, UK Feb81-85 - reg G-BLYW 3Jun85 - tfd D K Precision Inc, Fort Lauderdale, FL 1985-86 - rereg N800DK Apr86-87 - tfd Whittington Bros, Fort Lauderdale, FL 1988 - rereg N51SB to Steve Bolander/SWB Leasing, Libertyville, IL Jul92 - tfd Air Bear Corp, Libertyville, IL Apr94-98 - tfd Patten Aviation Inc, Wilmington, DE May99 to current.

P-51D-25NA Mustang   122-40033   44-73574
Richard Ransopher, NC   R

Reg N5478V to Marvin L Gardner, Mercedes, TX 1963 - tfd Gardner Flyers Inc, Brownwood, TX 1963-66 - tfd Beth Allen Truck Rental Inc, Stowe, PA 1969-70 - tfd Richard Ransopher, Kernersville, NC 1984-87.

P-51D-25NA Mustang   122-40196   44-73656   N2151D
Lenoch Engineering Inc, La Grange, IL   F

Sold surplus McClellan AFB, CA 1958 - tfd Delta A & E Parts Inc, NC Feb58 - tfd Michael E Coutches, American Aircraft Sales, Hayward, CA Nov58 - tfd Trans Florida Aviation,

Sarasota, FL 1958-63 - tfd Stanley Dunbar Studios, Charlotte, NC 1963 - tfd Howard Olsen, Midland, TX and raced as No.1 1963-66 - tfd Duncan Airmotive Inc, Galveston, TX 1968 - tfd to FA Salvadorena coded FAS 406 Dec68-74 - rereg N32FF to Flaherty Factors Inc, Monterey, CA 1Nov74 (adopted i/d of P-51K 44-12473 for import to USA) - tfd Gordon W Plaskett, King City, CA 1975; rebuilt 1976 and painted as 414237/HO-W Moonbeam McSwine - rereg N2151D to Gordon W Plaskett, King City, CA 1976-81 - tfd Chris Williams, Ellensburg, WA 1981-87 - tfd Vlado Lenoch, La Grange, IL 1988 to current.

P-51D-25NA Mustang   122-40223   44-73683
San Diego Aerospace Museum, San Diego, CA   M

Assigned FA d'L GN Nicaragua coded FAN GN 119 23May58-63 - reg N12064 to MACO Sales Financial Corp, Chicago, IL 1963 - tfd E D Weiner, Los Angeles, CA 1963-64 - tfd George W Drucker Jr, Los Angeles, CA 1966 - tfd George A Brown, Canoga Park, CA 1969 - tfd Meteorological Operations Inc, Hollister, CA 1969 - tfd John S Steinmetz, Londonderry, NH 1970-72 - rereg N5551D to Tri-T Aviation, Griffin, GA 1978 - tfd Heritage Aircraft Inc, Fayetteville, GA 1980-90; painted as Jumpin Jacques, later repainted as 414251/WZ-I Contrary Mary - tfd San Diego Aerospace Museum, CA 1992 - struck-off USCAR 12May92 - to San Diego-Gillespie Field, CA Mar93 to current.

P-51D-25NA Mustang   122-40233   44-73693   N35FF
Unlimited Air LLC, Van Nuys, CA   F

Assigned FA d'L GN Nicaragua coded FAN GN 116 23May58-63 - reg N6357T to MACO Sales Financial Corp, Chicago, IL Sep63 - tfd Ronald L Bryant, Jacksonville Beach, FL 1966 - tfd Alvin T George, Atlanta, GA 1969 - sold FA Salvadorena coded FAS 408 Jul69-74 - recovered and rereg N35FF to Flaherty Factors Inc, Monterey, CA 1Nov74 (adopted identity of 44-13253 on import to USA) - tfd Wilson C Edwards, Big Spring, TX 1978-87 and raced as No.45 Risky Business - tfd Mustang 4 Inc, Chino, CA 1988 - tfd Unlimited Air Racing LLC, Van Nuys, CA 1991 to current.

P-51D-25NA Mustang   122-40244   44-73704   N6168C
Musco Inc, Dallas, TX   F

Reg N6168C to Plauche Electric Inc, Lake Charles, LA 1963-69 - tfd Gardner Flyers Inc, Brownwood, later Mercedes, TX 1970-92 and raced as No.25 Thunderbird - tfd Musco Inc, Dallas, TX Feb94 to current.

P-51D-25NA Mustang   122-40291   44-73751   N5444V
PTI Inc, San Jose, CA   S

Reg N5444V to Robert Mitchum, Broomfield, CO 1963-64 - tfd Keith Larkin, Watsonville, CA 1966-69 - tfd PTI Inc, San Jose, CA Aug69 to current; stored externally on tie-down and in poor state of repair.

Jimmie Hunt of Heritage Aircraft, Tennessee, taxies P-51D-25NA 44-73683/N5551D painted as Jumpin-Jacques *in August 1984.*
William T Larkins

Originally painted as Jumpin Jacques *(but not to be confused with the similarly marked 44-72035/F-AZMU), 44-73683/N5551D is seen in 84th FS, 78th FG markings as 44-14251/WZ-I* Contrary Mary *when owned by Jimmie Hunt.*
Paul Hunt

A dramatic night shot of immaculately maintained P-51D-25NA 44-73543/N151TP Sweetie Face *with engineer John Pilkington exercising the aircraft's fire-breathing Merlin at its Tennessee base in 2000.* Uwe Glaser

Lefty Gardner's P-51D-25NA 44-73704/N6168C Thunderbird *wearing the colour scheme of the US Air Force Air Demonstration Squadron, better known as the 'Thunderbirds'.* Bob Munro

Photographed in September 1989 at Reno, Thunderbird *sits on the chocks and undergoes an engine run before taking part in another air race. The aircraft was sold to Lewis Shaw in February 1994.* Alan E Gruening

Following his acquisition of 44-73704/N6168C in 1994, long-time Mustang owner Lewis Shaw had Ezell Aviation rebuild the aircraft. It is seen here at the Gathering of Mustangs & Legends at Kissimmee, Florida in April 1999. Note the underwing (inert!) rockets. Tom Smith

P-51D-25NA Mustang   122-40372   44-73832   N117E
H E Hunewill Construction Co Inc, Wellington, NV   U

Reg N2873D - rereg N117E to Edward I Gilbert, Phoenix, AZ 1963-64 - tfd Frank C Sanders, Phoenix, AZ 1966 - tfd David Webster, Glendo, WY 1969-72 - tfd Scott Smith, Orlando, FL 1978 - acc Ellisville, MS 15Feb78 - tfd Gary McCann, FL as rebuild project 1983-85 - tfd Clarke Aviation Corp, Daytona Beach, FL 1987-88; was flown in 357th FG markings as *Hurry Home Honey* - tfd Bob Byrne Aviation, Bloomfield, MI 1989 - tfd H E Hunewill Construction Co, Wellington, NV 1989-95 - acc Wellington, NV 21Nov92 (destroyed; Hunewill killed) - i/d tfd Square One Aviation 1989.

P-51D-25NA Mustang   122-40383   44-73843   N10601
American Airpower Heritage Flying Museum, Midland, TX   F

Assigned RCAF as 9271, boc 11Jan51, soc 4Dec56 - reg N10601 to Stinson Field Aircraft, San Antonio, TX Oct56-57 - tfd Lloyd P Nolen of Mustang & Co, Mercedes, TX Oct57-77 - tfd Confederate Air Force, Harlingen, then Midland, TX Dec77 to current; mod as dual-control TP-51 by Ezell Aviation, Breckenridge, TX 1996.

P-51D-25NA Mustang   122-40396   44-73856   N7TF
Chino Warbirds Inc, Houston, TX   F

Reg N5077K to Jim Jeffers, Stateline, NV 1963 - tfd Contractors Equipment Co, Salem, OR 1963-64 - tfd Fowler Aeronautical Services, Burbank, CA 1966 - tfd Air Carriers Inc, Aurora, OR 1969 - rereg N711UP to Gale Aero Corp, Minneapolis, MN Aug69-70 - rereg N7TF to Cinema Air Inc, Houston, TX (based Carlsbad, CA) 1976-May01 - tfd Chino Warbirds, Houston, TX 8May01 to current.

Ezell Aviation took the Confederate Air Force's P-51D-25NA 44-73843/N10601 and fitted it with dual controls during a total restoration carried out at Breckenridge. Photographed at the San Marcos, Texas airshow in 1997. Chuck Gardner

Scott Smith taxies out in P-51D-25NA 44-73832/ N117E Colour Me Gone. The aircraft crashed on 21 November 1992. The Warbird Index

P-51D-25NA Mustang   122-40411   44-73871   N7098V
Mustang Air Inc, Wilmington, DE   F

Assigned RCAF as 9245, boc 6Dec50, soc 2May56 - ex-Whiteman Air Park, CA destined for Israel 1959 - to IDFAF coded ?? - tfd Israeli Aircraft Industries 1964 - rereg N7098V to Pioneer Aero Service, Burbank, CA 22Jun64-70 - tfd Cavalier Aircraft, Sarasota, FL 8Sep70-78 - tfd Albert McKinley, Hillsboro, OH 14Aug78 - tfd Elmer Ward/Pioneer Aero Service, Chino, CA 1990-91; rebuilt Chino, CA as TF-51D, ff 1991 as 473871/TF-871 - op by Warbirds of Great Britain Ltd, Biggin Hill; shipped to UK, ff Biggin Hill 19Mar92 - struck-off USCAR 5May94 - reinstated 1996 to current.

P-51D-25NA Mustang   122-40417   44-73877   N167F
Joda LLC, Town and Country, MO   F

Assigned RCAF as 9279, boc 23Jan51, soc 29Apr58 - reg N6320T (1st issue) to James H Defuria and Fred J Ritts of Intercontinental Airways, Canastota, NY 25Feb57-60 - tfd Aero Enterprises, Elkhart, IN 1960 - rereg CF-PCZ to Neil McClain, Strathmore, Alberta, Canada 1960-68 - rereg N167F to Paul D Finefrock, Hobart, OK 29Apr68-70 - acc

Euless, TX 1Sep69 - tfd Paul D Finefrock, Brownwood, TX Oct70-80 - tfd RLS 51 Ltd, CA Aug80-83 - ferried ex-USA to Oslo 27Jun86 - tfd Scandinavian Historic Flight, Oslo, Norway 1984-01 - tfd SHF San Francisco Ltd Jan01-Mar01 - tfd Joda LLC, Town and Country, MO 8Mar01 to current - Op by SHF Oslo, Norway as *Old Crow*.

P-51D-25NA Mustang   122-40442   44-73902   N38227
Wilson C Edwards, Big Spring, TX   S

Sold FA Guatemalteca coded FAG 315 16Dec54 - mod by Cavalier - reg N38227 to Don Hull, Sugarland, TX Aug72 - tfd Wilson C Edwards, Big Spring, TX 1978-96.

P-51D-25NA Mustang   122-40460   44-73920
Military Museum of the Chinese People's Revolution, Beijing, People's Republic of China   M

Assigned Chinese Nationalist AF 15Mar46 - to Chinese AF coded 03 1Oct49 - instructional airframe with Chinese AF - tfd Military Museum of the Chinese People's Revolution, Beijing, PRC; displayed as 03 1987 to current.

Assigned to the Chinese Nationalist Air Force on 15 March 1946, P-51D-25NA 44-73920 still survives; its current location is believed to be the Military Museum of the Chinese People's Revolution located in Beijing. The remnants of its '03' code are just discernable on the tail. Chris Armstrong

P-51D-25NA 44-73972 has for many years been mounted on a pylon at the 194th FS, 144th FW California Air National Guard Base at Fresno Air Terminal, California. Simon Brown

Tom Henley's P-51D-25NA 44-73990/N51TH is based in Geiger, Alabama. It was photographed in 1988 after being repainted. Tim Bivens

P-51D-25NA Mustang 122-40512 44-73972
USAFM, Fresno, CA   GG

USAFM, Fresno ANGB, Fresno, CA 1965 to current.

P-51D-25NA Mustang 122-40513 44-73973 N151DP
David G Price, Santa Monica, CA   F

Assigned RCAF as 9281 23Jan51, soc 29Apr58 - reg N6325T (2nd issue) to James H Defuria and Fred J Ritts of Intercontinental Airway, Canastota, NY 25Feb57-60 - tfd Aero Enterprises, Elkhart, IN 10May60-62 - tfd Peter Rosi, Notre Dame, IN Oct62-63 - tfd back to Aero Enterprises, Elkhart, IN 3Apr63-64 - tfd Farnum Brown, Michigan City, IN 4Mar64 - tfd Joseph D Wade, Houston ,TX 6Mar64-65 - tfd A E Lee, Atlanta, GA Oct65-66 - tfd James W Gentle, Birmingham, AL 16Jun66-67 - tfd Wendell K Trogden, Fort Lauderdale, FL 10Aug67-69 - sold to FAS coded FAS??? Jul69-74 - reg N35DD (ntu) - tfd Jack W Flaherty, Monterey, CA 1Nov74 - rereg N37FF to Flaherty Factors Inc, Monterey, CA 6Mar75 (adopted '44-10755' on import to USA) - rereg N51JC to Jerry C Janes, Vancouver, British Columbia, Canada 14Aug75-79; rebuilt (using ex-FAS aircraft) Chelan, WA 1976-77, del Vancouver Jan78 - rereg C-GJCJ (1st issue) to Grabber Screw Products, Vancouver, British Columbia,Canada Nov79-83 - reg N51JC and tfd David G Price, Los Angeles, CA Nov83 - rereg N151DP to David G Price, Santa Monica, CA Jan84 to current; raced as No.49 *Cottonmouth*.

P-51D-25NA Mustang 122-40519 44-73979
Imperial War Museum, London, UK   M

Assigned RCAF as 9246, boc 6Dec50, soc 16May51 - acc in RCAF service, grounded 16May51 - IA with serial A-612 10May55 - tfd College Militaire Royale, St Jean, Quebec, Canada - tfd RCAF St Jean, Quebec as gate guard 1960 - tfd Imperial War Museum, Duxford, UK Jun72-89; rebuilt by Duxford Aviation Society volunteers - tfd Imperial War Museum, Lambeth, London 1989 to current.

P-51D-25NA Mustang 122-40530 44-73990 N51TH
T W Henley, Geiger, AL   F

Assigned RCAF as 9282, boc 23Jan51, soc 14May59 - reg N8674E to James H Defuria of Intercontinental Airways, Canastota, NY 27Feb59-60 - tfd Aero Enterprises, Elkhart, IN 18Jun60 - tfd Kieran Aviation Sales, Birmingham, AL 14Aug60-62 - tfd Jack Adams Aircraft Sales, Walls, MS 3Feb62 - tfd Jackson Dental, Jackson, MS May62 - tfd Robert Graf, Tarkio, MO 13Aug62-65 - tfd Leonard A Tanner of Tan Air Industries Inc, North Granby, CT 19Jan65-70 - rereg N51LT to Len Tanner, North Granby, CT 1972-73 - rereg N2116 (2nd issue; ntu) - tfd John P Silberman, Sherborn, MA 8Apr73 - acc (struck car on landing) Yanceyville, NC 6Sep73 - rereg N51LT to Len Tanner, North Granby, CT 18Mar75-79; apparently rebuilt using parts from A68-175/N64824 - rereg N51TH and tfd to Tom W Henley, Emelle, AL 8Jan79 to current.

P-51D-25NA Mustang 122-40549 44-74009 N51KB
B & K Leasing Inc, Nantucket, MA   F

Assigned RCAF as 9275, boc 11Jan51, soc 17Sep57 - reg N6323T (1st issue) to James H Defuria and Fred J Ritts of Intercontinental Airways, Canastota, NY 25Feb57-60 - rereg N988C to Aero Enterprises, Elkhart, IN 1May60-61 - tfd Suncoast Aviation, St Petersburg, FL 8Jul61-62 - tfd A Fasken, Midland, TX 29Sep62-63 - tfd Houston Aircraft Sales, Houston, TX 1May63-65 - tfd William Fiore, Clairton, PA 30Apr65-68 - tfd Frank Cannavo Jr, Lester, PA 3Feb68-69 - tfd Robert J Shaver, Brigantine and Linwood, NJ 26Jun69-79 - tfd Robert L Ferguson, Wellesley, MA Apr79-Sep01 - rereg N51BK and tfd B & K Leasing, Nantucket, MA 17Sep01 to current.

The Scandinavian Historic Flight's P-51D-25NA 44-73877/N167F Old Crow was bought on charge by the RCAF (as 9279) in January 1951 and served until 1958. Restored for Anders Saether by Darrell Skurich of Vintage Aircraft Limited, Fort Collins, Colorado, it is one of the most original Mustangs extant. Birgit Altendeitering is checking out the cockpit for size. Anders K Saether

Jerry C Janes was responsible for the RAF-style paint scheme on P-51D-25NA 44-73973/N151DP, an ex-Fuerza Aerea Salvadorena aircraft seen here in September 1989 and now owned by David Price of Santa Monica, California. Thierry Thomassin

P-51D-25NA Mustang   122-40552   44-74012   N6519D
James E Smith, Fortine, MT   **F**

Assigned RCAF as 9243, boc 6Dec50, soc 17Aug59 - reg
N6518D (1st issue) to James H Defuria of Intercontinental
Airways, Canastota, NY 21Jul58-60 - tfd Aero Enterprises,
Elkhart, IN 15Aug60-63 - rereg (due to painting error) N6519D
(2nd issue) to Jerry McCutchin, Dallas, TX Oct63-64 - tfd
Gordon Travis/River Oaks Aircraft & Engine Brokers, Fort
Worth, TX 9Dec64-66 - tfd Robert R Redding, Houston, TX
13Jun66-68 - tfd Leroy B Penhall, Anaheim, CA and raced
as No.81 4Nov68-75 - forced landing Hudson, WI 4Aug74 -
tfd Gordon W Plaskett, King City, CA as hulk 30Sep75 -
rereg C-GPSI (1st issue) to Robert H Jens/Executive Aircraft
Ltd, Vancouver, British Columbia, Canada; rebuild project
(unfinished) 27Sep76-84 - rereg N6519D (2nd issue) to
Duane Williams, Kellogg, ID; completely rebuilt Feb84-87 -
tfd James E Smith, Fortine, MT Sep87 to current.

P-51D-25NA Mustang   122-40742   44-74202   N5420V
Robert H Coutches, Hayward, CA   **F**

Reg N5420V to Michael E Coutches, Hayward, CA
Dec66-83 - tfd Mike Bogue, Oakland, CA 1984-87 - tfd
Michael E Coutches, Hayward, CA 1990-Sep99 - tfd Robert
H Coutches, Hayward, CA 14Sep99 to current.

P-51D-25NA Mustang   122-40744   44-74204   N51U
William A Speer Jr, La Mesa, CA   **S**

Reg N5451V to Robert F Deweese, Newport Beach, CA
1963-64 - tfd David S Salerno, Santa Ana, CA 1966-70 - reg
N51U to David S Salerno, Santa Ana, CA 1972 - tfd George
Enhorning of Wolcott Air Service, Wolcott, CT 1978-90,
named *Passion Wagon* - crashed Cape Cod, MA
(destroyed; Enhorning killed) 29Sep90 - i/d tfd William A
Speer, La Mesa, CA 25Mar93-94, rebuilt as racer named
Deja Vu using ex-TNI-AU airframe - crashed Reno, NV (Bill
Speer killed) 12Sep94 - still on USCAR Mar2001; remains to
Keith Shell, sold to owner in Florida following Shell's death
in AT-6 accident 2000.

P-51D-25NA Mustang   122-40756   44-74216
USS *Alabama* Battleship Memorial, Mobile, AL   **M**

Allocated to USAFM - tfd USS *Alabama* Battleship
Memorial, Mobile, AL 1974 to current.

P-51D-25NT Mustang   124-44246   44-84390   N2869D
Douglas D Driscoll, American Falls, ID   **F**

Reg N2869D to Charles A Lyford, Belleview, WA 1963-72
and raced as No.8 *Bardahl Special* - tfd Life Science

Church, San Diego, CA 1978 - tfd Charles Hall, San Diego,
CA, racer No.3 1981 - tfd Bruce Ellis, San Diego, CA 1982 -
tfd Douglas D Driscoll, American Falls, ID Feb83 current.

P-51D-25NT Mustang   124-44345   44-84489
Peter N Anderson, Sydney, NSW, Australia   **S**

Assigned RAAF as A68-750, boc 6Aug45, soc 1Mar52 - tfd for
use as target RAAF Williamtown, NSW, Australia 1951 - rep
tfd American Aeronautics Corp., Burbank, CA Feb53 - tfd
Peter N Anderson, Sydney, NSW 1987 - reg VH-AMG (ntu) to
Peter N Anderson, Sydney, NSW 20Jun94 to current.

P-51D-25NT Mustang   124-44471   44-84615   N55JL
Bahia Oaks Inc, Ocala, FL   **F**

Sold to IDFAF (i/d unknown) - reg N7099V to Pioneer Aero
Service, Burbank, CA 1966 - tfd Larry R Strimple, Mansfield,
OH 1969-70 - rereg N9LR to Larry R Strimple, Mansfield, OH
- rereg N55JL to Jimmy Leeward of Bahia Oaks Inc, Ocala,
FL 1974 to current and raced as No.9 *Cloud Dancer*.

P-51D-25NT Mustang   124-44490   44-84634   N51ES
Laurie A Shipley, Malvern, PA   **F**

Assigned FA d'L GN Nicaragua as GN 96 - reg N6165U to
MACO Sales Financial Corp, Chicago, IL 2Sep63 - tfd
Thomas J Kuckinsky, Menomonee Falls, WI 1966-69 - tfd
Aviation Business Services Inc 1970 - tfd Air Sales Inc, Fort
Lauderdale, FL 1972 - tfd Max I Ramsay, Johnson, KS 1978 -
rereg N51JV to Associated Enterprises Inc, Painesville, OH
1979 - tfd Firebird Enterprises, OH 1983-89 - tfd Ohio
Associated Enterprises, Painesville, OH 1990 - tfd Edward H
Shipley, Malvern, PA 1991-92 - rereg N51ES to same owner
Feb92-95 - rebuilt Chino CA 1992-93; fffr Jul93.

Jimmy Leeward's P-51D-25NT 44-84615 Cloud
Dancer *in plain, fictitious USAF markings and
without its registration (N55JL) in August 1983.*
William T Larkins

*One of the handful of Mustangs to appear in
Royal Air Force colours, N55JL carried these
spurious marking for a few years in the 1980s.*
William T Larkins

A fine portrait of Ed Shipley's P-51D-25NA
44-84634/N51ES – one of many Mustangs
painted as Col John Landers' 78th FG Big
Beautiful Doll *over the years*. Robert S DeGroat

Jimmy Leeward brought 44-84615/N551JL to
*The Gathering of Mustangs & Legends at
Kissimmee, Florida in April 1999. It is reputed to
have begun its civilian career in Israel.* Author

Adorned with race number 9, Jimmy Leeward's
P-51D-25NT 44-84615/N55JL Cloud Dancer
*wears a plain race scheme as it basks in the
sun at Oshkosh in 1998.* John R Kerr

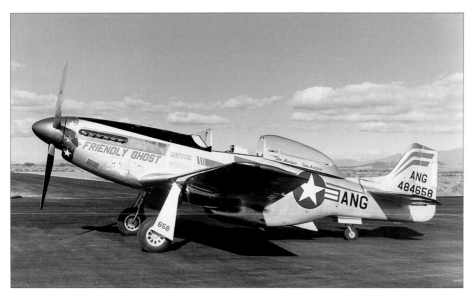

An original Temco TF-51D-25NT, 44-84658/N51TF Friendly Ghost *was rebuilt by Darrell Skurich at Vintage Aircraft Ltd, Fort Collins, Colorado for the late John MacGuire. It had been recovered from Indonesia in 1978 and was one of three Mustangs purchased by MacGuire.* Robb Satterfield

At the Korean War Museum in Seoul, South Korea is P-51D-25NT 44-84669, seen here in full ROKAF markings and in reasonable condition in the late 1970s. The Warbird Index

P-51D-25NT 44-84850/N850AH was another of the Mustangs retrieved from Indonesia by Stephen Johnson of VanPac Carriers. The aircraft was photographed in New Mexico in 1990 when registered as N87JB Ghost Rider *and owned by the late John MacGuire.* The Warbird Index

TF-51D-25NT Mustang 124-44514 44-84658 N51TF
John MacGuire, Santa Theresa, NM F

Assigned FA d'L GN Nicaragua as GN 99 20Feb58 - reg N851D (1st issue) to Trans Florida Aviation, Sarasota, FL 1963-64 - tfd Cavalier Aircraft Corp, Sarasota, FL 1966; mod as Cavalier TF-51D - sold to Indonesian AF/TNI-AU coded F-361 1968 - recovered by Stephen Johnson of Vanpac Carriers, Oakland, CA 1978 - tfd John MacGuire, El Paso, TX 1979-84; rebuilt by Vintage Aircraft Limited, Fort Collins, CO 1983-85 - rereg N51TF to same owner - del to War Eagles Air Museum, Santa Teresa, NM Jan85 - reg 1989 to current.

P-51D-25NT Mustang 124-44525 44-84669 M
Korean War Museum, Seoul, South Korea M

Temco TF-51: assigned Republic of Korea AF as 201 - exhibited Taegu AB, South Korea 1964-72 - tfd Korean War Museum, Seoul, South Korea 1988 to current.

TF-51D-25NT Mustang 124-44601 44-84745 N851D
Stallion 51 Corporation, Kissimmee, FL

Reg N5439V to Cline Cantarini, Lancaster, CA 1963-64 - mod as Cavalier TF-51D - tfd Stanley M Kurzet, Covina, CA 1966-69 - tfd Lindsay Newspapers, Sarasota, FL; dismantled and stored 1972-82 - rereg N851D (2nd issue) to David B Lindsay of Lindair Inc, Sarasota, FL Jun82 - tfd Gordon W Plaskett, King City, CA 1984; rebuilt King City and Chino, CA 1983-84 as TF-51D using fuselage from ex-FAS aircraft - tfd Bob Amyx, Oklahoma City, OK 1984-85 - tfd Bob Byrne Aviation, Bloomfield, MI 1987 - tfd Doug Schultz and Lee Lauderback of Stallion 51 Corporation, Kissimmee, FL Apr87 to current.

P-51D-25NT Mustang 124-44609 44-84753 N251BP
Bernie F Jackson Trustee, Poulsbo, WA F

Reg N5436V to Robert L Rodman, Fullerton, CA 1963-64 - tfd Les Grant, Santa Barbara, CA 1966-73 - reg N51TC (1st issue) to Ted E Contri of Contri Construction, Reno, NV 24Jun78-86 - reg N51BE (ntu) to Ted E Contri, North Highland, CA Nov86 - rereg N251BP to Planes of Fame East, Plymouth, MN Feb87-Mar99 - tfd Bernie F Jackson, Poulsbo, WA 18Mar99 to current.

F-6D-25NT 124-44642 44-84786 N51BS
Henry J Schroeder III, Danville, IL F

Original F-6D: sold surplus McClellan AFB, CA 25Nov49 - reported frustrated export to IDFAF - tfd Michael E Coutches, Hayward, CA - into storage 1952-61 - tfd Bill Myers, St Louis, MO; stored dismantled 1961-81 - discovered by Henry J Schroeder III, Danville, IL 1981 - rereg N51BS to Midwest Aviation Museum, Danville, IL Jan83 to current; fffr 17Jun93.

P-51D-25NT Mustang 122-44703 44-84847 N251RJ
James L Maroney, Kindred, ND F

Reg to Robert J Odegaard, Kindred, ND 15Jan99-00 - tfd James L Maroney, Fargo, ND 1Mar00 to current.

P-51D-25NT Mustang 124-44706 44-84850 N850AH
Anderson Aviation Inc, Ponte Vedra Beach, FL F

Sold Indonesian AF/TNI-AU as F-3?? - Cavalier field mod - recovered by Stephen Johnson of Vanpac Carriers, Oakland, CA 1978 - reg N87JB to John MacGuire, El Paso, TX Jan82-88; rebuilt, painted as 484850 *Ghost Rider* - exhibited at War Eagles Air Museum, Santa Teresa, NM 1988-94 - tfd Picacho Aviation 1994 - tfd Frank Borman, Las Cruces, NM 10Aug94-96 - rereg N15FS to same owner Aug95 - tfd Stan Musick 1998 - rereg N151BF to W H Freeman Aviation, Wilmington, DE 10Aug99-00 - rereg N850AH and tfd Anderson Aviation Inc, Ponte Vedra Beach, FL 18Apr00 to current.

Henry 'Butch' Schroeder at the controls of F-6D-25NT 44-84786/N51BS Lil' Margaret, *a rare photo-reconnaissance Mustang. This aircraft set new trends and standards for warbirds vying for the prestigious EAA Warbirds of America awards when it took the Grand Champion award at Oshkosh in 1993. This photograph was taken before all the stencilling was applied.* via Henry J Schroeder III

Two Mustangs, both Cavalier TF-51D-25NTs, have carried the registration N851D. It is believed this photograph shows 44-84658, which was modified by Cavalier in 1966 and went to the Indonesian Air Force (TNI-AU) as F-361 soon afterwards. The Warbird Index

Darryl Bond's TF-51D-25NT, 44-84860/N327DB Lady Jo at its Chino, California base. The aircraft, once part of the Piper Enforcer programme, flew for the first time following restoration on 19 May 1989. Author

Photographed when in an unrestored state some years ago, P-51D-25NT 44-84896/N5416V was unusual in that it sported an ADF ball on the rear fuselage. Trygve Johansson

P-51D-25NT 44-84900/N51YZ, the only Mustang ever to land on an aircraft carrier, looking magnificent after a lengthy, in-depth restoration by John Muszala and his Pacific Fighters team. Much of the original equipment carried by the aircraft during its NACA experimental test flights was retrieved and incorporated during the restoration process. Frank B Mormillo

Photographs on the opposite page:

P-51D-25NT 44-84933/N201F is owned by MA Incorporated of Oshkosh, Wisconsin and wears NACA titles. The Warbird Index

A rare photograph of Northeast Aircraft Associates' P-51D-25NT 44-84952/N210D in August 1989. Tim Bivens

TF-51D-25NT Mustang 124-44716 44-84860   N327DB
Aero Classics Inc, Chino, CA

Sold Indonesian AF/TNI-AU as F-3?? - recovered by Stephen
Johnson of Vanpac Carriers, Oakland, CA 1978 - reg N55509
to John MacGuire, El Paso, TX Aug84-88 - rereg N327DB to
Darryl Bond, Chino, CA Jan89; rebuilt Chino, CA as TF-51D
using ex-Australian mainplane and ex-Enforcer fuselage;
ffr 19May89

P-51D-25NT Mustang   124-44720 44-84864   N4223A
American Aircraft Sales Co, Hayward, CA   F

Assigned NACA coded NACA126, boc 27Aug45, soc 12Jul57
- designated ETF-51D, mod by NACA with tall vertical fin -
sold surplus ex-storage NAS Norfolk, VA 1957 - reg N4223A
to Kibler Bros 1957 - tfd Sidney A Franklin, Pacific
Palisades, CA 1963 - tfd Glenn Johnson Realty, Sacramento,
CA 1963-69 - tfd Michael E Coutches of Museum of
American Aircraft, Hayward, CA 1969 to current; exhibited
Wagons to Wings Museum, Morgan Hill, CA from 1979.

P-51D-25NT Mustang   124-44752 44-84896   N5416V
Kenneth M Scholz, Playa del Rey, CA   F

Reg N5416V to Lake Air Corp, Michigan City, IN 1963 - tfd
James C Keichline, Huntington Park, CA 1963-70 - tfd
Kenneth M Scholz, Playa del Rey, CA Apr73 to current.

P-51D-25NT Mustang   124-44756 44-84900   N51YZ
W C Allmon Jr, Las Vegas, NV   F

Only Mustang to land on aircraft carrier: assigned NACA
coded NACA127, boc 4Sep45, soc 5Jun52 - designated
ETF-51D - assigned USAFM, Greater Pittsburgh ANGB, PA
1973-94 on pylon, painted as 48490/'AJ-S - reg N51YZ tfd to
William Allmon Jr; rebuilt by Pacific Fighters, Idaho Falls.

P-51D-25NT Mustang   124-44789 44-84933   N201F
MA Inc, Oshkosh, WI   F

Sold surplus McClellan AFB, CA for $2,160 20Sep57 - reg
N2874D to Earl V Dakin, Sacramento, CA 20Sep57-58 - tfd
Douglas W Brown of Mustang Aviation, Great Falls, MT
Nov58-62 - tfd Kathleen C Murphy, Great Falls, MT - broken
down 8Oct62-64 - tfd Edward G Fleming, Calgary, Alberta,
Canada 10Mar64; roaded Great Falls to Calgary for rebuild -
reg CF-RUT to Edward G Fleming, Calgary, Alberta 4Aug65 -
tfd Donald F McGillivray of Nanaimo, British Columbia,
Canada 13Aug65-67 - tfd Charles E Roberts of Calg-Air
Sales, Calgary 4Nov67 - rereg N201F to Futrell Aircraft Sales,

Hot Springs, AR Dec67-69 - tfd Alexander J Edelman, Great
Neck, NY 1969 - tfd Suffolk Flight Associates, Huntington,
NY Jun69-72 - tfd John J Mark, Milwaukee, WI 1978-83 - tfd
John J Mark of MA Inc, Oshkosh, WI 1983 to current.

P-51D-25NT Mustang   124-44808 44-84952   N210D
Northeast Aircraft Association, Wilmington, DE   F

Reg N6495C - rereg N210D to Art Holst, Eugene, OR 1963-64
- tfd Contractor Equipment Co, Salem, OR 1966 - tfd Joseph
Hartney, Chino, CA 1978 - tfd Steve Tognoli, CA 1983-85 - tfd
Northeast Aircraft Associates, Wilmington, DE Aug86 to
current.

P-51D-25NT Mustang   124-44817   44-84961   N7715C
Steven J Hinton, Reno, NV   F

Sold as scrap McClellan AFB, CA Feb58 - reg N7715C to
Capitol Airways/Air Sales, Nashville, TN Feb58-64 - tfd
Charles F Willis, Frank Lynott and Charles R Hall, Seattle,
WA and raced as No.5 Jul64-67 - tfd Charles R Hall, Seattle,
WA 1967-71 - mod as racer No.5 *Miss R.J.* 1967 - tfd Gunther
W Balz, Kalamazoo, MI Jul71-73; heavy modification for
racing as No.5 *Roto-Finish* - tfd John M Sliker, Wadley, GA
Oct73-74 - tfd Ed Browning of Brownings Inc, Idaho Falls,
ID Feb74-79 - mod as 'RB-51' and rebuilt Van Nuys, CA with
RR Griffon 54 engine and contra-rotating props; fffr 3Jun75,
raced as No.5 *Red Baron* and gained world piston record at
499.018mph 14Aug79 - acc (forced landed during race)
Reno, NV 16Sep79 - wreck tfd Richard Ransopher,
Grapevine, TX 1980 - i/d tfd to Steven J Hinton of Fighter
Rebuilders, Chino, CA Sep85-96; rebuilt using ex-TNI-AU
structure at Chino, CA; ff Chino, CA Sep85 as stock P-51D
painted as 413334/G4-U.

P-51D-25NT Mustang   124-44818   44-84962   N9857P
Lee W Schaller, New Athens, IL   F

Assigned Republic of Korea AF - assigned Indonesian
AF/TNI-AU coded F-312 - recovered ex-Indonesia by
Stephen Johnson of Vanpac Carriers, Oakland, CA 1978 -
rebuilt Chino, CA; fffr 1983 - reg N9857P to Lee W Schaller,
Montville, NJ/New Athens, IL 13Aug81 to current.

P-51D-25NT Mustang   124-48144   45-11391   N51WT
Fly Rock Inc, Warrenton, VA   F

Reg N6170C to Thomas A Drummond, Ridgecrest, CA, 1963-64
- tfd to Jeffrey D Cannon, Los Angeles, CA 1966 - tfd Arthur R
Tucker, Norwood, NJ 1969-70 - rereg N5151N to same owner
1970 - rereg N51WT to John I Watson, Blackwood, NJ 1978-92
- tfd Fly Rock Inc, Warrenton, VA Feb94 to current.

P-51D-25NT Mustang   124-48248   45-11439   N51HY
Barbara Hunter, Lewisburg, WV   U

Reg N51HY to Barbara Hunter of Lewisburg, WV 14Jul98;
no further information known.

P-51D-25NT Mustang   124-48206   45-11453   N551MR
Sale Reported, Livonia, MI   R

Reg N5479V to John A Colling, Scottsdale, AZ 19 63 - to T A
Underwood, Buckeye, AZ 1963-64 - tfd Sanford Aviation,
Gardena, CA 1966 - sold FA Boliviana as FAB 511 10Jun66 -
recovered and rereg C-GXUP to Amy Carnegie, Edmonton,
Alberta, Canada; disassembled Dec77 - reg N59038 to George
Roberts, FL May 1978 - rereg N6310T (2nd issue) to
Whittington Bros, Fort Lauderdale, FL1978; rebuilt by Vintage
Aircraft Limited, Fort Collins, CO; fffr May85 (apparently
adopted identity 44-74832) - rereg N551MR to Herbert E Rupp,
Port Salerno, FL Jun85-96; flown painted as 414450 *Old Crow* -
acc (badly damaged by fire) Florida Feb96.

P-51D-25NT Mustang   124-48211   45-11458   N
Museo Aeronautico, Maracay AB, Venezuela

Assigned RAAF as A68-801, boc Sep45 - reg N4886V to
American Aeronautics Corp, Burbank, CA 23Feb53 - sold
FA Boliviana as FAB 504 c.Feb55 - possibly later Cavalier
field modification - tfd Museo Aeronautico, Maracay AB,
Venezuela 1987 to current.

TF-51D-25NT   124-48224   45-11471   N51U
Lady Alice Corporation, Wilmington, DE

Reg N5481V - rereg N332 to David Maytag, Colorado
Springs, CO; raced as No.9 1963-69 - tfd David J Zeuschel,
Van Nuys, CA 1970-78 - tfd James Barkley, AZ 1979 - acc
Borrego Springs, CA (Barkley killed) 21Aug79 - tfd Alan
Preston Air Racing Team, Dallas, TX 7Sep84-87; rebuilt
(fuselage of IDF69, mainplane from IDF28) as modified
racer No.84 *Stiletto* - tfd Sherman Aircraft Sales, West Palm
Beach, FL 1987-89 - tfd Liberty Aero Corp, Santa Monica, CA
Nov89-96 - mod as TF-51D conversion by Square One
Aviation, Chino, CA (Pete Regina completed work) - tfd
Lady Alice Corporation, Wilmington, DE 5Aug98 to current.

P-51D-25NT Mustang   124-48248   45-11495
Philip S Warner, Cheltenham, Glos, UK

To RNZAF as NZ2406 - to aviation museum; dismantled -
imported to UK from New Zealand 2Dec01 - restoration
under way to flying condition.

*The early 1970s saw Gunther Balz take on this
beautiful-looking air racer, N7715C No.5
(formerly* Miss R.J.) *and perform extensive
modifications, adopting a new paint scheme
and the name* Roto-Finish. *via William T Larkins*

*Charles 'Chuck' Hall taxies in the original
P-51D-25NT 44-84961/N7715C No.5* Miss R.J. *at
Reno in 1978. This went on to become the most
modified Mustang in history when owned by Ed
Browning who had considerable modification
work undertaken and a Rolls-Royce Griffon
engine installed – after which it was renamed*
Red Baron. *The Warbird Index*

On 14 August 1979 Mustang history was created again when this magnificent, Griffon-engined 'RB-51' (the heavily modified 44-84961/N7715C No.5 Red Baron) captured the World Speed Record for piston-engined aircraft at 499.018mph, piloted by Steve Hinton via William T Larkins

On 16 September 1979 the 'RB-51' was very badly damaged at Reno following an engine failure. Steve Hinton resurrected the airframe using many ex-Indonesian Air Force P-51 components acquired from Stephen Johnson. The new N7715C is seen here on its first air race outing at Reno in 1984. William T Larkins

In 1988 the same aircraft was photographed at Chino, California having been repainted once again, this time as 413334/G4-U of the 367th FS, 357th FG. Bob Munro

Dallas-built P-51D-25NT 45-11391/N51WT
Nervous Energy V *was first registered to
Thomas Drummon as N6170C in 1963. It is seen
here 33 years later as N51WT, taxying into
dispersal at Kissimmee for The Gathering of
Mustangs & Legends in April 1999.* Author

Photographed at the Reno Air Races in 1985,
45-11471/N332 was then a much-modified
racing Mustang conceived originally by the late
Dave Zeuschel. Raced as No.84 Stiletto, the
aircraft was notable for the lack of an air
scoop, the radiators being in the wing-mounted
gun bays. Alan Gruening

The same Mustang in March 1988 when owned
by Sherman Aircraft Sales of West Palm Beach
and raced by Scott Sherman. The aircraft was
eventually reworked back to stock as a
TF-51D-25NT and is now owned by the Lady
Alice Corporation of Wilmington, Delaware and
registered as N51UR. The Warbird Index

Owner Kermit Weeks taxies P-51D-25NT 45-11507/N921 Cripes A'Mighty 3rd *in its new bare metal scheme in 1987, having taken the EAA Warbirds of America Grand Champion Warbird award at Oshkosh.* Dick Phillips

DIY Mustang restoration? Not quite. An award should be presented to the gentleman who packed this lorry. Built as 45-11507, it served with the RNZAF as NZ2417 and is seen here shortly after being sold. The aircraft is a survivor, with Kermit Weeks at the Weeks Air Museum in Florida. Note the tail warning flag! Jim Winchester

P-51D-25NT Mustang   124-48260   45-11507   N921
Weeks Air Museum Inc, Miami, FL   F

Assigned RNZAF as NZ2417 (shipped to New Zealand) 6Sep45-58 - dismantled and stored at Ardmore 1945-52 - assembled Apr52 - wfu 11Aug55 and into storage Woodbourne AB 1955-58 - sold Ron E Fechney, Canterbury, NZ Apr58 - reg ZK-CCG to Ron E Fechney and Jack MacDonald, Aylesbury, NZ 31Aug64-74 - rebuilt Christchurch, NZ; fffr 29Nov64 (later stored) - flown to Christchurch 4Apr74 for shipping USA - rereg N921 to John F Schafhausen, Spokane, WA Oct74-75 - tfd Gene Stocker Chevrolet, State College, PA 1978-79 - tfd Von Weeks Flugwerke Inc, Tamiami, FL 1979-83 - tfd Weeks Air Museum, Tamiami, FL Jan83 to current - damaged by Hurricane Andrew 24Aug92 - rebuilt Salinas, CA 1993-94.

P-51D-25NT Mustang   124-48266   45-11513
John R Smith, Mapua, New Zealand   S

Assigned RNZAF as NZ2423 (shipped to New Zealand) 27Aug45-58 - dismantled and stored at Ardmore 1945-52 - assembled 1952 but not used; further storage at Rukuhia and Woodbourne 1952-58 - sold W Ruffell, Blenheim, NZ May58-64 - tfd John R Smith, Gardeners Valley, Mapua, NZ 1964-96 (dismantled and wingless).

P-51D-25NT Mustang   124-48271   45-11518   G-MSTG
Maurice Hammond Eye, Suffolk, UK   F

Assigned RNZAF as NZ2427 (shipped to NZ) 27Aug45 - dismantled and stored Ardmore 1945-52, assembled 1952 but not used; further storage Rukuhia and Woodbourne 1952-58 - sold Peter Coleman, Blenheim, NZ; stored May58-90 (incomplete airframe) - tfd Alpine Fighter Collection, Wanaka, NZ 1990-96 - tfd Maurice Hammond, Eye, UK 1997.

P-51D-25NT Mustang   124-48278   45-11525   N151AF
Heritage Flight Museum, Eastsound, WA   F

Assigned Indonesian AF/TNI-AU as F-3?? - Cavalier field mod - recovered by Stephen Johnson of Vanpac Carriers, Oakland, CA 1978 - reg N91JB to John MacGuire, El Paso and Fort Hancock, TX Mar82-88; based at War Eagles Air Museum, Santa Teresa, NM 1988-96 - tfd Apogee Flight, Bill Anders 15Apr96-5Feb99 - rereg N151AF and tfd to Heritage Flight Museum, Eastsound, WA 5Feb99 to current.

P-51D-30NT Mustang   124-48279   45-11526   VH-FST
Wyllie Aviation Pty Ltd, Canning Bridge, WA   F

To TNI-AU c.1959 - recovered by Stephen Johnson, Van Pac Carriers, Oakland, CA 1978 - tfd John Seevers, CA - tfd Rob Poynton, Panama Jacks (rebuilt to airworthy) - reg VH-FST.

P-51D-25NT Mustang   124-48293   45-11540   N151W
JRMC Inc, Chesterton, IN   F

Reg N5162V to James W Steverson, Littleton, CO 1963-64 - rebuilt Chino and Van Nuys, CA 1974 - tfd Dennis Schoenfelder, Santa Barbara, CA 1978 - reg N151W to Joe G Mabee, Midland, TX 1983-92 - tfd J A Michaels, Oconomowoc, WI May93 to current.

P-51D-30NA Mustang   122-40769   44-74229
Indonesian AF HQ, Jakarta, Indonesia   GG

Cavalier Aircraft Corporation - mod to Cavalier specification - to Indonesian Air Force/TNI-AU coded F-362 - tfd to Indonesian Air Force HQ, Jakarta where it has been exhibited on pylon 1990 to current.

P-51D-30NA Mustang   122-40770   44-74230   N5466V
David M Norland, Denver, CO   R

Reg N5466V to Robert G Bixler, San Jose, CA 1963-64 - tfd C L Caprioglio, Fresno, CA 1966 - tfd Frank R Davis, Beaverton, OR 1969-70 - tfd United States National Bank, Beaverton, OR 1972 - tfd David Norland, Denver, CO and raced as No.76 1973-89 - tfd James F Norland, Wasilla, AK 1990-92 - tfd David M Norland, Denver, CO May94 - rebuilt by American Aero Services Nov96 to -

Maurice Hammond imported Dallas-built P-51D-25NT 45-11518 from New Zealand (ex-NZ2427) in 1997 and rebuilt it himself at Eye in Suffolk. Registered as G-MSTG "Janie", this is only the second civil Mustang project to be imported to the UK and made flyable, the first being Robert Lamplough's P-51D-20NA 44-72216/G-BIXL which came from Israel. Richard Paver

The Heritage Flight Museum in Eastsound, Washington has ex-TNI-AU P-51D-25NT 45-11525/N151AF Val-Halla, seen here at Reno wearing racing number 68 in September 1999. Alan Gruening

P-51D-30NA Mustang   122-40802   44-74262   N515J
J A Milender, Fort Mojave, AZ F

Reg N515J to C H Henderson Jul92 - tfd J A Milender, Fort Mojave, AZ Nov92 to current.

P-51D-30NA Mustang   122-40851   44-74311   N151KM
Kenneth B McBride, Reno, NV F

Assigned RCAF as 9577, boc 7Jun47, soc 27Dec57 - tfd James H Defuria and Fred J Ritts of Intercontinental Airways, Canastota, NY Nov56-60 - tfd Aero Enterprises, Elkhart, IN; stored in crates 1960-62 - tfd Louis Hecklesberg, Bartlesville, OK; stored complete 1962-84 - reg C-GPSI (2nd issue) to Ritchie Rasmussen of Trans-Am Helicopters, Edmonton, Alberta, Canada Feb85-91; rebuild project, stored Edmonton, Alberta - tfd Kenneth B McBride, Reno, NV Aug98 to current.

P-51D-30NA Mustang   122-40929   44-74389   N64824
Arthur S Vance Jr, Sebastapol, CA F

Assigned RAAF as A68-175, boc Apr50, soc Jan59 - tfd Col Pay, Narromine, New South Wales, Australia 1960-65 - tfd Ed Fleming of Skyservice Aviation, Camden, NSW 1965-67 - reg CF-WWH to John C Kehler, Plumb Coulee, Manitoba, Canada 1May67-71; by ship to Vancouver, rebuilt Carman, Manitoba as four-seat conversion - reg N64824 to Frank Marcucci, Roslyn Heights, NY 18May71-73 - reg N5789 (ntu, though it flew with this registration) - reg N64824 to Frank Gruzman, West Babylon, NY 31Jan73 - tfd John P Silberman, Sherborn, MA 8Nov73-75 - tfd Arthur S and Dan Vance, Santa Rosa, CA 5Aug75-96 - identity transferred to rebuild using ex-TNI-AU airframe; rebuilt Shafter, CA 1975-82, fffr May82.

P-51D-30NA Mustang   122-40931   44-74391   N351MX
Woods Aviation LLC, Carefree, AZ R

Sold to FA Guatemalteca as FAG 351 (ex-Cavalier) - reg N38229 to Don Hull, Sugarland, TX Aug72 - tfd Wilson C Edwards, Big Spring, TX 1978 to 20Jun00 - tfd HEC Equipment Co, Oak Grove, LA 20Jun00 to current (for restoration) - tfd Woods Aviation LLC, Carefree, Arizona 30Oct00-May01 - rereg N351MX to same owner 24May01 to current.

P-51D-30NA Mustang   122-40944   44-74404   N151RJ
Robert J Odegaard, Kindred, ND F

Assigned RCAF as 9276, boc 11Jan51, soc 27Dec57 - reg N4132A (1st issue) to James H Defuria and Fred J Ritts

of Intercontinental Airways, Canastota, NY Nov56-60 - tfd M L Alson of Aero Enterprises, Elkhart, IN 1960 - acc (landing) Elkhart, IN - tfd Gary Harris, Half Moon Bay, CA (believed fuselage only) 1974-88 - tfd as rebuild project to William A Spear, San Diego, CA - tfd Tri-State Aviation, Wahpeton, ND 1990 - rereg N7129E to Robert J Odegaard, Kindred, ND Sep90-94 - rereg N151RJ to Robert J Odegaard, Kindred, ND 9Sep94 to current; rebuilt Kindred, fffr 1995.

P-51D-30NA Mustang   122-40947   44-74407
USAFM Collection, Fargo, ND GG

Allocated to USAFM, Hector Field ANGB, Fargo, ND 1965 to current; exhibited on pylon and painted as '474407' of North Dakota ANG.

Below: *Art Vance taxies out in N64824 at Reno in September 1999.* Kevin Grantham

Above: *Art Vance's P-51D-30NA 44-74389/N64824 Million Dollar Baby, seen here in 364th Fighter Squadron, 357th Fighter Group markings in September 1988.* Thierry Thomassin

P-51D-30NA Mustang   122-40949   44-74409   N51RT
Robert C Tullius, Sebring, FL   F

Assigned RCAF as 9235, boc 6Dec50, soc 30Dec58 - reg
N6319T to James H Defuria and Fred J Ritts of
Intercontinental Airways, Canastota, NY Dec58-60 - tfd Aero
Enterprises, Elkhart, IN 20Oct60 - tfd J H Cunningham,
Lexington, NC 14Jul61-62 - tfd Dean J Ortner, Wakeman, OH
19Aug62-68 - tfd Joe Bruce, Palm Springs, CA 15May68 - tfd
Cavalier Aircraft Corp, Sarasota, FL 3Jun68-69 - tfd Clint R
Hackney, Friendswood, TX 11Apr69-71 - tfd Frank D
Strickler, Denton, TX 2Nov71-77 - rereg N4409 and tfd to
Frank D Strickler, Grapevine, TX 30Dec77 - tfd Peter
Bottome, Caracas, Venezuela 1981 - rereg N555BM to
Gordon W Plaskett, King City, CA Jan81-82; rebuilt King City,
CA 1981-84 - rereg YV-508CP to Peter Bottome, Caracas,
Venezuela 1982-90 - tfd Robert C Tullius, Winchester, VA
(del Dec90 as N555BM) Mar91 - rereg N51RT Robert
Tullius/Group 44 Inc, Winchester, VA 9Apr91-19Apr99 - tfd
Robert C Tullius Trustee, Sebring, FL 19Apr99 to current.

P-51D-30NA Mustang   122-40957   44-74417   N6327T
Richard P James, Fennimore, WI   F

Assigned RCAF as 9586, boc 2Nov50, soc 1Nov60 - reg
CF-MWB to James H Defuria of Intercontinental Airways,
Canastota, NY Dec58-60 - rereg N6327T to Aero Enterprises,
Elkhart, IN 10May60-63 - tfd Garland R Brown, Freeland,
MI/Fort Wayne, IN 16Feb63-87 - acc Fort Wayne, IN 4Aug66
- tfd Robert Byrne, Bloomfield Hills, MI 1987-89 - tfd Richard
P James, Fennimore, WI Sep89 to current.

P-51D-30NA Mustang   122-40963   44-74423   N64CL
H Clay Lacy, Van Nuys, CA   F

Assigned RCAF as 9595, boc 8Nov50, soc 14Aug59 - reg
N6517D to James H Defuria of Intercontinental Airways,
Canastota, NY 21Jul58-59 - tfd Madison Aviation Corp,
Canastota, NY 11Nov59 - tfd Naylor Aviation Inc, Clinton,
MD 12Nov59 - rereg N182XF to North American Maritime
Corp, Cambridge, MA Nov59-62 - tfd Hamilton Aircraft Co,
Tucson, AZ 2Oct62 - Hillcrest Aviation Industries, Lewiston,
ID 1Nov62-64 - tfd California Airmotive Corp, Burbank, CA
1May64-70; operated and flown by Clay Lacy as No.64 *The
Purple People Eater* - rereg N64CL to H Clay Lacy, Van
Nuys, CA 1970 to current.

P-51D-30NA Mustang   122-40965   44-74425   N11T
Western Aviation Maintenance Inc, Mesa, AZ

Assigned RCAF as 9591, boc 8Nov50, soc 29Apr58 - reg
N6522D to James H Defuria and Fred J Ritts of

Intercontinental Airways, Canastota, NY 25Feb57-59 - tfd
Madison Aviation Corp, Canastota, NY 20Oct59 - tfd Naylor
Aviation Inc, Clinton, MD Oct59-63 - tfd Bonanza Inc,
Broomall, PA 3Jan63-64 - tfd Graubart Aviation, Valparaiso,
IN 25Jun64 - tfd Joseph W Bohmeir/New London Airport,
New London, PA 27Jul64 - tfd James Fugate, Oswego, OR
30Sep64 - tfd R A Hanson Co, Palouse, WA 8Dec64-66 - tfd
Superstition Air Service, Mesa-Falcon Field, AZ 6Jan66-68 -
tfd Larry N Mitchell, Hopkinsville, KY Oct68-71 - rereg
N51HB (ntu) - tfd Harold F Beal, Concord, TN 18Jun71 -
rereg N6522D to Flaherty Factors Inc, Monterey, CA 1Sep71
- tfd Harold F Beal, Concord, TN 1972 - acc (damaged,
landing) Knoxville, TN Oct72 - rereg N11T and tfd John
Herlihy, Half Moon Bay, CA, raced as No.8 1973 - acc
(ground collision) Half Moon Bay, CA 10Nov74 - tfd Johnny
Bolton Ford Inc, Maitland, FL 3Sep75 - tfd Pete Sherman
Exotic Cars, Maitland, FL 2Mar76-78 - tfd Ben R Bradley,
Oakland Park, FL 11Jan78 - tfd Gordon W Plaskett, King
City, CA 1981-82 - acc (damaged, forced landing)
Piedmont, OK 23Oct82 - tfd Bob Amyx, Oklahoma City, OK
1983 - tfd Robert Byrne, Bloomfield, MI 1984-85 - tfd World
War Two Enterprises Inc, Scotch Plains, NJ 1987-88 - tfd
John Goltra, Scotch Plains, NJ 1989 - tfd Western Wings
Aircraft Sales Co, Oakland, OR 1989 - tfd Planes of Fame
East, Minneapolis-Flying Cloud, MN 1990-92 - tfd Klaers
Aviation, Rialto, CA - tfd Western Aviation Maintenance Inc,
Mesa, AZ 94 - freighted to Netherlands, arrived Lelystad
6Apr94; operated by Stichting Dutch Mustang Flight,
Lelystad, Netherlands Apr94 to current.

P-51D-30NA 44-74425/N11T "Damn Yankee"
arrived at Lelystad, Netherlands on 6 April 1994
where it has remained ever since, operated by
Tom Vandermuelen. It is still on the USCAR to
Western Aviation Maintenance. Joe Cupido

P-51D-30NA 44-74423/N64CL (ex-RCAF 9595),
has been owned by Clay Lacy since 1962. It
became well known as The Purple People
Eater *due to its attractive purple paint scheme.*
The Warbird Index

Robert Tullius of Sebring, Florida has owned 336th FS, 4th FG-marked P-51D-30NA 44-74409/N51RT since December 1990 when it was imported from Venezuela. Note the dummy bombs on the underwing pylons. Tom Smith

This shot of Robert Tullius in 44-74409/N51RT clearly shows why there is a significant blind spot for the taxying Mustang pilot. Note also the wide undercarriage base. Tom Smith

P-51D-30NA Mustang   122-40967 44-74427   F-AZSB
JBS Aviation, Sommieres, France   F

Assigned RCAF as 9592, boc 8Nov50, soc 15Nov59 - reg N9148R to Trans Florida Aviation, Sarasota, FL 20May59-62 - tfd as N2251D to Robert A Hoover of North American Aviation, El Segundo, CA 19Mar62-67 - acc (damaged) Myrtle Beach, FL 20Jan65 - tfd North American Rockwell Corp, Los Angeles, CA Oct67-70 - acc (badly damaged, ground explosion) Oshkosh, WI 9Aug70 - tfd Steve Shulke and John B Bolton, Maitland, FL 1970-75; rebuilt Chattanooga, TN, using components of 44-74435/N130JT - tfd John J Stokes, San Marcos, TX 6Aug75-78 - tfd John T Baugh of Baugh Aviation, Nashville, TN 10Jan78-89; flown in civilian colours as *Miss Coronado* coded JT-B - tfd Paul C Romine, Indianapolis, IN 1990-94 - tfd Brian Hoffner/Kenair Inc, West Palm Beach, FL 18Aug94-Nov99 - tfd JBS Aviation, Sommieres, France Feb00 to current.

P-51D-30NA Mustang   122-40975 44-74435   N130JT
James J Chernich, Lake Zurich, IL   R

Assigned RCAF as 9221, boc 15Nov50, soc 29Apr58 - tfd James H Defuria and Fred J Ritts of Intercontinental Airways, Canastota, NY 29Apr58 - tfd Aero Enterprises, Elkhart, IN 1960 - rereg CF-LOQ to Lynn Garrison, Calgary, Alberta, Canada 26Sep61-63 - tfd Gerald W Wolton, Calgary, Alberta 13Mar63-66 - rereg N130JT to John W Temple, Signal Mountain, TN 26Apr66-70 - acc (minor damage) Calgary, Alberta 29Apr66 - acc (badly damaged)

23Oct70; some parts used in rebuild of 44-74427/N2251D in 1970 - remains to James J Chernich, Lake Zurich, IL 20Feb76 to current.

P-51D-30NA Mustang   122-40985 44-74445   N4132A
Bill H Hubbs, Pecos, TX   F

Assigned RCAF as 9594, boc 8Nov50, soc 4Dec56 - reg N4143A to Stinson Field Aircraft, San Antonio, TX Oct56-57 - tfd Truman E Miley/Big Piney Aviation, Roy, UT 3May57-59 - rereg N4132A (2nd issue) to M L Alson of Aero Enterprises, Elkhart, IN 1Oct59-61 - tfd George E Monea and Mario I Corbi, Alliance, OH 5Aug61-62 - tfd to Harold J Shelton, Belle Fourche, SD 28Mar62 - tfd Grazing Inc, Alzada, MT - mod for cloud seeding 9May62 - tfd M L Alson of Aero Enterprises, Elkhart, IN Oct62 - tfd Richardson Construction Co, Sterling, VA 2Nov62 - tfd Harold L Barkman, Indianapolis, IN 15Jan63-67 - tfd John E Dilley, Auburn, IN Nov67-69 - tfd Bill H Hubbs, Pecos, TX 5May69 to current.

P-51D-30NA Mustang   122-40986 44-74446   N1451D
Robert N Davis, Tipton, IN   F

Assigned RCAF as 9223, boc 15Nov50, soc 1Nov60 - tfd James H Defuria of Intercontinental Airways, Canastota, NY 30Dec58 - tfd Aero Enterprises, Elkhart, IN 1960 - rereg CF-LOR to Milt Harradance, Calgary, Alberta, Canada 1960-65 - tfd Gary L Oates, Weston, Ontario, Canada 1965-66 - tfd Gary L Oates and Mike Malagies, Toronto, Ontario, Canada 1968-69 - tfd Froates Aviation, Toronto, Ontario 1969-70 - tfd

P-51D-30NA 44-74427/N2251D painted as Major Leonard 'Kit' Carson's 44-11622/G4-C Nooky Booky IV of the 362nd FS, 357th FG. The aircraft is now F-AZSB of JBS Aviation. Ed Toth

Howard A Sloan 20Aug70 - tfd John W Temple and R L Robertson, TN 6Nov70 - rereg N1451D (2nd issue) to John W Temple, Signal Mountain, TN 14Mar75 - tfd John J Stokes of Cen-Tex Aviation, San Marcos, TX 13Nov75 - tfd Cecil H Harp, Lodi, CA 12Jan76-78 - tfd Michael Clarke, Prescott, AZ 26Mar78-92; flown as *Unruly Julie* coded MX-C - acc (forced landed) AZ Sep87 - rebuilt Chino, CA by Unlimited Aircraft Ltd 1988-94; ff 4Apr94, acc (forced landing) near Chino, CA 4Apr94, wreck tfd William A Speer, La Mesa, CA Apr94 - tfd Brian O'Farrell, Miami, FL 1995 - tfd Bill Jennings, Carson City, NV - tfd Barnett Investments Inc, La Verne, CA 11 Aug97 - tfd Robert N Davis, Tipton, IN 21Aug01 to current.

P-51D-30NA Mustang   122-40992 44-74452   N74190
Bruce L Winter, San Antonio, TX   R

Assigned RCAF as 9225, boc 15Nov50, soc 29Apr58 - tfd James H Defuria and Fred J Ritts of Intercontinental Airways, Canastota, NY 29Apr58-59 - sold to FA Guatemalteca coded FAG 366 Mar62-72 - recovered and reg N74190 to Don Hull, Sugarland, TX Aug72-76 - tfd Wilson C Edwards, Big Spring, TX 1976-Mar02 - tfd Registration Pending, San Antonio, TX 12Mar02 to current. NB: USCAR lists incorrect identity 44-75452.

Clark County, Indiana in 1993 and Paul Romine's 44-74427/N2251D raises its tailwheel on take-off. Later that year, ownership of this Mustang passed to Brian Hoffner of Kenair Inc based in West Palm Beach, Florida. Tom Smith

P-51D-30NA 44-74446/N1451D, complete with mirror-like polished metal exterior, outside Chino-based Square One Aviation's facility in January 1997 and about to be rolled out. Thierry Thomassin

John T Baugh, then President of Warbirds of America, flew P-51D-30NA 44-74427/N2251D Miss Coronado in this civilian paint scheme for many years. It was sold to Paul Romine in 1990 and adopted military marks soon afterwards, going on to France in February 2000. Author

P-51D-30NA Mustang 122-40993 44-74453 N251HR
Leestown Aviation Inc, Dover, DE F

Assigned RCAF as 9597, boc 8Nov50, soc 15Oct59 - reg N9150R to Trans Florida Aviation, Sarasota, FL 20May59-60 - rereg N1335 to E D Weiner, Los Angles, CA 29Jul60-61 - tfd Margaret and Frank Woodside, Lubbock, TX Oct61-62 - tfd Aero Enterprises, Elkhart, IN 12Mar62-63 - tfd John M Barker, Indianapolis, IN 25Feb63-70 - acc (landing) Indianapolis, IN (Barker killed) 17Mar63 - tfd (fuselage) Bill Destefani, Shafter, CA 1981-84; rebuilt Shafter using TNI-AU airframe, adopted i/d of 44-13903 - reg C-GJCJ (2nd issue) to Jerry C Janes, Vancouver, British Columbia, Canada 1987-89 - rereg N151JP to James R Priebe, Findlay, OH 1988-92, painted as *Glamorous Jan* - rereg N251HR to Kipnis Inc, Dover, DE May93-Apr98 - tfd KIPNIS, Chicago, IL 15Apr98-Feb02 - tfd Leestown Aviation Inc, Dover, DE 22Feb02 to current.

P-51D-30NA Mustang 122-40998 44-74458 N351DM
Barnstormers Aviation, Jacksonville, FL F

Assigned RCAF as 9226, boc 15Nov50, soc 15Oct59 - reg N9145R to Trans Florida Aviation, Sarasota, FL 20May59-61 - tfd Marine Maintenance Co, Galveston, TX 10Jan61- tfd Lorraine P Bodine, Texas City, TX 28Feb61-62 - tfd Aero Enterprises, Elkhart, IN 21Aug62 - acc (forced landed in cornfield) near Elkhart, IN 9Mar63 - hulk tfd Dave Zeuschel and Mike Geren, CA - tfd Aerospace Modifications, Van Nuys, CA 1970; rebuilt Van Nuys to TP-51 config 1970 - tfd John Marlin, Los Angeles, CA 1971 - reg N65206 to John Marlin 1973-87; rebuild continued at Compton, CA 1971-77, ff 1977 named *Green Machine* - tfd as N351DM to David Marco of Barnstormers Aviation, Jacksonville, FL Feb88; rebuilt by Glen Wegman, Fighter Enterprises, fffr 1991.

P-51D-30NA Mustang 122-41006 44-74466 N10607
Parmley Aviation Services Inc, Council Bluffs, IA F

Assigned RCAF as 9227, boc 15Nov50, soc 4Jan56 - reg N10607 to Stinson Field Aircraft, San Antonio, TX 26Oct56 - tfd George D Hanby, Evanston, IL 27Feb57 - tfd Thermal Belt Air Service, Tryon, NC 12May57 - tfd Northrop Carolina Inc, Ashville, NC 3Aug57 - tfd George D Hanby, Philadelphia, PA 1963-69 - tfd John M Sliker, Wadley, GA 19Mar69-76 - tfd to Madelaine H Sliker, Wadley, GA 24Mar76-84 - tfd Wiley C Sanders, Troy, AL 1985-92 - acc Reno, NV 14Sep85 as No.69 *Georgia Mae* - tfd Parmley Aviation Services Inc, Council Bluffs, IA Dec93 to current.

Michael Clark of Phoenix, Arizona, named P-51D-30NA 44-74446/N1451D Unruly Julie after the lady in his life. Seen in 78th FG markings in August 1984, it is now owned by Robert Davis of Tipton, Indiana. William T Larkins

P-51D-30NA 44-74452/N74190 is the last of the Mustangs once held in store by Wilson 'Connie' Edwards at Big Spring, Texas. At one time it was to have been shipped to Romania as part of an ambitious project to manufacture major new Mustang structures and even complete aircraft, The project was organised by a New York-based company calling themselves Milennium Classics, but in the end the plans failed to come to fruition. Chuck Gardner

A parched Oshkosh EAA Convention in 1998 saw P-51D-30NA 44-74466/N10607 Barbara Jean taxying out for take-off sporting a plain but highly polished scheme. John Kerr

The same Mustang displays its Nebraska ANG markings in 1999 while attending the Wings of the North Air Show. Bob Luikens

Dave Marco holds station in 44-74458/N351DM Sizzlin' Liz, beautifully restored by Glen Wegmann of Fighter Enterprises, Fort Lauderdale, Florida. Tom Smith

P-51D-30NA 44-74458/N31248 in pseudo 8th AF Scouting Force colours at Merced, California in June 1979. It later became Dave Marco's Sizzlin' Liz. William T Larkins

Reno, 1981: 44-74458, then registered N65206 to John Marlin of Los Angeles, raced as No.17 and wore the name Green Machine (but on the port side of the nose only). William T Larkins

P-51D-30NA 44-74474/N6341T "Rascal" in July 1988 when owned by Bob Byrne. It was subsequently restored for NASCAR owner Jack Rousch of Rousch Technologies and painted in an authentic 8th Air Force paint scheme as Old Crow. The Warbird Index

P-51D-30NA 44-74469/N7723C of Fighterbirds West in 1987. This ex-FAD Cavalier II Mustang was rebuilt following purchase from Brian O'Farrell in 1984. Thierry Thomassin

The same aircraft, now N51DJ, at Merced, California in June 1991 when owned by Dianne Dejacomo. It was transferred to Classic Air Parts in 1992. William T Larkins

P-51D-30NA Mustang 122-41009 44-74469 N1251D
Classic American Aircraft Inc, Poland, OH   F

Reg N7723C to Trans Florida Aviation, Sarasota, FL 1958-60 - mod as Cavalier Mk.2 - sold to FAD as FAD 1919 1960-84 - tfd Johnson Aviation, Miami, FL 19May84 - rereg N7723C to Jerry Miles of Fighterbirds West, Riverbend, AZ 1986-90; rebuilt Chino, CA; fffr 13Sep87, rereg N51DJ - tfd Classic Air Parts, Miami, FL 1992 - struck-off USCAR 27Jan93 - rereg N1251D to Classic American Aircraft Inc 20Jun00 to current.

P-51D-30NA Mustang 122-41014 44-74474 N6341T
Rousch Technologies Inc, Livonia, MI   R

Assigned RCAF as 9270, boc 11Jan51, soc 20Sep60 - reg N6341T to James H DeFuria and Fred J Ritts of Intercontinental Airways, Canastota, NY Nov56-60 - tfd Aero Enterprises, Elkhart, IN 10May60-62 - tfd Margaret Kahlow, Madisonville, KY 27Aug62-65 - tfd Audubon Service Inc, Henderson, KY 12Jun65-70 - tfd TAS Flight Services, Granville, OH 29Jul70-71 - tfd A C Lofgren, Hickory Corners, MI 3Nov71-81 - tfd Bob Byrne Aviation, Bloomfield Hills, MI 1981-92 - tfd Rousch Technologies Inc, Livonia, MI 26Sep94-95 - N51RZ reserved; USCAR quotes serial as 44-74774.

P-51D-30NA Mustang 122-41023 44-74483 N51GP
George Perez, Anchorage, AK   F

Assigned RCAF as 9228, boc 15Nov50, soc 17Aug59 - reg N6523D to James H Defuria of Intercontinental Airways, Canastota, NY 21Jul58 - acc (minor damage) Basking Ridge, NJ 4Feb60 - tfd Robert J Hartland of Dogwood Inc, Summit, NJ 7Jul60-61 - tfd Stencel Aero Engineering Corp, Ashville, NC 17Feb61 - tfd W R Lowdermilk, Greenville, SC 25Sep62-64 - tfd Airplanes Inc, Fort Worth, TX 31Oct64 - tfd John H Herlihy, San Mateo, CA Nov65-66 - tfd George Perez, Daly City, CA, race No.8 5Dec66-72 - rereg N51GP to George Perez, Sonoma, CA/Anchorage, AK 23Aug99 to current.

P-51D-30NA Mustang 122-41034 44-74494 N72FT
Vintage Aircraft Inc, Mountain View, CA   F

Assigned RCAF as 9237, boc 6Dec50, soc 1Nov60 - reg N6313T (1st issue, ntu) - tfd James H Defuria of Intercontinental Airways, Canastota, NY Dec58-60 (apparently ferried to USA as N6313T, not registered as this) - reg N6356T to Aero Enterprises, Elkhart, IN 10May60-63 - tfd Capital Steel, Baton Rouge, LA 13Jun63-64 - tfd Aero Enterprises, Elkhart, IN 20Mar64 - tfd Benjamin B Peck of Interocean Airways, Luxembourg and Munich, West Germany 20Feb64-66; flown USA to Luxembourg 28Jul64 - tfd Charles Masefield, Shoreham, UK Aug66-70; flown Shoreham for Spain 15Jan69 for film appearance in *Patton* (painted as 643147) - tfd Ed A Jurist of Vintage Car Store, Nyack, NY 15Mar70-72; shipped to USA Jan71, flew as 415271/OC-E - tfd Ed A Jurist of Vintage Aircraft International, Brownwood, TX 27Feb72-75 - Military Aircraft Restoration Company, Chino, CA Mar75-79 - tfd Wally McDonnell, Mojave, CA 1979 - tfd Bill Destefani, Bakersfield, CA 1979-81 - rereg N72FT to Bill Destefani, Shafter, CA Jan81-87; raced as 474494/LH-D No.2 *Mangia Pane* - tfd Vintage Aircraft Inc, Mountain View, CA Sep87 to current.

P-51D-30NA 44-74494/N6356T in the mid-1960s, believed to be in the UK before being painted in its Post Office Red paint scheme with white undersides, and then in its new paint scheme. The aircraft was flown by Charles Masefield during its stay in the UK. The Warbird Index

P-51D-30NA 44-74497/N6320T Vergeltungswaffe wore 361st FS, 356th FG markings but has since adopted 350th FS, 353rd FG markings following conversion to TF-51D configuration by Stallion 51 Maintenance Corporation. Tim Bivens

P-51D-30NA Mustang 122-41037 44-74497 N6320T
Lady Alice Corporation, Wilmington, DE   R

Assigned RCAF as 9230, boc 15Nov50, soc 1Nov60 - reg N6320T (2nd issue) to James H Defuria of Intercontinental Airways, Canastota, NY 30Dec58 - tfd Aero Enterprises, Elkhart, IN 1960 - tfd Ralph W Rensink, Lewiston, ID 10Jan66 - tfd Kenneth W Neal, Medford, OR 26Mar66-70 - acc Lancaster, CA 2Aug69 - tfd Glenn Cook, Seattle, WA 26Jan70 - tfd Mike Smith, Johnson, KS for rebuild 1970-72; fffr Mar71 - tfd I N Burchinall, Paris, TX 14Nov72 - tfd Kent Jones, Dallas, TX 3Jan73-75 - tfd John Rutherford, Fort Worth, TX Nov75-79 - tfd Heritage Aircraft Inc, Fayetteville, GA Jul79-98; painted as 415080/QI-B - tfd Lady Alice Corp Aug98 to current; new markings 2002.

P-51D-30NA Mustang 122-41042 44-74502 N351DT
Vintage Warbirds Inc, Louisville, KY   F

Assigned RCAF as 9232, boc 6Dec50, soc 1Nov60 - reg CF-MWC to James H Defuria of Intercontinental Airways, Canastota, NY 30Dec58 - rereg N6321T to Aero Enterprises, Elkhart, IN 1960 - reported seized en route to Cuba 1962 - tfd Otha D Aishman, Salina, KS 20Jul62-64 - tfd Edward

Fisher Flying Service, Kansas City, KS 2Jul64-73 - tfd Leroy Penhall, Balboa, CA 21Aug73 - tfd Military Aircraft International Inc, Miami, FL 2Nov73 - rereg N70QF to Ken Burnstine, raced as No.34 *Miss Foxy Lady* 1976 - tfd M D Pruitt Furniture Co, Phoenix, AZ 5Mar76 - tfd Gary Levitz of Western Aircraft Leasing, Scottsdale, AZ 4Jun76 - rereg N51VC to John V Crocker, Oakland, CA and Ione, CA 3Aug76-95; mod as air racer No.6 *"Sumthin' Else"* - tfd Vintage Warbirds Inc, Louisville, KY Jan 98, modified to TF-51 configuration - rereg N351DT 24Jan1998.

P-51D-30NA Mustang 122-41045 44-74505
Museum de la Revolucionaria, Havana, Cuba   M

Assigned RCAF as 9233, boc 6Dec50, soc 7Dec56 - reg N3990A to Stinson Field Aircraft, San Antonio, TX 26Oct56 - tfd Jack Adams Aircraft Sales, Memphis, TN 1956-57 - tfd Pat Moore, Hutchinson, KS 15Nov57 - rereg N68DR to David B Robinson, Miami, FL 6Jan58 - tfd Allen McDonald, Miami Springs, FL 20Nov58 - sold to FA Rebel de Cuba coded FAR401; del Nov58 to Museum de la Revolucionaria, Playa Giron, Havana; exhibited as FAR 401 1963 to current.

In 1976 Ken Burnstine raced P-51D-30NA 44-74502/N70QF as No.34 Miss Foxy Lady, *the aircraft wearing an all-white colour scheme and appropriate artwork on the aft fuselage.* The Warbird Index

"Sumthin' Else" in a dark blue and white paint scheme in 1993. This Mustang is one of several that has been completely rebuilt back to stock and is now in TF-51 configuration as N351DT with Vintage Warbirds in Louisville, Kentucky. The Warbird Index

Renumbered and repainted, 44-74502, reregistered N51VC to John Crocker, prepares for take-off during qualifying at Reno in 1976. The Warbird Index

Photographs on the opposite page:

Photographed at Merced, California in May 1982, P-51D-30NA 44-74494/N72FT Mangia Pane *basks in the hot sun following a display. This Mustang was operated in the UK in the late 1960s by Charles Masefield as N6356T.* William T Larkins

N72FT is now Iron Ass *and owned by Vintage Aircraft Inc of Mountain View, California. The aircraft is shown here at Santa Monica, California in August 1994.* Thierry Thomassin

P-51D-30NA Mustang   122-41046   44-74506   F-AZJJ
Rene Bouverat, Chambery, France   F

Assigned RCAF as 9231, boc 6Dec50, soc 1Dec60 -
reg CF-MWM to James H Defuria and Fred J Ritts of
Intercontinental Airways, Canastota, NY 30Dec58 - rereg
N6325T (ntu) - tfd Aero Enterprises, Elkhart, IN 1960 (ferried
to Elkhart as N6325T, not registered as this) - rereg N6317T
to Aero Enterprises, Elkhart, IN 1960 - rereg N335J (3rd
issue) to Ed Weiner, Los Angeles, CA; raced as No.14 and
No.49 24Mar63-73 - tfd Violet M Bonzer, Los Angeles, CA
8May73-79 - loaned to EAA Museum, Hales Corner, WI
1973-79 - tfd Max R Hoffman, Fort Collins, CO 1979 - tfd
Wolcott Air Services, Wolcott, CT 1980 - tfd Gary Norton of
Norton Aero, Athol, ID 1982-90 - tfd Sierra Aviation,
Boardman, OH 1992 - struck-off USCAR May93 - rereg
F-AZJJ to Rene Bouverat Ste., Air B Aviation, Chambery,
France 12Aug93 to current.

P-51D-30NA Mustang   122-41064   44-74524   N151HR
Henry L Reichert Jr, Bismarck, ND   F

Built by Bob Odegaard of Tri-State Aviation - reg N151HR to
Henry L Reichert Jr, Bismarck, ND 12May97 to current.

P-51D-30NA Mustang   122-41076   44-74536   N991R
Brent N Hisey, Oklahoma City, OK   R

Reg N5452V (1st issue) - tfd Donald G Singleton, Van Nuys,
CA; raced as No.19 1963-64 - tfd David S Allender, San
Aario, CA 1966 - rereg N991RC to Robert N Cleaves 1969 -
tfd Keefe Corp, Pacific Palisades, CA Jun69 - rereg N991R to
Howie Keefe of Keefe Corp, Van Nuys, CA 1970-78 - tfd Ron
and Janette Smythe, Everett, WA 1983-84 - tfd RGS Inc,
Edmonds, WA 1985-88 - tfd Hanover Aero Inc, Nashua, NH
Jun89-92 - tfd Brent N Hisey, Oklahoma City, OK Sep93 to
current - acc (badly damaged) Reno 11Sep02, on rebuild.

P-51D-30NA Mustang   122-41083   44-74543   N454
Richard M Vartanian, Los Angeles, CA   U

Assigned RCAF as 9252, boc 6Dec50, soc 17Sep57 - tfd
James H Defuria and Fred J Ritts of Intercontinental
Airways, Canastota, NY 25Feb57 - tfd Ray O Denman,
Brewerton, NY as scrap 28Jun61-65 - tfd Richard M
Vartanian, Pasadena, CA 30Jun65; roaded from Canastota
Jun74, stored Brewerton and Johnstown, NY 1980-82 -
rereg N4543 to Richard M Vartanian, Los Angeles, CA 1978;
thought to have been used in rebuild adopting identity
44-63655/N5500S.

P-51D-30NA Mustang   122-41122   44-74582   N6329T
Joseph H Thibodeau, Denver, CO

Assigned RCAF as 9253, boc 6Dec50, soc 19Aug59 - reg
N6524D to James H Defuria of Intercontinental Airways,
Canastota, NY 21Jul58 - rereg N6329T to Aero Enterprises,
Elkhart, IN Nov60-61 - tfd A G Ainsworth/A-Mack Co, Luling,
TX Oct61-63 - tfd Landon Cullum, Wichita Falls, TX
14Mar63-84 - tfd John C Hooper, Harvey, LA 1984-87 - tfd
Robert Byrne, Bloomfield Hills, MI 1988-90 - tfd N51JT (ntu)
- tfd Joseph H Thibodeau, Denver, CO Jan91 - rereg N6329T
to Joseph H Thibodeau, Denver, CO Feb91 to current.

P-51D-30NA Mustang   122-41142   44-74602   N358
Jack C Hovey, Ione, CA

Assigned RCAF as 9255, boc 6Dec50, soc 1Nov60 - reg
N6318T to James H Defuria of Intercontinental Airways,
Canastota, NY 30Dec58 - tfd Aero Enterprises, Elkhart, IN
19Aug61 - tfd Robert E King, South Bend, IN Nov61-63 - tfd
Aero Enterprises, Elkhart, IN 27Mar63 - rereg N35N to C E
Crosby, Bellingham, WA 20May63-67; raced as No.3 *Mr
Choppers* - rereg N3580 to Jack C Hovey of Hovey Machine
Products, Walnut Creek, CA and (later) Oakland, CA
10Jul67-95 - tfd Hovey Machine Products, Ione, CA 1996
to current.

44-74506/F-AZJJ arriving in France for Rene Bouverat of Air B Aviation in 1993. The aircraft is wearing fictitious 4th FG markings. Rene Bouverat

Long-time Mustang and air race pilot Skip Holm flying Henry 'Hank' Reichert Jr's P-51D-30NA 44-74524/N151HR Dakota Kid out of Oshkosh in August 1997. Dick Phillips

P-51D-30NA 44-74536/N991R Miss America sits out on the ramp at Reno in September 2000, ready to race. On 11th September 2002, Brent Hisey had to force-land the aircraft following engine failure at Reno. The aircraft was extensively damaged when the undercarriage collapsed, but it will be rebuilt. Tom Smith

Photographs on the opposite page:

Less than two years after being struck off charge as RCAF9233, P-51D-30NA 44-74505 was with the Fuerza Aerea Rebel de Cuba. It is now on display at the Museum de la Revolucionaria, Playa Giron, Havana, Cuba. Rod Kenward

Based in France for some ten years, P-51D-30NA 44-74506/F-AZJJ has recently been shipped back to the USA in the hope of finding a buyer. Thierry Thomassin

Landon Cullum of Wichita Falls, Texas owned P-51D-30NA Mustang 44-74582/N6329T when it was photographed in 1964. The Warbird Index

The same aircraft, location unknown, but looking very unloved! It is now with Joseph Thibodeau as N6329T in Denver, Colorado.

Enjoying a new lease of life, 44-74582/N6329T Crusader and Joseph Thibodeau take time out from the Breckenridge airshow in 1993 for a photo sortie. Ed Toth

P-51D-30NA Mustang 122-41167 44-74627
Philippine Air Force

Assigned Philippine Air Force as 73373 - tfd Basa
Air Base, Republic of the Philippines; exhibited as gate
guard 1977 to current.

P-51D-30NA Mustang 122-41279 44-74739 N51RH
John K Bagley, Rexburg, ID   F

Assigned RCAF as 9297, boc 16Mar51, soc 14May59 - reg
N8672E to James H Defuria of Intercontinental Airways,
Canastota, NY 27Feb59-60 - tfd Aero Enterprises, Elkhart, IN
18Jun60-61 - tfd Midwest Airways, Cincinnati, OH 10May61-
62 - mod to Cavalier by Trans Florida Aviation Inc, Sarasota,
FL Apr62 - rereg N151Q to Aerial Services Inc, London, OH
Oct62-63 - tfd Valair Aircraft, Cincinnati, OH 23May63 - tfd E
R Cantrell of Angels Aviation, Zephyrhills, FL 30May63-64 -
tfd Space Systems Laboratory Inc, Melbourne, FL 3Jul64-67
- tfd Trans Florida Aviation Inc, Sarasota, FL 28Mar67 - tfd
Cavalier Aircraft Corp, Sarasota, FL 4Aug67-71 (full Cavalier
conversion) - rereg N51RH to Robert A Hoover of North
American Rockwell Corp, El Segundo, CA 8May71 - tfd
Robert A Hoover/Rockwell International, El Segundo, CA
1974-85 - acc (damaged, wing fire) Marysville, OH 8Sep84 -
tfd Robert A Hoover, Los Angeles, CA Aug86-16Apr99 -
tfd John K Bagley, Rexburg, ID 16Apr99.

P-51D-30NA Mustang 122-41353 44-74813 N151KW
Ken J Wagnon, Danville, IL   F

Assigned RCAF as 9261, boc 10Jan51, soc 17Aug59 - reg
N6301T to James H Defuria of Intercontinental
Airways, Canastota, NY 21Jul58 - reported crashed and
destroyed Canastota, NY 27Jun60 - tfd Aero Enterprises,
Elkhart, IN 30Aug60 - tfd D C Mullery, Chicago, IL Nov62-66 -
tfd Richard D Burns, Hinsdale, IL 28Sep66-87 - tfd John D
Rodgers, Rockford, IL 1987-89 - tfd Richard D Burns,
Hinsdale, IL 1990-92 - tfd Jack D Rodgers, Rockford, IL
Jun93-95 as Air Classics Aircraft Museum, DuPage, IL 1995;
flown as *Cripes A'Mighty IV* - tfd Ken Wagnon, Danville, IL
Nov96 to current - rereg N151KW to Ken Wagnon, Danville, IL
3Mar01 to current; restored by Midwest Aero Restorations,
Danville, IL; fffr 17Apr02 as 44-14906 *Cripes A'Mighty*.

P-51D-30NA Mustang 122-41367 44-74827
RNZAF Museum, Wigram AB, New Zealand   M

To Trans Florida Aviation, Sarasota, FL (into storage)
1958-66 - mod as Cavalier Mustang (with serial 72-1541)
by Cavalier Aircraft Corporation, Sarasota, FL 1966 - to
Indonesian AF/TNI-AU coded F-367 1968-87 - stored at
Bandung TNI-AU base, Indonesia 1976-85 - tfd RNZAF
Museum, Wigram AB, New Zealand (exchanged for a
de Havilland Vampire) 1985 to current.

P-51D-30NA Mustang 122-41369 44-74829 ZK-TAF
P-51 Syndicate, Auckland, New Zealand   F

Assigned RCAF as 9265, boc 10Jan51, soc 14May59 - reg
N8675E to James H Defuria of Intercontinental Airways,
Canastota, NY 27Feb59-60 - ex-storage at
Winnipeg, Manitoba, Canada and ferried to USA 1959 - tfd
Aero Enterprises, Elkhart, IN 18Jun60 - rereg N169MD
(1st issue) to Dr Burns M Byram, Marengo, IA 18Aug60-66 -
acc (night, forced landing) near Des Moines, IA (Byram
unhurt, passenger baled out) 6Apr67 - rereg N769MD to
John E Dilley, Muncie, IN 11Jan68-73 - tfd to Max I Ramsay,
Johnson, KS 10Jan73-78; in storage Chino, CA 1977-??,
apparently used in rebuild of 45-11558/N6175C at
Chino, CA 1979 - tfd Consolidated Airways, Fort Wayne, IN
1981-84; rebuilt at Fort Wayne 1981-84 with ex-TNI-AU
P-51D, ff 13Nov84 - tfd Alpine Helicopters, Wanaka, NZ
1984 - rereg ZK-TAF to Alpine Deer Group, Wanaka, NZ
27May86-89 - shipped to NZ, reassembled, ff 23Jan85
painted as NZ2415 - rereg to NZ Historic Aircraft Trust,
Ardmore, NZ 1989 - tfd P-51 Syndicate 1995 to current.

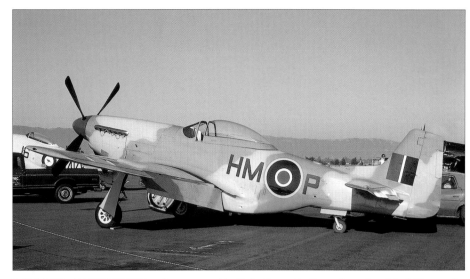

P-51D-30NA 44-74602/N3580 has been owned by Rolls-Royce Merlin engine wizard Jack Hovey of Hovey Machine Products – the only professional Merlin engine overhaul specialist to own his own Mustang – since 10 July 1967. The aircraft was photographed in July 1980. William T Larkins

Wearing the distinctive national insignia of the Philippine Air Force, P-51D-30NA 44-74627 Shark of Zambales now serves as the gate guard at Basa Air Base. The Warbird Index

For many years Bob Hoover would start the Reno Air Races with the immortal words 'Gentlemen, you have a race'. The aircraft used for the starts was P-51D-30NA 44-74739/N51RH "Ole Yeller", seen here in 1981 with Rockwell International titles on the highly visible canary yellow colour scheme. This Mustang still holds the Speed Record from Los Angeles, California to Daytona Beach, Florida – 5 hours 20 minutes – established on 29 March, 1985. William T Larkins

Bob Hoover's P-51D-30NA 44-74739/N51RH No.47 "Ole Yeller" *was perhaps the best-known civil-schemed Mustang and a Reno regular. It was transferred to John K Bagley of Rexburg, Idaho in April 1999.* Tom Smith

Built as P-51D-30NA 44-74825, this Mustang was converted by Cavalier and reserialled 72-1541. It went on to serve with the TNI-AU as F-367 and was traded for a Vampire in 1985. It is now displayed in the RNZAF Museum at Wigram AB. RNZAF Photograph

P-51D-30NA 44-74829/ZK-TAF in No.3 Sqn, RNZAF markings comes in to land at Wanaka, New Zealand. Dave McDonald

P-51D-30NA 44-74865/N8677E Mormon Mustang at The Gathering of Mustangs & Legends in April 1999. It was rebuilt by Pacific Fighters in Idaho for the Mallette family. Dick Phillips

Photographed during its service with No.402 'City of Winnipeg' Squadron, P-51D-30NA 44-74865 was taken on strength by the RCAF on 10 January 1951 as 9258 and served until 14 May 1959. The Warbird Index

Acquired by Tom Wood of Indianapolis in 1969, P-51D-30NA 44-74878/N6306T is yet another Mustang to have seen service with the RCAF (with whom it was serialled 9259) before being struck off charge in 1957. The Warbird Index

P-51D-30NA Mustang   122-41372   44-74832   N551MR
Sale Reported, Livonia, MI   U

Assigned RCAF as 9269, boc 10Jan51, soc 1Nov60 - reg CF-MWT to James H Defuria of Intercontinental Airways, Canastota, NY 30Dec58 - rereg N6310T (1st issue) to James H Defuria, Canastota, NY 1960 - tfd Aero Enterprises, Elkhart, IN 10May60 - tfd Clyde C Werner, Elkhart, IN 17Jun61-68 - tfd Courtesy Aircraft, Loves Park, IL 5Jun68 - tfd William J Allen, Greensboro, NC 13Sep68-69 - tfd Tipton Air Services, Tipton, GA 7Jun69-71 - tfd Max R Hoffman, Fort Collins, CO 4Mar71-78 - tfd Konig Spraying Service, Yuma, CO Oct76-78 - tfd Max R Hoffman, Fort Collins, CO 1Feb78-79 - tfd Ward Wilkins, Linden, IN 1980 - tfd Norton Aero, Athol, ID 1981; exhibited at Henley Aerodrome & Museum of Transportation, Athol, ID - acc (destroyed, fire) Athol, ID Aug81 - i/d tfd Micky Rupp, Port Salerno, FL (remains) 1983-85 - tfd to 45-11453 reg N551MR.

P-51D-30NA Mustang   122-41376   44-74836
Brian O'Farrell, Miami, FL   S

Assigned RCAF as 9260, boc 10Jan51, soc 4Dec56 - reg N3991A to Stinson Field Aircraft, San Antonio, TX 26Oct56 - tfd Jack Adams Aircraft Sales, Memphis, TN 30May57-58 - rereg N69X to James E Hall, Abilene, TX 1Apr58-63 - acc Dallas-Love Field, TX 1Jan59; wreck to scrap yard in Dallas, TX 1960 - tfd c.80 Walter Soplata Collection, Newbury, OH 1979-87 - tfd Brian O'Farrell, Miami, FL 1986 to current.

P-51D-30NA Mustang   122-41405   44-74865   N8677E
Mallette Family LLC, Provo, UT   F

Assigned RCAF as 9258, boc 10Jan51, soc 14May59 - reg N8677E to James H Defuria of Intercontinental Airways,

Canastota, NY 27Feb59 - tfd Aero Enterprises, Elkhart, IN 18Jun60-61 - tfd Walter H Erickson, Minneapolis, MN 11Apr61-65 - acc (take-off) Minneapolis, MN 1961 - tfd Don H Novas, Blackfoot, ID 5May65-97 - tfd CLB Corporation, Provo, UT Oct97; rebuilt by Pacific Fighters - tfd Mallette Family LLC, Provo, UT 8Jan01 to current.

P-51D-30NA Mustang   122-41418   44-74878   N6306T
Tom Wood Inc, Indianapolis, IN   F

Assigned RCAF as 9259, boc 10Jan51, soc 17Sep57 - reg N6306T to James H Defuria and Fred J Ritts of Intercontinental Airways, Canastota, NY 25Feb57-60 - tfd Aero Enterprises, Elkhart, IN 10May60-61 - tfd Suncoast Aviation, St Petersburg, FL 8Jul61 - tfd Florida Airmotive Sales, Fort Lauderdale, FL 14Nov61 - tfd Sherman Aircraft Sales, Fort Wayne, IN 7Jul62-64 - tfd Howard Olsen Development Co, Midland, TX 3Aug64-65 - tfd Huntley

Aviation Service, Leland, MS 7Jan65-69 - tfd Gardner Flyers Inc, Brownfield, TX 7Jan69 - tfd Tom Wood Aircraft Co, Kalamazoo, MI 6Mar69 - tfd Tom Wood Pontiac, Indianapolis, IN Oct71 to current.

P-51D-30NA Mustang   122-41448   44-74908   N151BP
Palm Springs Air Museum, Palm Springs, CA   F

Assigned RCAF as 9273, boc 11Jan51, soc 14May59 - crashed (landing) Winnipeg, Manitoba, Canada 17Jun56; into storage - reg N1070Z to James H Defuria of Intercontinental Airways, Canastota, NY 27Feb59 - tfd Aero Enterprises, Elkhart, IN 13May59-62 - tfd Charles P Doyle, Minneapolis, MN 15Mar62; rebuilt Winnipeg - rereg N965D to Charles P Doyle, Apple Valley, MN 1969-78 - rereg N151BP to Planes of Fame East, Spring Park, MN Jun80 - tfd R J Pond Foundation 9Apr96-23Apr99 - tfd Palm Springs Air Museum, Palm Springs, CA 23Apr99 to current.

P-51D-30NA 44-74908/N151BP wearing spurious military markings in 1987 when owned by Bob Pond's Planes of Fame (East) Air Museum. Thierry Thomassin

P-51D-30NA 44-74923/N6395, wrapped and in storage at Lelystad in The Netherlands in 1996, is owned by Shelley Levitz of Phoenix, Arizona. Willem Wendt via Coert Munk

- acc (reported destroyed) near Lancaster, CA 25Aug71; i/d transferred to Commonwealth Mustang Mk.22 c/n 1500 - tfd N20JS John P Silberman, Key West and Tampa, FL 1976-84 - rereg N7496W to Selby R Burch, Winter Garden, FL Nov84-93 - tfd Dick Thurman, Louisville, KY 1994-94; flown painted as USAF 200 - tfd Vintage War Birds Inc, Louisville, KY 22May95 - rereg N51DT to Vintage War Birds Inc, Louisville, KY Oct95-Aug1999 - tfd Tom Blair, Potomac, MD 25Aug1999 to current.

P-51D-30NA Mustang   122-41502   44-74962   N51DK
DK Aviation Inc, Fort Wayne, IN   F

Sold to Indonesian AF/TNI-AU as F-3?? - recovered by Stephen Johnson of Vanpac Carriers, Oakland, CA 1978 - tfd Consolidated Airways, Fort Wayne, IN 12Mar80 - rereg N51DK to Consolidated Airways, Fort Wayne, IN Nov80-84 - tfd Fort Wayne Air Service, Fort Wayne, IN Jan84-Oct01 - tfd DK Aviation Inc, Fort Wayne, IN 5Oct01 to current.

P-51D-30NA Mustang   122-41516   44-74976   N651JM
Jeffrey R Michael, Daytona Beach, FL   F

Sold to Indonesian AF/TNI-AU as F-311 Aug59-78 - poss Cavalier field modification - recovered ex-Indonesia by Stephen Johnson of Vanpac Carriers, Oakland, CA 1978 - tfd Ralph W Johnson, Oakland, CA 1979-81 - rereg N98582 to Ralph W Johnson, Oakland, CA 13Aug81-85 - rebuilt Chino, CA, fffr 1983 - tfd Jeffrey R Michael, Lexington, NC Mar86-Jun99 - rereg N651JM to Jeffrey R Michael, Daytona Beach, FL 28Jun99 to current.

P-51D-30NA Mustang   122-41450   44-74910   N74920
Charles F Nichols, Baldwin Park, CA   F

Sold for scrap McClellan AFB, CA 17Aug59 - tfd Cavalier Aircraft Corporation, Sarasota, FL - sold to Indonesian AF/TNI-AU coded F-351 - recovered by Stephen Johnson of Vanpac Carriers, Oakland, CA 1978 - reg N51SJ to Stephen Johnson, Oakland, CA Apr81-86 - tfd Yankee Air Corps, Chino, CA 1987-88 - rereg N74920 to Yankee Air Corps (later Yanks Air Museum), Chino, CA Feb88 to current.

P-51D-30NA Mustang   122-41463   44-74923   N6395
Shelley R Levitz, Phoenix, AZ   S

Reg N5438V to J J Wolohan, Livingston, CA 1963-64 - tfd Walter M Fountain of Hawke Dusters, Modesto, CA 1966-69 - sold FA Salvadorena coded FAS 410 Jul69 - recovered El Salvador, adopting identity 44-11353 on import to USA - rereg N132 to Donald R Anderson, Saugus, CA 1976 - rereg N100DD to Donald R Anderson, Saugus, CA 1978 - rebuilt by Dave Clinton and Don Anderson 1974-81 - tfd John R Sandberg, Robstown, TX 1981-84; raced as No.28 *Tipsy Too* - acc Reno, NV Sep83 - repaired and tfd as N345 to Gary R

Levitz, Dallas, TX Oct84-94; raced as No.38 *Miss Ashley* - tfd as N6395 to Shelley R Levitz, Phoenix, AZ Apr94 to current - Sodenal Group, Berne, Switzerland 1996; crated Kissimmee, FL Mar95, currently in storage Lelystad, Netherlands.

P-51D-30NA Mustang   122-41476   44-74936
USAFM, Wright-Patterson AFB, Dayton, OH   M

Allocated USAFM at Wright-Patterson AFB, Dayton, OH 1958 to current; originally painted as *Shimmy IV*, later repainted as *Sharpshooter*.

P-51D-30NA Mustang   122-41479   44-74939
NASM, Washington, DC   M

Allocated NASM, Washington DC 1965 to current.

P-51D-30NA Mustang   122-41490   44-74950   N51DT
Tom Blair, Potomac, MD   F

Reg N5464V - rereg N511D to Melvyn Paisley, Great Falls, MT 1963 - tfd Mustang Pilots Club Inc, Van Nuys, CA 1963-72

Stephen Johnson recovered several airframes and tons of P-51 spares from Indonesia in 1978; one of the first aircraft to fly following retrieval was his personal aircraft, P-51D-30NA 44-74910/N51SJ, seen here in 1983. Following his untimely death in a biplane accident the Mustang was sold to the Yankee Air Corps in 1987, who re-registered it as N74920. The Warbird Index

Peter and Richard Lauderback (now of Stallion 51 Maintenance Operations) restored P-51D-30NA 44-74950/N7496W initially for Selby Burch of Winter Garden, Florida. The aircraft was later sold to Dick Thurman of Louisville, Kentucky who had it painted as Slender, Tender & Tall. *Though the 352nd Fighter Group's Mustangs would never have looked as pristine as this, the aircraft is a sight to behold – a true jewel.* Tom Smith

P-51D-30NA 44-74978/N74978 is reputed to have served with the Fuerza Aerea Costarricense, being delivered in 1955. It joined the USCAR in 1964 and is now with Cal Pacific Airmotive at Salinas, California. William T Larkins

Seen at Shafter, California in 1981, this fuselage section (minus afthouse) was incorporated into the rebuild of the Reno Racer 44-74996/N5410V Dago Red. The Warbird Index

P-51D-30NA Mustang 122-41517 44-74977 N5448V
Christopher Gruys Trustee, Santa Fe, NM   F

Reg N5448V to Earl Dodge, Anchorage, AK 1963-66 - tfd Michael E Coutches of Museum of American Aircraft, Hayward, CA 1969-93 - stolen from Tonopah, NV 5May84 - found Merced, CA Sep84 - tfd Christopher Gruys, Sante Fe, NM May94 to current.

P-51D-30NA Mustang 122-41518 44-74978 N74978
Cal Pacific Airmotive Inc, Salinas, CA   F

To Fuerza Aerea Costarricense coded 4, del 16Jan55 - reg N6169U to Will W Martin/MACO Sales Financial Corp, Chicago, IL 31Mar64 - tfd Richard M Vartanian, Pasadena, CA 1966-70 - rereg N74978 to Richard M Vartanian, Arcadia/Shafter, CA 1972-88 - tfd Arthur W McDonnell, Mojave, CA 26Feb88 - allegedly destroyed in hangar fire, Shafter, CA Jul88 - rereg N74978 to Cal Pacific Airmotive, Salinas, CA 23Mar00 to current.

P-51D-30NA Mustang 122-41536 44-74996 N5410V
Dago Red LLC, Gladstone, OR   F

Reg N5410V to Prevost F Smith Parachute Co, Santee, CA 1963-69 - tfd Donald E Walker, Orinda, CA 1970 - tfd Michael E Coutches, Hayward, CA 1978 - tfd Bill Destefani, Bakersfield, CA 1981-83; rebuilt Shafter, CA 1981-82, modified to race as No.4 *Dago Red* - tfd Frank Taylor Racing Inc, Bakersfield, CA 1983-85 - tfd Alan Preston, Dallas, TX 1987-88 - tfd Sherman Aircraft Sales, West Palm Beach, FL 1988 - tfd Liberty Aero Corporation, Santa Monica, CA 1988-95 - tfd Dago Red LLC.

P-51D-30NA Mustang 122-41547 44-75007 N3451D
EAA Aviation Foundation, Oshkosh, WI   F

Reg N5462V to Trans Florida Inc, Sarasota, FL 1963-64 - mod to full Cavalier 2000 - rereg N3451D to Trans Florida Aviation, Sarasota, FL 1966 - tfd Tempress Research Corp, Sunnyvale, CA 1969 - tfd Jerry G Brassfield of Pacific Military Air Museum, San Jose, CA and raced as No.96 1970-73 - tfd EAA, Oshkosh, WI Mar77 to current.

P-51D-30NA Mustang 122-41549 44-75009 N51TC
Contri Family LLP, Yuba City, CA   F

Reg N5474V to David L Rountree, Anderson, CA 1966-69 - tfd Homer Rountree, Anderson, CA 1970-78 - tfd Ted E Contri, Reno, NV 1984-87 - rereg N51TC (2nd issue) to Ted E Contri, Yuba City, CA Mar87-Mar01 - Reg'n Pending Yuba City, CA Apr01 - tfd Contri Family LLP 9May01 to current.

P-51D-30NA Mustang 122-41564 44-75024 N96JM
John MacGuire, Santa Teresa, NM   F

Sold to Indonesian AF/TNI-AU as F-3?? Aug59-78 - poss Cavalier field modification - recovered ex-Indonesia by Stephen Johnson of Vanpac Carriers, Oakland, CA 1978 - tfd John MacGuire, Fort Hancock, TX 1984-89 - rereg N4261U to John MacGuire 7Jun91 - rereg N96JM to War Eagles Air Museum, Santa Teresa, NM May94 to current.

P-51D-30NT Mustang 124-48306 45-11553 N51VF
Blue Sky Aviation, Streetman, TX   F

Sold as surplus McClellan AFB, CA 20Sep57 - reg N5414V - rereg N713DW to Richard D Weaver, Van Nuys, CA; raced as No.6, later No.15 1963-69 - tfd Thomas A Neal, Pasadena, CA 1970 - rereg N22DC to Anthony J D'Alessandris, Reno, NV 1972 - rereg N51T (1st issue) to same owner 1977 - rereg N51TZ to same owner Jun77 - rereg N5415V (2nd issue) to same owner, Reno, NV Nov77 - tfd Richard Smith, Bradbury, CA 1977-88 - rebuilt using parts from 45-11571 alias N5415V - tfd RWR Development, Las Vegas, NV 1989 - tfd Erin Rheinschild of Unlimited Air Racing Inc, Van Nuys, CA 1990-92; raced as No.553 serialled 511553/FF-553 *Miss Fit* - rereg N38JC to NA-50 Inc, New York, NY Jun93-Jul97 - rebuilt Rialto, CA; ffff Jul93 - tfd Blue Sky Aviation, Streetman, TX and rereg N51VF 15Jul97 to current.

Racing Mustang 44-74996/N5410V Dago Red *with Bruce Lockwood at the helm during the Reno Unlimited Air Races, September 1998.* Dago Red's successful career as an air racer continued on 14 September 2002, when Skip Holm piloted it victory in the Unlimited Gold finals at the Reno Air Races at a recorded speed of 466.834mph (751.27km/h). Tom Smith

N5410V Dago Red *at Reno in 1988. Note the profusion of sponsors logos in comparison to the other two photographs.* The Warbird Index

Bruce Lockwood running-up Dago Red *at Reno in September 1998. Today, if not finished in authentic 8th Air Force colours, Mustangs are often dressed to race.* Kevin Grantham

EAA Founder Paul H Poberezny attending the Reno Air Races in the late 1970s, in Cavalier Mustang 44-75007/N3451D Paul I. *The EAA have owned this Mustang since March 1977. William T Larkins*

P-51D-30NA 44-75009/N51TC has belonged to Ted Contri since 1984. It is seen here in California in December 1986 wearing a striking red and black paint scheme. The Warbird Index

P-51D-30NT 45-11553/N5415V No.553 Miss Fit *makes its air racing debut with RWR Development at Reno in September 1988. Thierry Thomassin*

The late Bill Dodds flies Jeff Clyman's Dallas-built P-51D-30NT 45-11553/N38JC The Jacky C. *in company with Ed Shipley in another Dallas-built Mustang, P-51D-25NT 44-84634/N51ES* Big Beautiful Doll *in 1996. Ed Toth*

N38CJ went on to become Blue Sky Aviation's N51VF Shangrila, *registered in 1997 after a rebuild at Rialto, California in 1993. Tim Bivens*

Henry 'Butch' Schroeder prepares to depart Oshkosh and head back to his base at Danville, Illinois in Cavalier F-51D 45-11559/N51MX North American Maid *which saw service with the Fuerza Aerea Salvadorena before being recovered by Flaherty Factors in November 1974. It was later restored by Fort Wayne Air Service and became TF-51D* Mad Max *in 1996.* The Warbird Index

Max Chapman's TF-51D-30NT 45-11559/N51MX Mad Max *sits out on the ramp at Kissimmee in April 1999. This aircraft was modified to TF-51D status when it was restored. Note the tall Cavalier fin and longer, more bulbous canopy that for some make the Mustang even sexier.* Eric Quenard

The Air Museum's P-51D-30NT 45-11582/N5441V No.1 "Spam Can", codeless but sporting a variety of sponsors logos at Chino in September 1995. Thierry Thomassin

P-51D-30NT Mustang   124-48311 45-11558   N514DK
DK Warbirds Inc, Las Vegas, NV   **F**

Reg N6175C to Aerodynamics Inc, Pontiac, MI 1963-64 - tfd James C Gorman, Mansfield, OH 1966 - tfd Herbert E Rupp, Port Salerno, FL 1966 - acc (crashed) Georgia 1967; rebuilt and tfd John E Dilley, Auburn, IN 1969-72 - tfd John Rutherford, Fort Worth, TX 1978-79 - tfd Mark Clark of Courtesy Aircraft, Rockford, IL 1982 - tfd Joseph Kasparoff, Van Nuys, CA May83-95; raced as No.39 *The Healer* - acc Van Nuys, CA - tfd William E, Jones, Sun Valley, CA Jun97-Sep99 - tfd DK Warbirds Inc, Las Vegas, NV 8Sep99-May00 - rereg N514DK to same owner NV 31May00 to current.

P-51D-30NT Mustang   124-48312 45-11559   N51MX
Gardner Capital Management Inc, New York, NY   **F**

Reg N5469V to Jim B Tregoning, Bakersfield, CA 1963-64 - tfd Burford Co International Corp, Maysville, OK 1966 - rereg N6451D to Levitz Furniture Co, Dallas, TX 1969 - tfd Volkmer Manufacturing Co, Dallas, TX Jun69 - sold to FA Salvadorena coded FAS 401 Jul69 - field modification by Cavalier Aircraft Corporation - recovered and rereg N30FF to Flaherty Factors Inc, Monterey, CA 1Nov74 - i/d also reported as 44-11153/FAS 409 - tfd Ward Wilkins, Linden, IN 1978 - tfd Henry J Schroeder III of Midwest Aviation Museum, Danville, IL 1982-95; painted in Cavalier markings as 5-11559 *North American Maid* - tfd Warbird Operators Inc, Indianapolis, IN May95; rebuilt as TF-51D - Gardner Capital Management Inc, New York, NY May96 to current.

P-51D-30NT Mustang   124-48324 45-11571   N51T
Anthony J D'Alessandris, Reno, NV   **F**

Reg N5415V (1st issue) to Arni L Sumarlidason, Nice, France 1963-64 - tfd Marvin Parker, Shelton, CT 1966-69 - tfd South Delta Aviation, Rolling Fork, MS Aug69 - tfd Jet America Inc, Wilmington, DE 1970 - tfd Anthony J D'Alessandris, Reno, NV Apr71-77; raced as No.15, rebuilt adopting i/d 45-11553 - rereg N51T (2nd issue) to Anthony J D'Alessandris, Reno, NV Jul77 to current.

P-51D-30NT Mustang   124-48335 45-11582   N5441V
Air Museum, Chino, CA   **F**

Reg N5441V - sold surplus McClellan AFB, CA Nov57 - tfd The Air Museum, Claremont, CA, later Ontario, CA and Chino, CA 6Nov57; painted as 413334/G4-U *Spam Can*, repainted as 414888/B6-Y *Glamorous Glen III*, raced as No.8 *Spirit of Phoenix*.

P-51D-30NT   124-48339 45-11586   N51HT
Gerald S Beck, Wahpeton, ND   **F**

Sold surplus McClellan AFB, CA Jan57 - reg N5423V to Walter D Oakes, Chicago, IL 1963-70 - tfd Albert Shirkey, Tulsa, OK 1978 - rereg N51HA then N13LF to Lynn L Florey, FL 1983-85 - tfd Harry E Tope, Mount Pleasant, MI Nov86 - rereg N51HT to same owner Feb87-90 - acc (crashed) Ottawa, Ontario, Canada (Tope killed) 1Jul90; i/d tfd Gerald S Beck, Wahpeton, ND 1998 to Aug02 - tfd Paul C Ehlen, Bloomington, MN w/e 27Aug02 to current.

P-51D-30NT Mustang   124-48381 45-11628   N151X
Ho Hun Inc, Mesa, AZ   **F**

Reg N5446V to Michael E Coutches, Hayward, CA 1961 - tfd Thomas P Mathews, Monterey, CA 1963-64 - rereg N151X to Walter E Stewart, Monterey 1966-72 - tfd Jack W Flaherty, Monterey, CA and raced as No.8 1973 - tfd John T Johnson, Rexburg, ID 1975-81 - tfd William L Hane, Mesa, AZ Nov81 to current; exhibited Champlin Fighter Museum, Mesa, AZ

P-51D-30NT Mustang   124-48386 45-11633   N151MW
Lady Alice Corporation, Wilmington, DE   **F**

Reg N5413V to William G Lacy of Lacy Steel Inc, Honolulu, HI 1963-Aug99 - tfd Lady Alice Corporation, Wilmington, DE 26Aug99 to current - rereg N151MW 28Jan00.

The Air Museum's two-seater 45-11582/N5441V
Spam Can (note revised artwork) airborne out
of Planes of Fame Air Museum, Chino. The pilot
is Robby Patterson. Phillip Wallick

P-51D-30NT 45-11582/N5441V has been in the
custody of The Air Museum (now located at
Chino, California) since 6 November 1957. It is
seen here in August 1981 coded G4-U, the code
being that of the 357th Fighter Squadron, 362nd
Fighter Group. William T Larkins

Registered N51HA, P-51D-30NT 45-11586 was
reregistered N13LF to Lynn L Florey in 1983. The
aircraft later passed to Harry Tope who named
it Death Rattler; it crashed in Ontario, Canada
on 1 July 1990 with the loss of Harry. It is now
registered N51HT to Gerry Beck in Wahpeton,
North Dakota. The Warbird Index

P-51D-30NT 45-11628/N151X at Concord Airport, California in December 1975 during an engine run by owner John T Johnson of Rexburg, Idaho who owned the aircraft until 1985 when it was purchased by Bill Hane, its current owner. William T Larkins

P-51H-5NA 44-64314/N551H is owned by American Aircraft Sales Co of Hayward, California and was built using parts from scrap dealers and a P-51 crash site. The aircraft sports non-standard long-range underwing fuel tanks. Bob Munro

Lackland Air Force Base, San Antonio, Texas is the location of P-51H-5NA 44-64376 Petie 2nd, *photographed in 1998. Not only is it criminal to leave this scarce H model outside exposed to the elements, but its markings are inaccurate – those for a P-51D of the 352nd FG.* Chuck Gardner

P-51D-30NT Mustang 124-48389 45-11636 N11636
Michael W Bertz, Broomfield, CO F

Reg N5467V Tallmantz Aviation Inc, Glenview, CA 1963-64 - tfd Rosen Novak Auto Co, Omaha, NB - rereg N11636 to John E Dilley, Fort Wayne, IN 1968 - tfd Michael W Bertz, Cheyenne, WY/Nashville, TN Aug68-78 - tfd Michael W Bertz, Broomfield, CO 1978 to current.

XP-51G Mustang 105-25931 43-43335
John Morgan, La Canada, CA R

Utilised as cockpit electronics trainer - tfd Reynolds Aluminum for scrap 1975 - large sections recovered from scrap dealer 1975 - tfd John Morgan, La Canada, CA 1975 to current.

P-51H-5NA Mustang 126-37691 44-64265
Octave Chanute Aerospace Museum, Chanute, IL M

Allocated USAFM, Chanute AFB, Rantoul, IL 1965-94 - reported dismantled and into store 1995 - to Octave Chanute Aerospace Museum, Chanute, IL to current.

P-51H-5NA Mustang 126-37740 44-64314 N551H
American Aircraft Sales Co, Hayward, CA F

Reg N1108H to William E Hogan, Hamilton, OH 1963-64 -tfd Michael E Coutches, Hayward, CA 1966; rebuilt using parts ex-scrap dealers and wreck recovered from Utah crash site 1962 - reg N551H to Michael E Coutches of American Aircraft Sales Co, Hayward, CA 1968 to current.

P-51H-5NA Mustang 126-37801 44-64375 N67149
James R Parks, Bend, OR R

Wreck salvaged from Alaska - reg N67149 to Paul Shoemaker, Orting, WA 1978-90 - tfd James R Parks, Bend, OR May90 to current.

P-51H-5NA Mustang 126-37802 44-64376
USAFM Collection, Lackland, TX M

Allocated USAFM Collection - tfd Lackland AFB, TX 1965 to current.

P-51H-5NA Mustang 126-37841 44-64415 N49WB
Sale Reported, Fort Lauderdale, FL F

Assigned NACA coded NACA130, boc 18Dec46, soc Apr61 - to NACA at Moffett Field, CA - to USN as salvage 1961 - reg N313H to William E Hogan, Hamilton, OH and raced as No.3 1966-78 - rereg N49WB to Bill and Don Whittington of World Jet Inc, Fort Lauderdale, FL and raced as No.94, later No.08 Jun78 to current.

P-51H-10NA Mustang 126-38120 44-64697 S

Aircraft hit a mountain at night 30Dec57 - wings and battered fuselage retrieved 1961 - in store and up for sale Mar02 to current.

P-51K-5NT Mustang 111-29940 44-11807 N30991
MDS Enterprises, Mesa, AZ R

Assigned USAFM, McEntire Field ANGB, Florence, SC 1973-92 - tfd MARC, Chino, CA - tfd Courtesy Aircraft, Rockford, IL 1993-94; stored Rockford for sale - tfd Shauver Bros, AZ 1994 - rereg N30991 and tfd to Amjet Services International, Minneapolis, MN 22Feb94 - tfd MDS Enterprises, Mesa, AZ Mar94 - tfd Meryl J Shawver, Mesa, AZ 29Mar96 to current.

P-51K-10NT Mustang 111-30249 44-12116
Frederick Crawford Museum, Cleveland, OH M

Reg NX79161 to Robert Swanson 1946 and raced as No.80 *Second Fiddle* - to Thompson Products Museum, Cleveland, OH 1958 - tfd Frederick Crawford Museum, Cleveland, OH 1979 to current.

Mike Bertz has owned P-51D-30NT 45-11636/N11636 since 1968. It was originally registered N5467V to Tallmantz Aviation of Glenview, California in 1963. Named 'Stang Evil it is seen flying out of Breckenridge, Texas en route its Colorado base in 1993. Ed Toth

Bill Hane (plus passenger) taxies in following a flight in P-51D-30NT 45-11628/N151X Ho! Hun in August 1984. William T Larkins

North American F-6K 44-12840/N51EW Montana Miss *was voted Best P-51 at Oshkosh 1998 and was rebuilt minus the photo reconnaissance camera gear.* Dick Phillips

Aadu Karemaa and his wife rebuilt P-51K-10NT 44-12140/N119AK from 1981 to 1989. The aircraft was reregistered N119VF to the same owner in April 1992. The Warbird Index

P-51K-10NT Mustang   111-30247   44-12118   N60752
Mark Tisler, Wahpeton, ND   R

Reg N60752 to Mark Tisler, Wahpeton, ND 14Sep00 to current - no further information known.

P-51K-10NT Mustang   111-30258   44-12125
Militaire Luchtvaart Museum, Soesterberg AB,
Netherlands   M

Assigned to Royal Netherlands AF as H-307 - tfd Delft Technical School, Delft, Netherlands 1965 - tfd Militaire Luchtvaart Museum, Soesterberg AB 1968 to current.

P-51K-10NT Mustang   111-30259   44-12126
Israeli Air Force Museum   M

Reg N9140H - tfd to Israeli Defence Force 1950 - tfd Israeli Air Force Museum c.1983 to current.

P-51K-10NT Mustang   111-30273   44-12140   N119VF
Aadu Karemaa, San Diego, CA

Reg NX66111 (2nd allocation) to Al Hanes 1963 - tfd Charles E Yost, Granada Hills, CA 1963 - tfd Frank J Moore, Los Angeles, CA 1963-64 - tfd Glenn Hussey, Carmichael, CA

1966-70 - acc (crashed) 7Jul68 - tfd Aadu Karemaa, San Diego, CA; rebuild project 1981-89 - rereg N119AK to Aadu Karemaa, San Diego, CA Oct89-92 - rereg N119VF to same owner Apr92 to current.

P-51K-10NT Mustang   111-30591   44-12458
People's Liberation Army Air Force Museum,
Datangshan AB, People's Republic of China   M

Assigned to Republic of Korea AF (serial undetermined) - captured by Chinese Air Force and pressed into service coded 3003 - recov and tfd to Peking People's Museum, Peking, PRC c.1965 - tfd Beijing Aeronautical Institute, Beijing, PRC 1988 - tfd People's Liberation Army Air Force Museum, Datangshan AB, PRC 1990 to current.

F-6K-15NT Mustang   111-36100   44-12817   N5151T
Lindair Inc, Sarasota, FL   S

Reg N4963V - rereg N85BW - rereg N5151T to Trans Florida Aviation, Sarasota, FL 1963-64 - tfd Bob Abrams (flew painted as N5151) 1965 - crashed (racing) Las Vegas, NV (Abrams killed) 1965 - tfd Cavalier Aircraft Corp, Sarasota, FL 1966-70 - tfd Lindsay Newspapers, Sarasota, FL 1972-80 - tfd Lindair Inc, Sarasota, FL 31Jul80 to current.

F-6K-15NT Mustang   111-36123   44-12840   N51EW
Valhalla Aviation Inc, Los Angeles, CA   F

To Victory Air Museum, Mundelein, IL 1968-76 - tfd Bill Conner 1982-84 (stored dismantled) - tfd Joseph Kasparoff, Montebello, CA 1987-90; restored by B & D Enterprises - tfd Ed Wachs 2Oct97-Mar02 - tfd Valhalla Aviation Inc, Los Angeles, CA 7Mar02 to current.

P-51K-10NT Mustang   111-36135   44-12852   N357FG
James E. Beasley, Philadelphia, PA   F

Reg NX66111 and raced as No.80 *Full House* c.1946 - modified F-6K - acc (forced landed) Cleveland, OH 1946 - rereg as N90613 and tfd to Intercontinental Airways, Canastota, NY Dec52-54 - rebuilt by Jack Hardwick, El Monte, CA 1954 with dual controls; FAA list identity as ICA-5131 - rereg N22B to B L Tractman of Aviation Corp of America 15Mar54 - reported to Cavalier then to FAD as FAD 1900 26Apr54-84 - recovered by Johnson Aviation, Miami, FL 19May84-89 - rereg N21023 to James E Beasley, Philadelphia, PA Jul89 to current; trucked to Fort Wayne, IN for restoration, ff 1990, painted as 413318/C5-N *Frenesi* - rereg N357FG Oct95 to same owner.

CA-17 Mk.20 Mustang 1326 A68-1 N51WB (2nd issue)
Wiley C Sanders Jr, Troy, AL   F

Assigned RAAF, boc Jul45 - ff Fisherman's Bend, Victoria, Australia May46 - used for atomic blast tests, Emu Junction, South Australia Oct53; at test site 1953-67 - sold Stanley Booker - Stan Air Inc, Fresno, CA Aug67; del Emu to Adelaide-Parafield 31Oct-1Nov67, stored Parafield, reg VH-EMQ (ntu) - tfd Tony Schwerdt, Adelaide, South Australia 1969 - damaged Adelaide to USA Jun69 - reg N7773 to Stan Air Inc, Fresno, CA 1970 - tfd Ed Jurist of Vintage Aircraft Int'l, Nyack, NY - tfd Randy Sohn and Gary Levitz, Dallas, TX - rereg N51WB (2nd issue) to Bill and Don Whittington, Fort Lauderdale, FL 1979-81; rebuilt Vintage Aircraft Ltd, Fort Collins, CO 1979-80, ff Nov80, adopted i/d 44-15757 - tfd Wiley C Sanders Truck Lines, Troy, AL 1981 to current.

CA-17 Mk.20 Mustang 1364   A68-39   N551D
Erickson Group Ltd, Beaverton, OR   F

Assigned RAAF, boc Dec45, soc Dec53 - reg VH-BOY to Fawcett Aviation at Illawarra Flying School, Bankstown, New South Wales; used as civilian target-towing aircraft Oct59-78 - acc (take-off) Bankstown, New South Wales 5Jun76; repaired - tfd Warbirds of Great Britain Ltd, Blackbushe, UK 1978 (ntu) - tfd Gordon W Plaskett, King City, CA 1979 - tfd Flying Tiger Farms, Bakersfield, CA 1981 - rereg N551D (3rd issue) to Bill Destefani, Bakersfield, CA 1983; rebuilt adopting i/d 45-11489, fffr 5Oct83, new i/d used to register aircraft as 44-14826 - tfd Erickson Air Crane, Medford, OR Nov83 to current.

CA-17 Mk.20 Mustang 1396   A68-71
Derek A Macphail, Perth, Western Australia   S

RAAF, boc 16Apr46 - acc in RAAF service (damaged, landing) at Pearce, Western Australia 24Apr49 - to RAAF as instructional airframe No.14, RAAF Pearce, Western Australia; soc Oct52 - tfd Midland Technical School Aeronautical Annexe, Perth Airport, Western Australia as instructional airframe Oct52-72 - tfd RAAF Association Aviation Museum, Perth, Western Australia 22Mar72-84; stored disassembled - sold to Derek A Macphail, Perth, Western Australia 28Jun84 to current.

CA-18 Mk.21 Mustang 1425   A68-100   N51AB
Inpatient Dental Service Inc, Ashland, OR   F

Assigned RAAF, boc 6Nov47, soc Apr58 - tfd A J R Oates, Sydney, New South Wales, Australia 23Apr58 - tfd Fawcett Aviation, Sydney-Bankstown, NSW 1960-61 - reg VH-BOW (ntu) 25Aug61-67 - mod for high-altitude survey work; ff Bankstown, NSW 8Dec61, last flight 1Mar62; external storage Bankstown - tfd Ed Fleming of Skyservice Aviation, Camden, NSW 1967- tfd James Ausland, Seattle, WA 20Nov67 (by ship to Seattle); rebuilt 1968-71 adopting i/d 44-14777- reg N51AB to James Ausland of Sports Air, Seattle, WA Jul71 - tfd Joe Arnold, Greenville, MS 20Feb74 - tfd Robby R Jones, Minter City, MS 25Aug75-89; painted as 414777/J-RR *Miss Escort* - tfd Norman Lewis of Lewis Aviation, Louisville, KY 1990-Jan00 - tfd Inpatient Dental Service Inc, Bend, OR 3Feb00 to current.

CA-18 Mk.21 Mustang 1429   A68-104   VH-BOB
Robert L Eastgate, Moonee Ponds, Victoria, Australia F

RAAF, boc Nov47, soc Apr58 - tfd Taren Point Non-Ferrous Metals Pty Ltd, Sydney, New South Wales, Australia 23Sep60 - tfd A J R Oates, Sydney, NSW 1960 - tfd Adastra Airways, Sydney-Mascot, NSW Nov62-64; open storage here 1962-64 - tfd Tony Fisher, Jerilderie, NSW ex-Mascot 2Aug64-70 - reg VH-BOB to Robert L Eastgate, Melbourne, Victoria; del 26Mar73 but registered Oct70, fffr 26Feb76 painted as A68-104, to current.

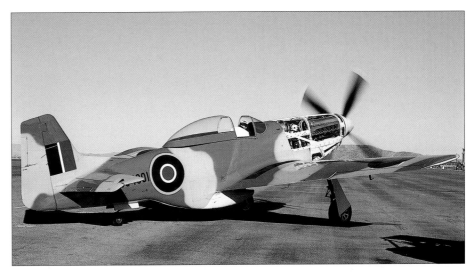

CAC Mustang Mk.20 A68-1/N51WB is owned by Wiley Sanders of Troy, Alabama. It was restored to flying condition by Darrell Skurich of Vintage Aircraft Limited, Fort Collins, Colorado and flew for the first time in November 1980. It is seen here in a pseudo RAF paint scheme at Reno the following year during an engine test. William T Larkins

CAC Mustang Mk.20 A68-39/N551D is owned by the Erickson Group in Beaverton, Oregon. Rebuilt by Bill 'Tiger' Destefani, it made its first post-restoration flight in October 1983. The Warbird Index

CAC Mustang Mk.21 A68-100/N51AB Flying Dutchman was painted in fictitious military markings for many years, but now wears 15th Air Force colours and underlines the current trend for authentic wartime Mustang paint schemes and markings – apart that is from air racing Mustangs, which are a law unto themselves! The Warbird Index

A fine air-to-air study of CAC Mustang Mk.21 A68-104/VH-BOB in 1988. This aircraft was struck off charge with the RAAF in April 1958 and went through three owners before being registered to Bob Eastgate in March 1973. He has owned the aircraft ever since, flying it for the first time in February 1975 following restoration work. RAAF Official

Owner Bob Eastgate taxies in A68-104/VH-BOB in November 1990. The Warbird Index

CAC Mustang Mk.21 A68-107/VH-AUB taxies for take-off in January 1985. Col Pay operated the aircraft from 1975 to 2001; it is now registered to Ross Pay of Moree, New South Wales. The Warbird Index

CA-18 Mk.21 Mustang 1430   A68-105   VH-JUC
High Performance Aviation Pty, Mt Eliza, Australia   F

Assigned RAAF, boc 21Nov47, soc 23Apr58 - tfd R H Grant
Metals, Tocumwal, NSW, Australia Apr58 - tfd Peter
Freason, Laverton, Victoria Aug60-64; displayed externally
at Fleetwings Garage, Laverton, Victoria Aug60-65 - tfd
Richard E Hourigan, Melbourne, Victoria Nov64 - exhibited
at Moorabbin Air Museum, Melbourne, Victoria Nov64-74 -
tfd RAAF Museum, Point Cook, Victoria (on loan) Jul77-90 -
reg VH-JUC to Richard E Hourigan, Melbourne, Victoria
1990-94; aircraft transported to Tyabb, Victoria 24Mar90 for
rebuild to fly - ownership tfd Dick Hourigan and Judy Pay,
Tyabb, Victoria 1994 to current, fffr 18Dec98.

CA-18 Mk.21 Mustang 1432   A68-107   VH-AUB
Ross Pay, Moree, NSW, Australia   F

RAAF, boc Dec47, soc May58 - reg VH-AUB to A J R Oates,
Bankstown, NSW, Australia 24Apr58-66 - tfd Ewan McKay,
Rosedale Station, Jericho, Queensland Apr66-74 - wfu and
stored Rosedale Station 1966-74 - tfd Col Pay, Scone, NSW
1975-01 - tfd Ross Pay, Krui Airstrip, Moree, NSW 7Jun01 to
current - painted as '44-14837' for film work 2002.

CA-18 Mk.21 Mustang 1435   A68-110   VH-MFT
Warplanes P/L, Caboolture Airfield, Qld, Australia   F

Reg Ed Field of Mustang Fighter Trust, Hong Kong Mar94
to current - composite restoration project, by ship ex-USA
to Caboolture, Queensland for assembly, arrived 26May95;
i/d quoted as CA-18 c/n 1335 serial A68-110 (recorded by
RAAF as scrapped RAAF Tocumwal, NSW 1957), fffr
24Jan02 - painted as '42-86621' for film work 2002.

CA-18 Mk.21 Mustang 1443   A68-118   VH-AGJ
Jeffrey P Trappett, Morwell, Victoria, Australia   F

Assigned RAAF, boc 10May48, soc Apr58 - tfd Wilmore
Aviation Services, Moorabbin, Victoria, Australia 23May58 -
reg VH-WAS to Joe R Palmer of Wilmore Aviation Services
7Aug59-78 - wfu at Bankstown, NSW 6Aug60 - stored
outside 1960-73 - tfd Camden Museum of Aviation, New
South Wales (on loan), arrived 7Jul73-78 - rereg VH-AGJ to
Jeffrey Trappett, Morwell, Victoria; Camden to Morwell
2Jan79 for rebuild, fffr Morwell 19Apr81 painted as A68-118.

CA-18 Mk.23 Mustang 1462   A68-137
RAAF Museum, RAAF Townsville, Qld, Australia   M

Assigned RAAF, boc 26Nov48, soc Feb60 - Aeronautical
Research Labs, Melbourne, Victoria, Australia 1960-70 - tfd
RAAF Museum, Point Cook, Victoria; rescued from fire
dump 1974 - reg VH-PPV (ntu) - tfd Vic Perry at RAAF
Townsville, Queensland 1974-80 - tfd RAAF Museum, RAAF
Townsville, Queensland 1980-96.

CA-18 Mk.23 Mustang 1495   A68-170   VH-SVU
RAAF Museum, Point Cook, Victoria, Australia   F

Assigned RAAF, boc Feb50 - tfd RAAF Stores Depot,
Toowoomba, Queensland; exhibited 1960-70 - tfd RAAF
Museum, Point Cook, Victoria Oct70 - reg VH-SVU to RAAF
Museum, Point Cook 28Aug95 for rebuild to fly, fffr 1999.

CA-18 Mk.22 Mustang 1512   A68-187   N50FS
Picacho Aviation LLC, Fairacres, NM   F

Assigned RAAF, boc Oct50, soc Apr58 - tfd A J R Oates, Sydney,
NSW, Australia 23Apr58 - tfd Adastra Airways Pty Ltd, Mascot,
NSW 1960-61 - tfd Fawcett Aviation, Sydney-Bankstown, NSW
1961-67; open storage Bankstown, NSW 1961-67 - Chieftain
Aviation Pty Ltd, Bankstown, NSW 1967-69; used as pylon-
mounted advertising display at Bankstown Airport - tfd Hockey
Treloar, Sydney, NSW Jul69-95 - reg VH-UFO (ntu) with owner
- rebuilt at Canberra, ACT with RR Dart turboprop installed
1976-77; not flown, conversion incomplete - into storage at
Toowoomba, Qld 1990-95 - to USA 1995 - reg N919WJ to World
Jet Inc, Fort Lauderdale, FL Aug95 - tfd Frank Borman, NM,
converted to TF-51D by Square One Aviation, Chino, CA - rereg
N50FS to Picacho Aviation LLC, Fairacres, NM 7Oct 1997.

CAC Mustang Mk.21 A68-105 was exhibited at the Moorabbin Air Museum, Melbourne, Victoria between 1964 and 1974 before being loaned to the RAAF Museum. It was registered VH-JUC and is now owned by High Performance Aviation Pty of Mt Eliza, Victoria, flying for the first time after a lengthy restoration on 18 December 1998. The Warbird Index

Given the identity A68-110, CAC Mustang Mk.21 VH-MFT flew for the first time in 2002 and is painted in an attractive RAAF colour scheme, seen here at Caboolture in Queensland, April 2002. Peter N Anderson

CAC Mustang Mk.23 A68-170 is owned by the RAAF Museum and registered VH-SVU to them at RAAF Williams, Point Cook, Victoria. Painted as A68-750, the aircraft is airworthy and flown regularly but within strict RAAF budgets. Courtesy RAAF Museum

CAC Mustang Mk.22 A68-187 was registered N919WJ to World Jet Inc before being sold to Colonel Frank Borman who decided to have Square One Aviation restore the aircraft and modify it to TF-51D standard. It is now registered N50FS to Picacho Aviation LLC in Fairacres, New Mexico. Square One Aviation

Victor Haluska and passenger in CAC Mustang Mk.22 A68-198/N286JB The Best Years of Our Lives in February 1991. The Warbird Index

CA-18 Mk.22 Mustang   1523   A68-198   N286JB
William Bruggeman, Minneapolis, MN   F

Assigned RAAF, boc Jul51, soc Apr58 - tfd Fawcett Aviation, Sydney-Bankstown, NSW, Australia 1961-68; open storage Bankstown 1961-68 - tfd Arnold J Glass, Sydney, NSW 1966-68 - tfd Ed Fleming of Skyservice Aviation, Camden, NSW 1968 - tfd Stanley Booker of Stan Air Inc, Fresno, CA 1968 - by ship to USA; Bakersfield, CA by Nov68 - reg N65198 to Joe F Banducci and Elmer Rossi, Bakersfield, CA 1968-77 - rereg N4674V (2nd issue) to them, adopted i/d 45-11483 ex-A68-813 and raced as No.86 *Ciuchetton* - reg N607D (ntu) - rereg N86JB to Joe F Banducci, Bakersfield, CA and raced as No.86 Oct77-82 - rereg N286JB to same Mar82 - tfd Don Whittington, Fort Lauderdale, FL 1984 - tfd Frank Strickler of Fox 51 Ltd, Denton, TX 1985-90 - to Lewis Shaw of Fox 51 Ltd, Dallas, TX 1989-90; finished as 511483/FF-483 - Victor Haluska of Santa Monica Propeller, CA 1991 - tfd Flying Eagles Inc, Wilmington, DE 1991 - tfd Franklin Devaux of Apache Aviation, Dijon, France May91; by ship to France ex-Chino, CA 1991 - rereg F-AZIE to Lafayette Aviation then

Flying Legend Association, Dijon-Longvic 1Sep92-96; painted as 511483 *The Best Years of Our Lives* - acc (damaged: in-flight fire, forced landing) Dijon, France 5Sep93; rebuilt by Historic Flying, Audley End, UK 1994 and repainted as 415622/AJ-T *Short-Fuse Sallee* - tfd William Bruggeman, Minneapolis, MN 9Apr96 to current, rereg N286JB.

CA-18 Mk.22 Mustang   1524   A68-199
Graham Hosking, Mt Eliza, Victoria, Australia   R

Assigned RAAF, boc Jul51, soc Apr58 - tfd A J R Oates, Bankstown, NSW, Australia 1960 - reg VH-BOZ to Fawcett Aviation at Illawarra Flying School, Bankstown, NSW for target-towing contract Nov60-79 - reg G-MUST (ntu): Warbirds of Great Britain Ltd, Blackbushe 20Dec79 - impounded by HM Customs Australia following attempted export Dec79-84 - tfd RAAF Museum 1984-95; into storage RAAF Stores Depots, Sydney then Dubbo, NSW 1979-92 - roaded to RAAF Williamtown, NSW 15Feb92 for Fighter World Museum, RAAF Williamtown, NSW 1994-98 - tfd Graham Hosking, Mt Eliza, Victoria Nov98 to current.

Cavalier Aircraft Corporation Mustangs

Some of the aircraft reworked by Cavalier completely lost their original manufacturer's identities and FY USAAF serial numbers and were allocated new FY 67/68 USAF serials.

Cavalier T Mk.2 Mustang   67-14865

Built by Cavalier Aircraft Corp, Sarasota, FL 1967 as T Mk.2 - Project 'Peace Condor' for FAB coded FAB 522 Oct67 - stored by FAB for planned museum 1985 to current.

Cavalier T Mk.2   67-14866   N20TF
Chino Warbirds Inc, Houston, TX   F

Built by Cavalier Aircraft Corp, Sarasota, FL 1967 as T Mk.2 - Project 'Peace Condor' for FAB coded FAB 521 19Jan68-77 - recovered and reg C-GXUR to Arny Carnegie, Edmonton, Alberta, Canada Dec77 - tfd Neil J McClain of McClain Flight Service, Strathmore, Alberta Nov78-91 - rereg N20TF to Tom Friedkin of Cinema Air, Houston, TX Oct91-Dec01 - tfd Chino Warbirds Inc, Houston, TX 17Dec01 to current.

Cavalier T Mk.2 Mustang   67-22579   N251RM
Russell McDonald, Heber City, UT   F

Built by Cavalier Aircraft Corp, Sarasota, FL 1967 as T Mk.2 -
Project 'Peace Condor' for FAB coded FAB 519 Oct67-77 -
reg C-GXRG to Arny Carnegie of Edmonton, Alberta,
Canada Dec77 - tfd to Neil J McClain of McClain Flight
Service, Strathmore, Alberta Nov78-84 - rereg N52BH to
Robert E Hester, Bladenboro, NC Sep85-92 - rereg N251RM
to Russell McDonald, Park City, UT Apr92 to current.

Cavalier Mk.2 Mustang   67-22580   N2580
Charles R Hall Jr, Boulder, WY   F

Built by Cavalier Aircraft Corp, Sarasota, FL as T Mk.2
24Nov67 - Project 'Peace Condor' for FAB coded FAB 520
19Jan68-77 - rereg C-GXUQ to Arny Carnegie, Edmonton,
Alberta, Canada Dec77 - tfd Neil J McClain of McClain Flight
Service, Strathmore, Alberta Aug78-84 - rereg N151RK to
Richard F Korff, Lockport, NY Oct86-92 - tfd Aero Classics
Inc, Daytona Beach, FL May92-96.

Cavalier T Mk.2 Mustang   67-22581   N151MC
Gardner Capital Management Corp, Briarcliff Manor, NY

Built by Cavalier Aircraft Corp, Sarasota, FL 1967 as T Mk.2 -
Project 'Peace Condor' for FAB coded FAB 523 9May68-77 -
reg C-GMUS to Arny Carnegie, Edmonton, Alberta, Canada
Dec77 - tfd Ross F Grady, Edmonton, Alberta Aug78-91;
flown in FAB colours as *What's Up Doc* - tfd Fort Wayne Air
Service for rebuild Nov98 - rereg N151MC 9Feb98 to current.

Cavalier Mustang II 67-22579/N52BH when
owned by Bob Hester in 1988. The aircraft was
subsequently reregistered N251RM when
ownership passed to Russ McDonald in April
1992. Thierry Thomassin

Richard F Korff of Lockport NY owned Cavalier
II Mustang 67-22580/N2580 (an ex-Project
'Peace Condor' aircraft) in the summer of 1987
when this photograph was taken. It is now with
Chuck Hall. The Warbird Index

Cavalier T Mk.2   68-15795
Minnesota ANGB, Minneapolis, MN   M

Built by Cavalier Aircraft Corp, Sarasota, FL 1967 as T Mk.2 -
tfd US Army for trials 1967 - tfd RAF Museum; airfreighted to
RAF Mildenhall, UK 22Jun76, refurbished RAF Upper
Heyford, UK 1976-77, rejected by RAF Museum and into
store, RAF Henlow, UK Nov77-80 - tfd USAFM 1980 - tfd
Minnesota ANGB, Minneapolis, MN 1982 to current.

North American F-82 Twin Mustangs

F-82B Twin Mustang   123-43748   44-65162   N12102
??   R

Tfd USAFM Collection, Lackland AFB, TX 1956-65 - tfd
Confederate Air Force, Mercedes, TX 1966-68 (flown
Lackland to Mercedes) - reg N12102 to Confederate Air
Force, Mercedes, TX, later Harlingen, TX and Midland, TX

31Jan68 - acc (landing) Harlingen, TX 10Oct87 - rebuilt to
fly (commenced) - tfd San Diego-Gillespie Field, CA 2001
for American Airpower Flying Heritage Museum - reported
as traded/sold by CAF to new owner Nov02.

F-82B Twin Mustang   123-43754   44-65168
USAFM, Wright-Patterson AFB, Dayton, OH

Assigned NACA as NACA132, boc Sep50, soc Jun57 - tfd
USAFM, Wright-Patterson AFB, Dayton, OH 21Jun57 to
current.

F-82E Twin Mustang   144-38142   46-256   N142AM
??

Assigned NACA as NACA133, boc Jan50, soc Mar54 - EF-82E
Walter Soplata Collection, Newbury, OH 1965-85 - reg
G-BXEI and tfd David Arnold - rereg N142AM to AMJET
Aircraft Corporation Blaine, MN - tfd James P Harker,
Birchwood, WI 27Sep00 to current.

Ross Grady purchased sharkmouthed Cavalier II Mustang 67-22581/C-GMUS What's Up Doc *in the summer of 1978 and for many years it was kept in its original Fuerza Aerea Boliviana colour scheme as FAB523, with the addition of the Bugs Bunny artwork and catchphrase. It was photographed in August 1984 complete with Canadian flag on the tail.* William T Larkins

The camouflage, sharkmouth and tall Cavalier tail on 67-22581 gave way to this stunning paint scheme and a revised tail to conceal the aircraft's history very nicely. Reregistered N151MC and named American Beauty *for USAAF flyer Major John T Voll, it was also named "Lovely Lila" on the starboard side for its crew chief. The aircraft is now registered to Gardner Capital Management of New York.* Tom Smith

F-82B Twin Mustang 44-65162/N12102 was badly damaged in a landing accident at Harlingen, Texas on 10 October 1987 and is seen here a few months later. Chris Williams

Following its accident N12102 was airlifted to San Diego-Gillespie Field by C-5A Galaxy. It is seen here in 1998, over ten years after its accident but with restoration well advanced. In October 2002 the CAF agreed to trade the aircraft (to an as yet unidentified new owner) as part of a deal to acquire flyable P-38L Lightning 44-26981/N5596V. Chuck Gardner

F-82E Twin Mustang 46-256/N142AM was assigned to NACA in January 1950. After many years in the private collection of Walter Soplata it was briefly registered G-BXEI to Wizzard Investments, but the aircraft itself was never imported to the UK. Present owner James 'Pat' Harker is having the aircraft restored to flying condition. Dick Phillips

F-82E Twin Mustang   144-38148   46-262
?? M

Tfd USAF Museum Collection, Lackland AFB, TX 1956 to current.

F-82G Twin Mustang   150-38268   46-382
??

Assigned 4th F(AW)S May52 named *Night Takeoff* - recovered from smelter's yard by Dick Odgers, Soldotna, Alaska 1989; substantial remains recovered, now in store.

F-82G Twin Mustang   150-38277   46-391
Dick Odgers, Soldotna, Alaska S

Accepted by USAAF 17Sep48 - tfd 68th FW 6Aug50 coded 'M' - scrapped USA - recovered from smelter's yard by Dick Odgers, Soldotna, Alaska 1989; substantial remains recovered, now in store.

F-82G Twin Mustang   150-38279   46-393
Dick Odgers, Soldotna, Alaska S

Accepted by USAAF 20Sep48 - assigned for reclamation Ladd Field, Alaska 18Dec53 - recovered from smelter's yard by Dick Odgers, Soldotna, Alaska 1989; substantial remains recovered, now in store.

F-82H Twin Mustang   150-38272   46-386
??

To Ladd AFB coded 'J' 16Mar49 - recovered from smelter's yard by Dick Odgers, Soldotna, Alaska 1989; substantial remains recovered, now in store.

Mustangs with unknown identities

P-51D   FAG 336
La Aurora AB, Guatemala City, Guatemala GG

Assigned FA Guatemalteca coded FAG 336 Mar56 - exhibited Guatemala City - tfd La Aurora AB, Guatemala City, Guatemala; exhibited as FAG 360 1979 to current.

P-51D

Assigned IDFAF - tfd Israeli AF Museum, Hatzerim AB 1991 (fuselage only, composite) - exhibited as IDF 01.

P-51D
Halim AB, Jakarta, Indonesia

Mounted on pylon at Halim AB, Indonesia.

P-51D
Indonesian Air Force HQ, Jakarta, Indonesia

P-51D Cavalier
Indonesian Air Force Museum, Yogyakarta, Indonesia

P-51D
Museum Palagan, Jawa Tengah, Indonesia

P-51D
Kalijati AB, Indonesia

P-51D
Philippine Air Force Museum, Manila, Philippines

P-51D
Royal Air Force Museum Hendon, London, UK M

Eagle Squadron Association, San Diego, CA 1986 to current - static restoration Chino, CA (believed based on ex-TNI-AU airframe, with parts from 44-73415 alias N6526D) - tfd RAF Museum, Hendon; airfreighted to RAF Lyneham 13Feb89.

Photographs on the opposite page:

F-82E Twin Mustang 46-262 was transferred to the USAF Museum Collection at Lackland AFB, Texas in 1956 and is still there today. Chuck Gardner

Major structure elements of F-82G 46-382 and F-82H 46-386 were recovered from a smelter's yard by Dick Odgers of Broke Aircraft & Salvage in Alaska in 1989. Though the airframes are badly damaged following 'storage' at a scrap yard they could yield an enormous amount of usable airframe parts for an F-82 rebuild project. The co-pilot's cockpit from 46-382 is clearly recognisable. Dick Odgers

Photographs on this page:

Almost enough to break your heart; two Cavalier Mustangs sat atop concrete pylons outside the headquarters of the TNI-AU in Jakarta, Indonesia. They carry TNI-AU serials F-338 and F-367. The Warbird Index

Now owned by Ken McBride, the identity of this seldom seen Mustang – photographed at Rialto during the Air Fair in October 1993 – remains a mystery. Trygve Johansen

Parts of P-51D-25NA 44-73415/N6526D are believed to have been used to make up this static example which is now on display in the RAF Museum, Hendon, London. Bob Munro

Photograph on the following page:

The sun sets on P-51D-30NA 44-74536/N991R Miss America at the end of another day's air racing at Reno in 1988. Damaged at Reno in 2002, it will be rebuilt to fly again, thus adding to the Mustang story over 60 years after the prototype NA-73X first flew. Thierry Thomassin

GERMAN SECRET FLIGHT TEST CENTRES TO 1945

H Beauvais, K Kössler, M Mayer and C Regel

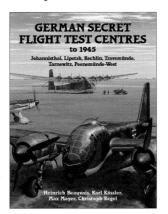

A group of German authors, some of whom were involved at the time have brought together a history and overview of the establishment and activities of government flight-test centres in Germany from its resumption in the 1920s until the end of the Second World War. Major locations included are the research facilities at Johannisthal, Lipetsk, Rechlin, Travemünde, Tarnewitz and Peenemünde-West.

Hardback, 282 x 213mm, 248 pages
270 b/w photos, sketches, 8pp of col
1 85780 127 X **£35.00**

AMERICAN AIR MUSEUM DUXFORD

A Tribute to American Air Power

Roger A Freeman

The American Air Museum, designed by Sir Norman Foster, was opened the Queen at Duxford on 1st August 1997. This book sets out the story behind the museum, its major exhibits and conservation programmes.

It includes an overview of US airpower and its connections with the UK. The narrative concentrates on the 20+ aircraft in the collection, giving the origin of each exhibit and details of the aircraft's current representation.

Hardback, 280 x 215 mm, 128 pages
130 colour and 65 b/w photos
1 85780 119 9 **£19.95**

AIR WAR ON THE EDGE

A History of the Israel Air Force and its Aircraft since 1947

Bill Norton

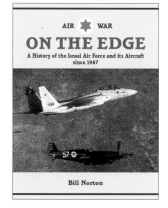

An in-depth book on the aircraft, units and exploits of the Israel Air Force. Detailed type-by-type coverage supported by a barrage of photographs follows the IAF from the mixed bag of aircraft of its formative days, through the Suez Campaign, the Six Day War, Yom Kippur and on to today's sophisticated, well-equipped force. Included for the first time are all of the badges and heraldry of the units of the IAF, in full colour.

Hbk, 282 x 213 mm, 432pp, 470 b/w, 60 colour photos, 147 unit markings
1 85780 088 5 Winter **c£45.00**

LUFTWAFFE SECRET PROJECTS

Fighters 1939-1945

Walter Schick & Ingolf Meyer

Germany's incredible fighter projects of 1939-45 are revealed in-depth – showing for the first time the technical dominance that their designers could have achieved. With access to much previously unpublished information the authors bring to life futuristic shapes that might have terrorised the Allies had the war gone beyond 1945. Full colour action illustrations in contemporary unit markings and performance tables show vividly what might have been achieved.

Hardback, 282 x 213 mm, 176 pages,
95 full colour artworks, over 160 diagrams and over 30 photos
1 85780 052 4 **£29.95**

LUFTWAFFE SECRET PROJECTS

Strategic Bombers 1935-45

Dieter Herwig and Heinz Rode

In this companion to the enormously popular volume on fighters, Germany's incredible strategic bomber projects 1935-45 are revealed showing the technical dominance that their famed designers could have achieved if time had allowed. The authors bring to life futuristic shapes that might have terrorised the Allies had the war gone beyond 1945. Careful comparison with later Allied and Soviet aircraft show the legacy handed on, right up to today's stealth aircraft.

Hbk, 282 x 213 mm, 144pp, 100 colour artworks, 132 b/w photos, 122 dwgs
1 85780 092 3 **£24.95**

BRITISH SECRET PROJECTS

Jet Fighters Since 1950

Tony Buttler

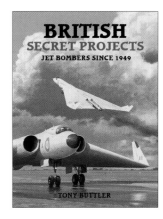

A huge number of fighter projects have been drawn by British companies over the last 50 years, in particular prior to the 1957 White Paper, but with few turned into hardware, little has been published about these fascinating 'might-have-beens'. Emphasis is placed on some of the events which led to certain aircraft either being cancelled or produced. Some of the varied types included are the Hawker P.1103/P.1136/ P.1121 series, and the Fairey 'Delta III'

Hbk, 282 x 213 mm, 176 pages
130 b/w photos; 140 three-views, and an 8-page colour section
1 85780 095 8 **£24.95**

BRITISH SECRET PROJECTS

Jet Bombers Since 1949

Tony Buttler

This long-awaited title forms a natural successor to the author's successful volume on fighters. The design and development of the British bomber since World War II is covered in similar depth and again the emphasis is placed on the tender design competitions between projects from different companies. The design backgrounds to the V-Bomber programme, Canberra, Buccaneer, Avro 730, TSR.2, Harrier, Jaguar and Tornado are revealed.

Hbk, 282 x 213 mm, c224pp, c130 b/w photos; 3-views, 8pp colour section
1 85780 130 X Winter **c£24.99**

FALKLANDS AIR WAR
A Chronological Account of Air Operations
During the Falklands War of 1982

Chris Hobson with Andrew Noble

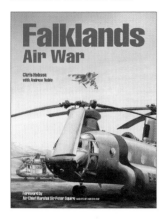

This is the first serious in-depth
analysis of the the role of air power in
the Falklands conflict, as opposed to
'instant' history. The narrative is
enhanced with extracts from interviews
with personnel involved. Many of the
book's illustrations, from the collections
of participants rather than official sources,
are published here for the first time.

Details of individual aircraft and ships
are given to complement a detailed
chronology of the course of the conflict.

Hbk, 282 x 213 mm, 208 pages
160 colour and b/w photographs
1 85780 126 1 **£24.99**

GERMAN STARFIGHTERS
The F-104 in German Air Force
and Naval Air Service

Klaus Kropf

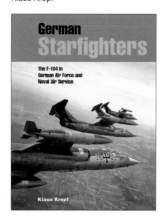

The F-104 equipped 12 Luftwaffe and
two Bundesmarine front-line fighter
groups and formed the backbone of
NATO air power during a career that
lasted over 30 years. This authoritative
study by a former Luftwaffe F-104 pilot,
will evoke many memories of West
Germany's Starfighter era and includes
technical details, F-104 bases,
individual aircraft notes, lists of F-104
pilots, a breakdown of F-104 losses,
special paint schemes.

Sbk, 282 x 213 mm, 176pp, 298 b/w &
85 colour photos, 42 colour badges
1 85780 124 5 **£19.99**

VIETNAM AIR LOSSES
USAF, Navy and Marine Corps Fixed-Wing
Aircraft Losses in SE Asia 1961-1973

Chris Hobson

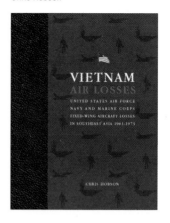

A most thorough and detailed review of
all the fixed-wing losses suffered by the
USAF, USN and USMC; basically a
chronological recording of each aircraft
loss including information on unit,
personnel, location and cause of loss.
Information is also provided on the
background or future career of some of
the aircrew involved.

Interspersed with the text is
background information on campaigns,
units, aircraft and weapons etc.

Softback, 280 x 215 mm, 288 pages
113 b/w photographs
1 85780 115 6 **£19.95**

THE X-PLANES X-1 to X-45
New, totally revised third edition

Jay Miller

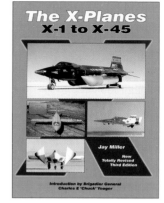

This new, totally revised and updated
version of 'The X-Planes' contains a
detailed and authoritative account of
every single X-designated aircraft.
There is considerable new, and newly-
declassified information on all X-Planes.

Each aircraft is described fully with
coverage of history, specifications,
propulsion systems and disposition.
Included are rare cockpit illustrations.
Each X-Plane is also illustrated by a
detailed multi-view drawing.

Hardback, 280 x 216mm, 440 pages
c980 photos incl colour,c250 drawings
1 85780 109 1 **£39.95**

WRECKS & RELICS
18th Edition

Ken Ellis

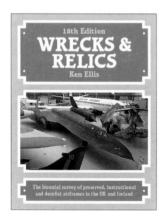

This standard reference work takes the
reader on a county-by-county and
province-by-province journey through
the fascinating world of museums,
military stores and dumps, 'geriatric'
airliners awaiting the axe, restoration
workshops, technical schools, treasures
in garages and barns and much more.
Within the wealth of detailed information
supplied on thousands of aircraft can be
found commentary, items to raise the
eyebrow!

Hardback, 210 x 148mm, 320 pages
192 colour photographs
1 85780 133 4 **£15.99**

VICKERS VALIANT
The First V-Bomber

Eric B Morgan

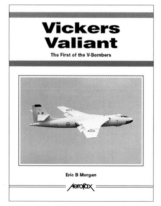

The Valiant was the shortest-lived of the
post-war V-bombers, first flying in 1951
and with production of 104 aircraft
ending in 1957, and official withdrawal
in January 1965 after investigation had
shown that the main wing spars were
suffering from metal fatigue. Valiants
participated in British atomic bomb tests
and made noteworthy long-distance
flights, principally operating from
Marham and Gaydon. Includes a full
listing of each aircraft history.

Softback, 280 x 215 mm, 128 pages
155 black/white and colour photos,
plus b/w line and schematic drawings
1 85780 134 2 **£14.99**

Red Star Volume 7
TUPOLEV Tu-4
SOVIET SUPERFORTRESS

Yefim Gordon and Vladimir Rigmant

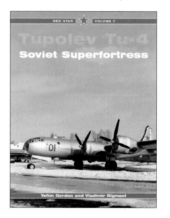

At the end of WW2, three Boeing B-29s
fell into Soviet hands; from these came
a Soviet copy of this famous bomber in
the form of the Tu-4. This examines the
evolution of the 'Superfortresski' and its
further development into the Tu-70
transport. It also covers the civil airliner
version, the Tu-75, and Tu-85, the last
of Tupolev's piston-engined bombers.
Also described are various experimental
versions, including the Burlaki towed
fighter programme.

Softback, 280 x 215 mm, 128 pages
225 b/w, 9 col photos, plus drawings
1 85780 142 3 **£18.99**

TARGET ROLLING
A History of Llanbedr Airfield

Wendy Mills

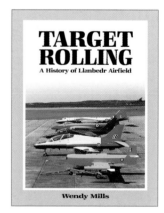

Llanbedr airfield near Harlech in North
Wales was established in 1941 and
after wartime operations providing air-
firing facilities for visiting front-line
squadrons, continued to specialise in
aerial target operations. This unusual
role continues today with brightly
painted Jindivik drones and various
control aircraft types.

This book covers the history of the
airfield, but places the emphasis firmly
on the target flying, including first-hand
accounts of how it is all achieved.

Softback, 216 x 152 mm, 128 pages
125 b/w and colour photographs
1 85780 136 9 **£10.99**